**ORACLE**® *Oracle Press*™

Oracle Networking

About the Author

Hugo Toledo, Jr. consults primarily on Oracle client/server and internetworking technologies for SSC, a systems management consultancy headquartered in Chicago, Illinois, USA. He has over fourteen years of experience, primarily focused on the successful design and deployment of distributed software solutions. His experience on the Internet dates to 1982 when, as an undergraduate at Duke University, he was an early member of the Usenet community.

Mr. Toledo is a frequent speaker at industry conferences including IOUW, COMDEX, ECO, Uniforum/Enterprise Solutions Conference, and CODA. He is also a technical editor and writer for books and periodicals including *Teach Yourself Unix Shell Programming*, *Oracle Informant Magazine*, and the journal, *Oracle Developer*.

His e-mail addresses are **72700,1705** on CompuServe and **hugo@mcs.com** on the Internet.

ORACLE® Oracle Press™

Oracle Networking

Hugo Toledo, Jr.

Osborne **McGraw-Hill**

Berkeley New York St. Louis San Francisco
Auckland Bogotá Hamburg London Madrid
Mexico City Milan Montreal New Delhi Panama City
Paris São Paulo Singapore Sydney Tokyo Toronto

Osborne **McGraw-Hill**
2600 Tenth Street
Berkeley, California 94710
U.S.A.

For information on translations or book distributors outside the U.S.A., or to
arrange bulk purchase discounts for sales promotions, premiums, or fundraisers,
please contact Osborne **McGraw-Hill** at the above address.

Oracle Networking

1234567890 DOC 99876

ISBN 0-07-882165-7

Acquisitions Editor
Wendy Rinaldi

Project Editor
Emily Rader

Copy Editor
Gary Morris

Proofreader
Linda Medoff

Indexer
David Heiret

Computer Designer
Lance Ravella

Illustrator
Leslee Basin

Series Design
Jani Beckwith

Quality Control Specialist
Joe Scuderi

To my parents, Hugo and Miriam, for fostering my sense of curiosity; to my sister, Ileana, for her graceful support and assistance; and, especially, to Barb, my very own angel on Earth.

Contents At A Glance

1   Oracle and Distributed Processing   1
2   Oracle Connectivity Products Montage   15
3   SQL*Net   37
4   TNS Applications: Oracle Names, MPI, SNS, and SNMP   69
5   Oracle Network Manager   99
6   Application Interfaces   119
7   Transparent Gateways and Other Open System Integration
      Technologies   139
8   TNS Network Design and Deployment   153
9   Oracle Connectivity Troubleshooting   169
10 Oracle Enterprise Manager   193
11 Oracle Mobile Agents   217
12 Oracle and the Internet   235
13 Oracle WebServer   265
14 Oracle PowerBrowser   287

15   Keeping Up with Oracle Technology **305**

Index **343**

Contents

ACKNOWLEDGMENTS, XVII
INTRODUCTION, XXI

1 Oracle and Distributed Processing **1**
Middleware   2
        Client/Server Processing   3
Open Systems   5
        Structured Query Language (SQL)   5
        Standard LAN and WAN Protocols   8
        Open Database Connectivity (ODBC)   9
        Simple Network Management Protocol (SNMP)   9
Oracle Distributed Database Technology   10
        Local Database System   10
        Remote Database System   10
        Distributed Database System   11
        Oracle7 Server   11
Date's 12 Rules for Distributed Databases   12
        Distributed Database Characteristics   12

2 Oracle Connectivity Products Montage **15**
ACME PLC   16
SQL*Net   18

Oracle Network Manager   20
Multiprotocol Interchange   21
Oracle Names   21
Secure Network Services   22
Simple Network Management Protocol (SNMP)   23
Native Drivers and OCI   24
Open Database Connectivity (ODBC)   25
Oracle Open Client Adapter for ODBC   26
Open Gateway Technology   27
Transparent Gateways   28
Procedural Gateways   28
Oracle XA Library   29
Oracle Access Manager   29
Oracle Mobile Agents   30
TCP/IP for Internet Applications   32
OpenDOC and OLE   33
Heterogeneous Networked Environments   34

3 SQL*Net **37**
What Is SQL*Net?   38
What Does SQL*Net Do?   39
How Does SQL*Net Work?   40
User Programmatic Interface (UPI)   41
Two-Task Common   42
SQL*Net   42
Transparent Network Substrate (TNS)   45
Oracle Protocol Adapters   48
Listener   48
Oracle Programmatic Interface (OPI)   52
SQL*Net QuickStart   52
Confirm Network Availability   52
SQL*Net Configuration   54
Checking the Configuration   58
Troubleshooting a Failed Connection   60
Using Your New SQL*Net Configuration   65
What More Is There to SQL*Net?   66

4 TNS Applications: Oracle Names, MPI, SNS, and SNMP **69**
TNS Network Components   70
Oracle Names   71
Resolving Service Names   72
Name Space   72
Resolving Service Names   75
Scalability   76

Oracle Network Manager   77
Configuring Oracle Names Servers   78
Dynamic Discovery Option   79
NAMESCTL   81
Oracle Native Naming Adapters   82
Enterprise Naming Services   82
Configuring Oracle Native Naming Adapters   83
MultiProtocol Interchange   83
Configuring Interchanges   84
Data Pumps   85
INTCTL   86
Secure Network Services   86
Configuring SNS Parameters   87
Oracle Authentication Adapters   89
Oracle SNMP   90
Message Information Base   90
Configuring SNMP Parameters   91
SQL*Net OPEN   92
Developing SQL*Net OPEN Applications   92
SQL*Net OPEN API Functions   93
SQL*Net OPEN API Errors   95
SQL*Net OPEN Sample Applications   95
Conclusion   96

5   Oracle Network Manager **99**
Oracle Network Manager   101
Network Configuration Files   102
File or Database Storage?   104
The Oracle NetPrint Utility   105
The Oracle NetConv Utility   105
The Oracle NetFetch Utility   106
QuickStart for Oracle Network Manager   107
Advanced Network Management   117

6   Application Interfaces **119**
Heterogeneous Access Needs   120
Oracle Bridging Technologies   121
Heterogeneous Communications Considerations   121
Access to Non-Oracle7 Databases   122
Access to Oracle7 Data from
a Non-Oracle Application   123
Access to Oracle7 Stored Procedures
from a Non-Oracle Application   124

Access to Non-Oracle7 Procedures
  from an Oracle Application   125
Heterogeneous Access Means   126
  Oracle Call Interface (OCI)   126
  Oracle Precompilers   128
  Oracle SQL*Module   129
  Native Drivers   130
  Open Database Connectivity (ODBC)   131

**7 Transparent Gateways and Other Open System Integration
  Technologies** **139**
Access to Legacy Data and Code   142
Open Gateway Technology   142
  Oracle Transparent Gateways   143
  Oracle Procedural Gateways   148
  Transaction Integration Technology   149
  Migration Technologies   149
The Open Road   150

8 TNS Network Design and Deployment **153**
Architecting Oracle Connectivity   154
  Community Involvement   154
Planning Your TNS Network   157
  Present Status Assessment   157
  Design Goals   158
  Designing Your TNS Network   162
Techniques   164
  Optimal Flexible Architecture   164
  Segmentation   165
Implementation   165

9 Oracle Connectivity Troubleshooting **169**
Problem Resolution Policy   170
  Documentation   171
  Proactive Measures   172
  Reactive (or Ad Hoc) Measures   178
Troubleshooting Connectivity Problems   179
Products   179
  ODBC Drivers   180
  Open Client Adapter for ODBC   182
  Oracle Objects for OLE (OO4O)   184
Operating System-Specific Problems   188
  Windows 3.1, 3.11, and
    Windows for Workgroups 3.11   189

Windows NT and Win95   190
NetWare   190
Solaris   191
Macintosh   191

10   Oracle Enterprise Manager **193**
Network Management   194
Why Do You Need Network Management Technology?
    195
ISO Network Management Framework   196
Network Management Implementations   200
Management Stations   203
Oracle Enterprise Manager   206
OEM Components   208
OEM Network Management Operations   209
Conclusion   214

11   Oracle Mobile Agents **217**
What Is a Mobile Application?   219
Types of Mobile Applications   219
Why Not a Client/Server Solution?   222
Limitations of a Client/Server Architecture   222
The OMA Advantage   223
Mobile Application Design   223
Message-Based Mobile Applications   224
Limit Interaction Between Client and Server   224
The Structure of OMA Systems   225
OMA and Client/Agent/Server   226
Limitations of Mobile Computing   229
Oracle Power Objects and OMA   230
Using the Class   230
Conclusion   231

12   Oracle and the Internet **235**
A Brief History of the Internet   237
ARPANET   237
Internet Protocols   239
Standards   239
Telnet   240
FTP   242
Archie   243
Wide Area Information Search (WAIS)   245
Gopher   247
Multipurpose Internet Mail Extensions   249

The World Wide Web   249
HTTP   251
HTML   251
Uniform Resource Locators   252
Dynamic Web Pages   253
Server-Side Includes   254
CGI   254
The Oracle World Wide Web Interface Kit   256
Overview of the Kit   257
Acquiring the Kit   258
Installing the Kit   258
WOW   259
A Demonstration of WOW Using SQL*Plus   260
wowstub: the Agent Component   261
The wow Shell Script   261
Extending WOW Using PL/SQL   262
WOW's Limitations   263
The Future of Oracle and the Web   263

13   Oracle WebServer **265**
Oracle WebServer 1.0   267
Oracle Web Listener   267
Oracle Web Agent   271
Oracle7 Server   275
Optimizing WebServer 1.0 Applications   276
Converting WOW Applications to WebServer 1.0   276
Oracle WebServer 2.0   278
Secure Sockets Layer (SSL)   279
Proxy Support   280
Web Request Broker   281
Extended PL/SQL Function Library   282
Conclusion   283

14   Oracle PowerBrowser **287**
Browser Technology   288
Oracle PowerBrowser Quick Start   289
Setting Preferences   291
Using PowerBrowser   297
Personal Server   297
PowerBrowser Programming   299

15   Keeping Up with Oracle Technology **305**
A Wide Variety of Sources   306
Etiquette   306

Types of Information Sources   307
     Electronic Information Sources   307
     Nonelectronic Information Sources   308
Oracle Corporation   308
     Product Documentation   309
     Oracle Press   316
     Oracle Education   317
     Oracle Services   318
     Alliances Marketing   319
     Oracle WorldWide Customer Support   320
Extra Oracle Information Sources   327
     Commercial Online Services   327
     Independent BBSs and Local Users Groups   334
     The Internet   335
     User Groups and Conferences   338
     Osborne/McGraw-Hill's Oracle Press Series   339
     The Fourth Estate   340
     Anything Missing?   341

Index **343**

Acknowledgments

If I have seen further than others, it is because I have stood on the shoulders of giants.

–Sir Isaac Newton

I have a sense, now, of what this means. You cannot write a book without tremendous support from your colleagues, friends, and family. And, now, rather than take a stand at the end of the Acknowledgements, I'd like to start off by stating that all errors, omissions, and deviations from the way things really are, are solely my fault. Heaven knows everyone listed here did his or her darnedest to make sure I got it right!

The Oracle Press–Osborne/McGraw-Hill

The person responsible for seeing this tome to the shelves of your local bookseller is the book's Acquisitions Editor. *Oracle Networking* is Wendy Rinaldi. Although she inherited this project, she nurtured it to maturity as if it were her own—even through the terrible teens (i.e., thirteen, fourteen, fifteen...weeks behind schedule that is)! I cannot say enough to express my gratitude to Wendy for her support, assistance, and unflagging perseverance. I only hope I haven't put too many years on her.

I also want to thank Heidi Poulin, Emily Rader, Polly Fusco, Janet Walden, Daniela Dell'Orco, Brad Shimmin, and Scott Rogers. And thank you, Kelly Young, for prodding me when I call!

Oracle Corporation

This book developed as a tremendous amount of change was taking place in the Oracle product lines. WebServer, Oracle7 release 7.3 Universal Server®, PowerBrowser, and Oracle Enterprise Manager all came out as the book was being written. Through it all, one person, Wynn White, Group Manager, Networking Product Management, Server Technologies, made certain I had the latest releases and kept me informed of the status of products covered in the book. Without his continual assistance this book could not have been produced. Wynn, I am forever in your debt.

The culprit behind my writing this book is the globe-trotting Mark Jarvis, V.P., Marketing, Server Technologies. While at the Network Products Division he was an early supporter, assisting me in my quest for total Oracle connectivity. Thanks Mark, wherever you are today!

To Julie Gibbs, Oracle Press, and her staff I express my appreciation for the opportunity to work on this project. I thank you all also for your continued support of my writing on and off the web.

Specific support and access to information on the various technologies covered were graciously provided by each the following individuals: Oracle Mobile Agents—Conway Snyder and Jay Verkler; Oracle Enterprise Manager—Neeracha Taychakunavuyd; Secure Network Services—Mary Ann Davidson; Oracle Alliances/BAP—Tim Wong; Personal Oracle7 and Oracle Objects for OLE—Craig Yappert and Keith Majkut; Oracle Power Objects—Max Schireson, Rick Schultz, Matt Bennett, Ronny Lashaw, and Jeremy Burton; Battlestar/Oracle Software Manager—Mark Gaydos; PowerBrowser—Jeff Menz and John McCormack; WebServer—Randy Hodge, Aileen Jaitin, and Magnus Lönnroth; Mainframe and Integration Technologies—Dave Dargo and Vivian Nalbone; Oracle Worldwide Customer Support—Robert Pearson; Network Products—Julie Belluomanie; Oracle Enterprise Manager—Lillian Gordon.

A special round of applause goes to the folks in the Web and Workgroup Systems Division. Oracle Senior Vice President Marc Benioff amassed an incredible wealth of talent and fun in one place. To him and others in the group not previously mentioned—including Shari Simon, Doug Laird, Laura Pauli, Donna Coates, Debbie Harrison, Neil Morgan, Elizabeth Donahue, and Vernon Keenan—I appreciate your support and assistance in all our other work together. Thanks for the chance to participate with you in such wonderful developments. I look forward to more joy and success.

Thank you also Leith Anderson. I appreciate the time you took to help me best share my thoughts and effort with the folks at Oracle. Without your assistance and introductions, I would never have established many of the relationships I am now fortunate to have.

Saraswati Systems Corporation (SSC)

Continually supporting our professional development and always reminding us to maintain quality in our personal lives through balance are two of the ways in which William Hinman, founder of SSC, leads his organization. A longtime independant consultant, I never thought I would find a home working for any company. I consider myself truly fortunate to experience both the stimulation and the warmth which SSC and its stellar ensemble provides. I truly appreciate your accommodating my work on the book and, especially, your consideration in ensuring I maintained my sanity while I did!

A most fortuitous fringe benefit from my association with SSC is my friend and mentor, Steven Feuerstein, Director/Oracle Practice, SSC. Thank you for your (usually) sober counsel on the development of this book. You set a very high example both personally and professionally that I will always strive to emulate.

To my other friends and colleagues at SSC and our clients, thank you for your support and assistance. I hope you are pleased with what I have accomplished with your help.

And to the Ones Who Tried to Warn Me

So, let's see. Each chapter is about the length of one and a half Oracle technical journal articles, right? So, OK, 15 chapters at 1.5 articles/chapter...that's like 22.5 articles, right?

—Hugo Toledo, Jr.

Well, no, not really. Now, don't get me wrong, it's not as if I didn't ask other authors for advice. Here is a sampling of their sagacious commentary:

"Are you crazy?" Kevin Loney, *author* Oracle DBA Handbook *and* The Complete Oracle Reference, 3rd Edition

"You're kidding, right?" Michael Corey, Past-President IOUG-Americas, author of
Oracle: A Beginner's Guide and Oracle Tuning Handbook

"Why don't you just write the 22.5 articles and then come talk to me?" Steven
Feuerstein, Director/Oracle Practice, SSC, author of Oracle PL/SQL Programming

Ah, well, hope springs eternal! Wise-cracks not withstanding, I very much appreciate Kevin Loney, Kasu Sista, Michael Corey, and Rick Greenwald taking the time to share with me their insights on authoring, helping me understand what I was about to undertake.

Thank you also, Tony Ziemba, editor of Pinnacle Press' *Oracle Developer*, for publishing my first article on Oracle technology. Look at what you started!

To my financee, Barbara Bolin, I thank you, sweetheart, for all of the time and effort you put into helping me with so much of this book, for accommodating my frequent unavailability as another application was being chronicled, and, most importantly, for allowing me to clutter up your lovely house with all matter of unwieldy hardware and media. Just a few more paragraphs and I'll be able to start putting it all away. (At least until it is time for the next edition!)

Finally, lifetime thank yous go to, in order of appearance: My parents, Hugo and Miriam, for allowing me to clutter up their lovely house with hardware and media as well; Ms. Filter for teaching me BASIC; Mr. Banull for my first microcomputer class; Tom Truscott and Lauren Weinstein for purely altruistic assistance in the early days of Usenet (ah, the days of high signal-to-noise ratio!); Dr. David Smith for my first client; Kenneth Zimmerman for 15 great years of friendship and business partnership; Chuck Casper, my first mentor; and Mel Ivey and Flip Nehrt, for professional and personal guidance and support.

Thank you all for aiding me in the pursuit of my craft.

Introduction

This software was not developed for use in any nuclear, aviation, mass transit, medical, or other inherently dangerous applications. It is the customer's responsibility to take all appropriate measures to ensure the safe use of such applications if the programs are used for such purposes.

—Standard Disclaimer in Oracle Documentation

Clearly, you had better read this book. Oracle technology and inexperienced personnel are a recipe for disaster, if this disclaimer is to be believed.

Networked Computing

In *Ideas and Information* [Simon & Schuster, 1989], Arno Penzias, head of research for AT&T's Bell Laboratories, and a Nobel Prize-winning physicist, says

As work becomes increasingly information intensive, I see organizational success depending more and more on giving each individual contributor needed information at the right place, at the right time, and in the right form. The

degree to which this requirement can be met depends crucially on the information architecture used, the organization's "nerve system."

How right he was. Before the rest of the world came to see that the "network is the computer," AT&T, SRI International, and Xerox were working on ways to improve the timely distribution of data. It took others to take the fruit of their labors and create commercially viable implementations of those ideas. This book is intended to teach you means of crafting such a "nerve system" in which to effectively cultivate your Oracle technology.

What is Oracle Networking?

About a year ago I undertook the development of a book to be called *Oracle Networking*. Whenever anyone heard of the book they'd say "Oh, yeah, SQL*Net." I'd then have to explain, "No, no, the connectivity considerations for an Oracle infrastructure call for more than just SQL*Net. Why just the..." About then they'd begin to mumble about having to get home to walk the dog or something. Well, I gather you've read this far because you are interested in getting that question answered. Simply put, Oracle Networking is about connectivity.

Information Anywhere

Oracle gives you Information Anywhere. It did so first by creating the earliest commercial implementation of a SQL database. Soon after it did so again, releasing the first commercial SQL database implementation on Unix. From there Oracle has gone on to perfect the distributed relational database system. Whether in the office, on the Internet or across wireless networks, Oracle has the technology to connect everyone to every "bit" securely and efficiently. This book will help you determine which technology to use and when to use it.

Intended Audience

I recently received a solicitation from the *Harvard Business Review*. On it were listed the following roles: Strategist, Mentor, Champion, Architect, Builder, Coordinator, Talent Scout. The promotion is geared to management executives. However, it did lead me to think about the various roles technologists, especially those charged with the interconnection of unrelated product lines, have to play.

The database networking expert—more precisely, the database connectivity expert—must wear the same hats for a variety of reasons:

- Strategist—Information strategies have at their heart the goal of providing information to anywhere at anytime. Clearly, tradeoffs must be made to achieve the spirit of this goal when it cannot reasonably be achieved due to constraints imposed by time, money, or space. This is where the tough decisions must be made. This is where the connectivity expert helps craft information strategy by enabling understanding of the issues involved.

- Mentor—The connectivity expert fosters excellence in an organization by enhancing application of technologies and providing assistance in the proper incorporation of disparate technologies.

- Champion—The best solution is rarely everyone's favorite. An important role in achieving operational success is that of champion for proper planning, implementation, and oversight.

- Architect—You have an idea, you put it to paper, and then you craft a plan. Each step of the way, remember what you've learned in class, what you've been taught on the job, and what you learned from your failures. Apply engineering principles to ensure your solution meets the test.

- Builder—Well, now that you've designed it, it's time to prove it will work. Not sure? Go back to the last role.

- Coordinator—The modern enterprise is rife with tool-of-the-month junkies. You cannot always prevent unanticipated implementations from making their way onto the corporate infrastructure. You can, however, prevent the often inappropriate solution from snarling up the rest of the corporate network cloud, kudzu-like.

- Talent Scout—Uh, talent scout? Hey, like I said, the ad was geared to management executives. Your plate is full as it is. However, you cannot do it all yourself. Continually keep an eye open for those whose talents and desires seem to encompass the preceding roles as well.

What Hat Do You Wear?

This book is intended to help anyone involved in Oracle connectivity solutions understand, design, craft, implement, and maintain appropriate interfaces between technologies. Software developers will learn the situations for which each Oracle connectivity technology is appropriate. Software designers and network architects will learn, and perhaps be pleasantly surprised by, the ways in which Oracle technology makes their job easier through transparent multiprotocol connections and gateways. System implementers will learn the "how-tos" of putting Oracle solutions in place through the Quick Start sections found throughout the book.

How This Book Is Organized

This book has five sections. The first section, Chapters 1 and 2, is introductory, providing overviews of distributed processing issues and of Oracle's connectivity technologies. The next section, Chapters 3 through 5, cover SQL*Net, Oracle's primary networking application. The third section, Chapters 6 through 10, covers network integration issues including interoperability with foreign technologies and network design and deployment. Section Four covers the newer network media, wireless communications, and the Internet. Finally, the last chapter of the book, Chapter 15, informs you of other sources of reliable information on Oracle.

A Brief Overview of the Chapters

Here is a brief description of each chapter's contents broken down by section. This information should help you determine where to look for information on new topics.

Distributed Databases and Oracle Technology

The first section provides a broad view of the state of distributed database processing and Oracle's place in the world of networked database technology. This section contains much information referred to throughout the rest of the book.

Chapter 1, "Oracle and Distributed Processing," will teach the reader about Oracle's database technology, its role in the modern enterprise, and the direction of distributed database processing. It also provides information on principles related to Oracle connectivity including C.J. Date's "12 Rules of Distributed Database Systems."

Chapter 2, "Oracle Connectivity Products Montage," provides an overview of each of Oracle's connectivity technologies and discusses where each is appropriately applied. It contains pointers to the appropriate chapter for each technology covered.

SQL*Net

SQL*Net is Oracle's primary networking application. The only means of getting to the Oracle database server is through SQL*Net.

Chapter 3, "SQL*Net," discusses that product's role in Oracle connectivity and provides the background for subsequent chapters on Transparent Network

Substrate (TNS) applications. Chapter 3 also provides the first of several Quick Start sections intended to show the user how to get up and running on an Oracle connectivity product quickly. The Quick Start subjects for Chapter 3 are SQL*Net Easy Configuration and the SQL*Net Listener.

Chapter 4, "TNS Applications," provides an introduction to each of Oracle's TNS applications, the Oracle MultiProtocol Interchange, Oracle Names, Secure Network Services, and Oracle SNMP.

Chapter 5, "Oracle Network Manager," provides the reader with an overview of the Oracle's premier network configuration tool, Oracle Network Manager. The Quick Start for Oracle Network Manager parallels the example provided in Chapter 3 for Easy Configuration providing an opportunity to compare the two methods.

Enterprisewide Integration

It is not possible in the modern enterprise to succeed without providing access to the past and future technologies as well as to foreign technologies. This section describes the various means of dealing with legacy data and with foreign data sources and applications.

Chapter 6, "Application Interfaces," covers the means of communicating to Oracle technologies through other technologies. Although SQL*Net is always present as it is the only means of communicating with the database server, there are a number of circumstances where another set of software completes the link to Oracle. The featured Quick Start is on Open Client Database Connectivity (ODBC).

Chapter 7, "Transparent Gateways and Other Open System Integration Technologies," focuses on Oracle's Transparent Gateways and Procedural Gateways. The gateways use SQL*Net to provide a bridge to non-Oracle data sources and applications. This is the essential technology for mainframe connectivity.

Chapter 8, "TNS Network Design and Deployment," takes the products you learn about in the preceding chapters and puts them to work in the configuration and deployment of an Oracle network. The emphasis is on achieving the goals put forth by Chris Date in his "12 Rules of Distributed Database Systems."

Chapter 9, "Oracle Connectivity Troubleshooting," teaches you how to find the source of your connection trouble and how to correct it. Additionally, performance improvement techniques and "gotchas" to avoid are outlined.

Chapter 10, "Oracle Enterprise Manager," describes Oracle's new single console solution to managing resources in a distributed database environment. Using SNMP and TNS technology, Oracle Enterprise Manager provides a means of incorporating application and server management into the same framework that is so successfully used to manage current enterprise network infrastuctures.

Extending Your Reach

The modern enterprise is rarely contained in a single building. The need to communicate globally is no longer the province of multinational corporations, either. This section covers both the wide area networking technologies Oracle provides and other means of broadening communication.

Chapter 11, "Oracle Mobile Agents," provides a thorough introduction to Oracle's primary technology for mobile users. Featuring multi-mode communication, OMA's client/agent/server technology enables developers to provide a single interface to users regardless of the medium employed to connect to the enterprise, be it wireless, circuit-switched (telephone), LAN-based, or while disconnected for deferred processing.

Chapter 12, "Oracle and Internet," describes the role of Oracle's technologies in the rapidly growing Internet. A survey of the key Internet protocols and an explanation of how Oracle has been used with the Internet across the years are provided. This is a very important chapter, a prerequisite to understanding the contents in the two chapters that follow. It ends with a chronicle of the Oracle WWW Interface Kit, the ground-breaking precursor to the Oracle WebServer.

Chapter 13, "Oracle WebServer," covers the server side of Oracle's chief web integration technology; its components are Oracle WebServer, WebAgent, Web SDK, and Oracle7 Server. Both WebServer release 1.0, bundled with Oracle7 release 7.3 and later, and the optional WebServer release 2.0 are covered.

Chapter 14, "Oracle PowerBrowser," describes Oracle's own web browser technology. Not just a way of viewing pages on the World Wide Web, however, PowerBrowser features market-leading technology providing connections to local databases and client-side processing through Java and Oracle's own PowerObjects Basic. The chapter concludes with a Quick Start on configuring PowerBrowser.

Chapter 15, "Keeping up with Oracle Technology," provides not an end but a beginning to the next leg of the quest to Oracle excellence. This chapter covers the variety of Oracle resources available from Oracle and other sources, through the Internet and off. These include on-line services, publications, user groups, Oracle Services consulting, Oracle Education, and worldwide conferences. A Quick Start section on setting up support with Oracle's WorldWide Customer Support's CompuServe-based SupportLink is provided.

Conventions Followed in This Book

To facilitate your understanding of important points, several different icons are employed.

TIP
This icon indicates a Tip. Tips are features to improve performance or utility.

NOTE
This icon indicates a Note. Notes provide additional information and direct you to other sources of information on the material just covered.

CAUTION
This icon indicates a Caution. Cautions are items which cannot be stressed enough and will save you time, effort, money, and, of course, aggravation. Save you, that is, if only you heed the warnings!

DEFINITION
This icon indicates a Definition. Uncommon terms or those specific to Oracle technology are defined here.

CHAPTER 1

Oracle and Distributed Processing

Something there is that doesn't love a wall,
And wants it down.

—Robert Frost

At one time software and data were always on the same computer. These were local, or centralized, systems. This was necessary given the state of the technology. Now, however, most nontrivial systems are networked and decentralized. As a result there is often a gulf between data and the application or applications that manipulate it. This gulf is simply a geographic separation and may be easily bridged. You do so across your local area networks (LANs) regularly.

Certain walls remain, however. These include vendor incompatibilities, data representation differences, and dissimilar network protocols. Fortunately, Oracle's connectivity technologies eliminate or surmount barriers between data and applications. These technologies are a broad range of software that bridges data and applications, leaving you free to architect an open system without worrying about incompatible components.

DEFINITION

Open systems: Systems that rely on industry standards and are not limited to a single vendor's proprietary, or closed, technology. The availability of open technology components enables the selection of the best component for each aspect of a complex system.

Middleware

Suppose after reengineering a business process you find that you must connect a legacy Visual Basic application to an Oracle7 database. Although Visual Basic cannot innately communicate with an Oracle7 database, you know you can safely design and deploy a solution because Oracle has technologies to complete the connection. In fact, in the case of Visual Basic and Oracle7 together, Oracle provides two solutions, the first based on the Open Database Connectivity standard (ODBC), and the second a component object technology, Oracle Objects for OLE (OO4O). Such bridging technology is generally referred to as *middleware*.

DEFINITION
Middleware: The enabling technology that bridges a communications-level technology with an application-level technology. An example of middleware is ODBC, which enables database-independent client applications to communicate with an Oracle7 database. The client application does not have to be network aware and does not need to directly communicate with SQL*Net, Oracle's primary server communications technology.

Most of Oracle's networking and data communications technologies function as middleware. Other Oracle connectivity technologies, however, do not serve to bridge applications but may provide applications services, as does Oracle's WebServer; facilitate the design Oracle networks, as does Oracle's Network Manager; or enable real-time management of distributed database networks, as does Oracle Enterprise Manager.

NOTE
Not all of Oracle's connectivity technologies are network related. Oracle Objects for OLE, for example, while clearly bridging communications barriers, is not a network application. It functions at a different layer without regard to the presence of a network. However, for simplicity, the term *networking* will be used synonymously with connectivity, to describe both interapplication and network connectivity.

Client/Server Processing

The evolution of user/machine architecture, which led to the need for middleware, is called *client/server processing.* Client/server takes advantage of cheap and plentiful processing power available on the desktop and attempts to combine the best of batch and online processing to leverage each side's resources more efficiently. In client/server processing, much of the data manipulation is performed using local CPU cycles. Server-side processing exists to support centralized functions, including data repository management, business rules, and computer-intensive processing requiring mainframe- or server-class systems. The desired result is more flexible processing at a lower cost per transaction.

Gartner Group's Definition of Distributed Processing

The partitioning of client/server processes has been segmented into the following five forms by the Gartner Group, a prominent technology analysis firm:

- Remote presentation
- Distributed presentation
- Distributed logic
- Remote data management
- Distributed data management

Remote Presentation   In *remote presentation,* the original form of client/server processing, the client process is responsible solely for presentation or display and screen navigation functions. Examples include character-based applications run from a terminal session using Telnet.

Distributed Presentation   In *distributed presentation,* the next form of client/server processing, the client process is again responsible solely for presentation or display functions. However, the processing of any display and all navigation functions are handled by the server. Examples include X Window applications.

Distributed Logic   In *distributed logic,* some processing is performed on the client side and some on the server side. Examples include database applications where the client application is responsible for the final merging of data from multiple remote servers. Each server is responsible for running the query; only the client is responsible for combining the result sets.

Remote Data Management   Probably the most common client/server model, a typical *remote data management* implementation has GUI client applications interacting with a sole server application, such as an Oracle7 server.

Distributed Data Management   *Distributed data management* requires clients and servers to function cooperatively and autonomously. Each can coordinate with others but none is in charge of all processing. Oracle7 does this.

One-Stop Shopping

You may have noted the words "attempts" and "desired" in the first paragraph in this section. This is because client/server processing is not yet an engineering discipline. To this day, architecting client/server solutions often involves artistry and some fast footwork. Why? Because the wealth of solutions often prevents the wise selection of truly compatible platforms. Users are overwhelmed by claims of superiority as they attempt to combine best-of-breed components. Sticking with a consistent architecture from end to end will help avoid this problem.

Oracle alone offers such a consistent architecture. From Blaze, Oracle Power Objects local data store, upwardly compatible with the Oracle7 database, all the way through Personal Oracle7 and the Oracle Workgroup Servers to the Oracle7 Enterprise Servers, a clear migration and interoperability path exists. Because it is such a broad product line, it is important to know which tool to apply to which task. This book will illustrate examples of correct and erroneous applications of Oracle technology.

Open Systems

Open systems are a key factor in the successful design and deployment of information systems solutions today. Oracle's success is in large part due to the establishment and acceptance of standards. This ensures that Oracle products can interoperate with the broadest range of technologies as the market requires. The major standards Oracle embraces include

- Structured Query Language (SQL)
- Standard Local Area Network (LAN) and Wide Area Network (WAN) Protocols
- Open Database Connectivity (ODBC)
- Simple Network Management Protocol (SNMP)

Structured Query Language (SQL)

The single most important standard Oracle helps set and supports is the Structured Query Language (SQL). SQL is the standard language for relational database systems. It is also the primary technology that enables Oracle to interoperate with other vendors' databases and vice versa. Oracle developed the first commercially available SQL implementation in 1979. Now all of the major relational database systems support SQL.

At the heart of SQL is the relational model. Arising from work done in the early 1970s by IBM scientist E. F. Codd, SQL defines the instructions to which a relational database server responds and the process each instruction invokes. Relational databases are one of several database models including hierarchical and network databases. The others predate relational databases but were actually more complicated in design. Relational databases are much simpler and more intuitive but require greater processing power than the others. As a result, it took some time for SQL to go from concept to product.

NOTE
The SQL standard is maintained by both the International Standards Organization (ISO) and the American National Standards Institute (ANSI). The latest SQL standard is ANSI-SQL X3.135-1992 or ISO 9075(1992).

SQL Basics

Much of the power of Oracle7 technology comes from the effective implementation and extension of the SQL standard. This is the means by which most data access occurs in Oracle environments. Key to understanding the optimal implementation of Oracle technology is knowing how the Oracle7 server operates. The following sections will briefly describe SQL language basics. How Oracle technology makes it possible to simultaneously support hundreds of users and millions of rows of data is covered later in the section on the Oracle7 Server.

Tables, Rows, and Columns
Relational databases organize their data in tables. Each table contains rows of data. For a given table, each row in that table contains the same number and type of columns. Each row contains columns of values. All SQL operations result in rows being returned, added, modified, or deleted. Table 1-1 is an example of a SQL table showing the organization of the data into rows and columns.

The following listing shows a simple SQL query that results in two columns from each row being returned.

```
SELECT emp_number, emp_name, emp_salary
FROM employee
WHERE emp_salary > 20000
ORDER BY emp_name;

EMP_NAME   EMP_SALARY
--------   -----------
ALLEN         32010
JONES         21000
SMITH         20050
```

Row	EMP_NUMBER	EMP_NAME	EMP_SALARY
1	101	JONES	21000
2	102	SMITH	20050
3	103	ALLEN	32010

TABLE 1-1.   *Representation of a Relational Database Table*

Schemas   Multiple tables belong to a single schema. Typically, each schema
refers to a single database user, or owner. The owner can grant or revoke access
to database objects in his schema to other users. A database object is a subset of
a database such as a table. Other database objects include those described in
Table 1-2.

For example, in a complex database system, all of the Payroll tables may
belong to the PR schema. All of the Human Resources tables may belong to the HR
schema. Tables from different schemas may be combined in queries. For example,
when analyzing workloads, the HR.POSITION table may be used to get the
employees' job classifications, while tables in the PR schema contain the actual
hours-worked data. To retrieve all of the hours each employee works by job
classification, you could use a simple SQL statement such as this one:

```
SELECT job_class, emp_number, SUM(PR.hours)
FROM HR.position, PR.employee
WHERE emp_salary > 20000
GROUP BY job_class, emp_number;
```

Database Object	Description
Indexes	Used to speed up searches by using a key value for each row
Sequences	Used to generate serial numbers within the database
Views	Subsets of tables or joined tables
Database links	Pointers to external databases
Synonyms	Used to create transparent local aliases to external objects
Packages	Sets of programs stored within the database

TABLE 1-2.   *Partial List of Oracle7 Database Objects*

Notice how the schema name was specified for each table. This allows users other than the owner of the table to view information in that table. This applies to all database objects, not just tables.

NOTE
The schema itself is stored in tables. If you look inside the Oracle7 catalog, or system tables, you will see that each database object created has rows in the database describing it.

SQL Language   The SQL language used to interact with the database is as simple as its structure. When an application communicates with the Oracle7 server, it generally performs one function: it supplies a SQL statement and waits for a result set. There are a relatively small number of SQL statement types that are performed:

- Data Manipulation Language (DML), including SELECT, INSERT, UPDATE, and DELETE
- Data Definition Language (DDL), including CREATE, DROP, and ALTER
- Transaction control statements, such as COMMIT, ROLLBACK, and SAVEPOINT
- Session control statements, such as ALTER SESSION and SET ROLE
- System control statements, of which only ALTER SYSTEM currently exists
- Embedded SQL statements, including CONNECT, OPEN, CLOSE, FETCH, and EXECUTE

Standard LAN and WAN Protocols

Oracle supports all of the major Local Area Network (LAN) protocols, including

- *TCP/IP*   The standard Internet protocol, this is the most popular open LAN protocol.
- *SPX/IPX*   This is Novell's native protocol for its NetWare technology.
- *LU6.2*   This is one of IBM's System Network Architecture Peer-to-Peer protocols.
- *OSI*   Open Systems Interconnect is the canonical, layered protocol standard.

■   *Named Pipes*   This is the primary technology used by Microsoft Windows networks.

Additionally, Oracle supports multiple LAN protocols simultaneously. This is necessary to provide a truly distributed database system. Technology such as that in Oracle's MultiProtocol Adapter and Oracle Names facilitate cross-protocol operation.

To facilitate global processing across Wide Area Network (WAN) protocols, products such as Oracle Mobile Agents support

■   *X.25*   This is the most common packet switching protocol in use.

■   *Mobitex*   This is the international mobile data communications packet protocol.

■   *Cellular Digital Packet Data (CDPD)*   This is standard for packet data over cellular networks.

Open Database Connectivity (ODBC)

Regardless of whether a relational database supports SQL, there is no standard application program interface (API) for databases. Each vendor generally provides a proprietary interface that is optimized to interact with its data stores. There is an open, if incomplete, solution, however, and that is the Open Database Connectivity Standard (ODBC).

ODBC provides an effective, two-part data access technology that is supported by all major database vendors. Applications that support ODBC have a single, standard means of interacting with data sources rather than multiple, possibly incompatible, means of communication to various vendors' products. ODBC is not limited to SQL databases. ODBC can be used to manage simple databases stored in flat files. By the same token, key features of Oracle7 are not available through ODBC. Regardless, ODBC provides a simple and effective solution to many data access needs. ODBC is covered in detail in Chapter 6.

Simple Network Management Protocol (SNMP)

As network components increase in quantity and complexity, it becomes necessary to centralize their monitoring. Such support is enabled through the Simple Network Management Protocol (SNMP) standard. As the use of distributed databases grew, it became apparent that centralized monitoring of distributed application technologies was also required. Standards were developed to enable SNMP to support more complex hardware and software systems.

Oracle is a key player in the development of SNMP standards for distributed database system monitoring. In fact, Oracle authored the RDBMS Management Information Base (MIB). The MIB is the data structure SNMP uses to represent a network component's management capabilities and characteristics. SNMP is covered in detail in Chapter 4.

TIP
As with many standards, SNMP is in flux. At this time, there are two competing flavors of SNMPv2, not to mention SNMPv1, vying for market share. Review your product literature to ensure that the implementation of SNMP you seek is supported by both your Oracle releases and your other vendors' technologies.

Oracle Distributed Database Technology

The goal of this book is to inform and guide you in the successful design, deployment, and maintenance of networked and distributed Oracle systems. Database systems fall into one of three categories: local, remote, and distributed. Each is supported by Oracle's technologies. Understanding the difference between them will help you avoid the problems that may arise when implementing each one.

Local Database System

The simplest database system is the stand-alone or local Oracle application system running on a single computer. A typical example is an Oracle Power Objects application accessing data stored in a Personal Oracle7 database. No other users are competing for access to the database.

A slightly more complex example is one where the application and the database are not homogeneous technologies. For example, Visual Basic is designed to accommodate simple Access databases. To communicate with the same Personal Oracle7 database, a bridging technology such as ODBC or Oracle Objects for OLE (OO4O) must be employed.

Remote Database System

More complex workgroup solutions involve networks. Remote database systems introduce complexity in the form of network protocols, routing, and name resolution.

Routing is how an application or operating system determines how to reach another application or computer. Name resolution is how an application or operating system determines where another computer or application is located on a network by looking up the destination's name.

If you extend the previous example, you have an application communicating with an Oracle7 Server located on another computer. SQL*Net, Oracle's primary networking technology, is now employed to help with routing and name resolution through use of the Oracle Names server.

Distributed Database System

Finally, in the most complex of distributed environments, multiple database servers are employed. Each functions autonomously but also cooperates with other database servers to implement a distributed database. A *distributed database* is one in which the database objects may exist across multiple computers and networks but appear to the user as a single database. Actually, there are 12 rules for a distributed database described later in this chapter.

Distributed database architects often have to contend with different network protocols. In such cases, Oracle's MultiProtocol Interchange technology may be used to bridge the different networks. The combination of these technologies provides for the most complex of layouts—a distributed database system.

Oracle7 Server

Oracle7 is the latest generation in a long history of leading relational database technologies. It features the most sophisticated database technology and broadest connectivity of any major database vendor. Oracle7 is a SQL-based technology featuring

- Unmatched performance
- Laptop to mainframe scalability
- Portability across platforms
- Transparent access to non-Oracle7 data sources
- Transparent distributed processing

Most importantly, the Oracle7 Server meets Date's 12 Rules for Distributed Databases.

Date's 12 Rules for Distributed Databases

E. F. Codd first conceived of the relational database when he was a researcher at IBM. C. J. (Chris) Date worked with Codd to extend the influence of the RDBMS in the business world. One of Date's more important contributions to the field was the development of 12 defining rules for a true distributed RDBMS. First and foremost, Date believes that the ideal distributed RDBMS in all other respects should behave like a nondistributed RDBMS. This is sometimes called Rule 0. Following are each of the 12 rules, what they mean, and how Oracle's technology meets these conditions.

NOTE
The source of the original 12 rules is C. J. Date, *An Introduction to Database Systems, Volume 1,* Addison-Wesley Publishing Company, Reading, MA 1990.

Distributed Database Characteristics

According to Oracle, these are the database characteristics and how Oracle7 technology meets each point:

- *Local autonomy* The data is owned and managed locally. Local operations remain purely local. One site (node) in the distributed system does not depend on another site to function successfully.

- *No reliance on a central site* All sites are treated as equals. Each site has its own data dictionary.

- *Continuous operation* Incorporating a new site has no effect on existing applications and does not disrupt service.

- *Location independence* Users can retrieve and update data independent of the site.

- *Partitioning [fragmentation] independence* Users can store parts of a table at different locations. Both horizontal and vertical partitioning of data is possible.

- *Replication independence* Stored copies of data can be located at multiple sites. Snapshots, a type of database object, can provide both read-only and updatable copies of tables. Symmetric replication using triggers makes readable and writable replication possible.

■ *Distributed query processing* Users can query a database residing on another node. The query is executed at the node where the data is located.

■ *Distributed transaction management* A transaction can update, insert, or delete data from multiple databases. The two-phase commit mechanism in Oracle ensures the integrity of distributed transactions. Row-level locking ensures a high level of data concurrency.

■ *Hardware independence* Oracle7 runs on all major hardware platforms.

■ *Operating system independence* A specific operating system is not required. Oracle7 runs under a variety of operating systems.

■ *Network independence* The Oracle's SQL*Net supports most popular networking software. Network independence allows communication across homogeneous and heterogeneous networks. Oracle's MultiProtocol Interchange enables applications to communicate with databases across multiple network protocols.

■ *DBMS independence* DBMS independence is the ability to integrate different databases. Oracle's Open Gateway technology supports ODBC-enabled connections to non-Oracle databases.

CHAPTER 2

Oracle Connectivity Products Montage

When all you have is a hammer, every problem looks like a nail.

—Anonymous

To craft a successful solution, you need the appropriate tools and an understanding of the role each fulfills. And, as today's networks must provide a high degree of interoperability, supporting multiple network protocols and unpredictable segment loads, you need components that can cooperatively provide multiple application solutions. Fortunately, Oracle's product line meets the challenge with a variety of products with which to connect network resources reliably and securely.

However, sometimes even the most appropriate network component may constrain communications. For example, Internet technology requires a Transmission Control Protocol/Internet Protocol (TCP/IP) network to operate. In an otherwise Open Systems Interconnect (OSI) network, this could limit interoperability. To mitigate such potential limitations, you need tools to facilitate the management of disparate communications channels. With features such as a GUI metaphor for visualizing the network, and drag-and-drop manipulation of network components, Oracle also provides products to enable effective communications channel modeling and management.

Various types of components make up a networked Oracle environment. You must know the role each type plays in order to harness its capabilities. The types of components to be discussed, along with examples of each type, are described in Table 2-1.

ACME PLC

You are probably familiar with ACME, Inc.—the fictitious company in Oracle's product documentation. ACME is used in examples to illustrate how Oracle's products are used within the enterprise. Well, times have changed and ACME has changed with them. Now the organization is a multinational conglomerate called ACME PLC, and its data communications needs have expanded. Oracle's products, of course, continue to ensure reliable and secure communications among all of its nodes.

However, now ACME PLC finds it must support many non-Oracle products in addition to ACME, Inc.'s existing Oracle technology. In the following section, you will see how in an enterprise, such as ACME PLC, foreign technologies may be accommodated and even embraced using Oracle's networking products.

Client applications	Programs such as those written with Developer/2000, third-party tools such as spreadsheets, and other end user applications.
Server applications	Server-side processing including database triggers and stored procedures for use in remote procedure calls (RPCs). Oracle7 server stored procedures are written in PL/SQL.
Data sources	Oracle7, Oracle Power Object's Blaze data store, file systems, and foreign databases.
Gateways	Entry points to data sources and server technologies. Oracle's Open Gateway Technology and Oracle Mobile Agents contain gateway components.
Network protocols	Network communications standards such as TCP/IP, LU6.2, NetWare (SPX/IPX), and OSI.
Network applications	Programs that facilitate communication between clients and servers. Not usually directly accessed by end users, examples include the Oracle Protocol Adapters, Oracle Names, and the Oracle Multiprotocol Interchange (MPI).
Network management tools	Tools to design, implement, and manage network components. Examples include the Oracle Network Manager and the Oracle Software Manager. Non-Oracle examples include HP OpenView and IBM NetView.
Access managers	Transaction processing (TP) monitors such as Tuxedo, Top End, and Encina, and the Oracle Access Managers for CICS and IMS/TM.

TABLE 2-1.   *Oracle Network Components*

The connectivity technologies available to Oracle products include

- Oracle SQL*Net
- Simple Network Management Protocol (SNMP)
- Native drivers and the Oracle Call Interface (OCI)
- Open Database Connectivity (ODBC) drivers
- Oracle Open Client Adapter for ODBC
- Oracle Open Gateway Technology
- Oracle XA library

■ Oracle Access Manager

■ Oracle Mobile Agents

■ TCP/IP for Internet applications

■ OpenDOC and OLE

One or more of these technologies is used to enable communication among both Oracle and non-Oracle data sources and software. Figure 2-1 shows how ACME PLC uses each of these in its enterprise.

SQL*Net

SQL*Net is Oracle's flagship networking technology. When most Oracle users think of Oracle Networking, they think SQL*Net. Although it is only one of several important network applications, it is the most commonly used Oracle connectivity component.

SQL*Net's primary role is to connect Oracle products to each other. While other networking technologies handle communications with non-Oracle nodes,

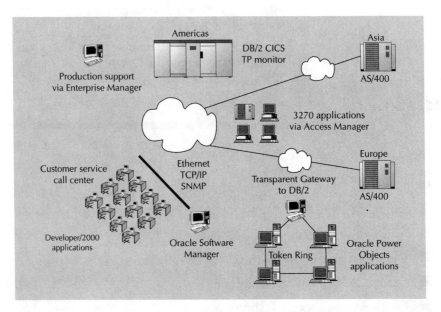

FIGURE 2-1. *ACME PLC and Oracle networking technology*

SQL*Net enables Oracle products to communicate regardless of physical location or disparate communications protocols. It does so by providing both run-time and design-time applications. The run-time components include the software that performs the features for which SQL*Net is used, the Protocol Adapters and the Transparent Network Substrate (TNS). The design-time components include Oracle Network Manager and its associated utilities that are used to lay out and manage the logical network. One way in which SQL*Net's technologies are used is shown in Figure 2-2.

Within SQL*Net's product line are additional applications that facilitate communications management. These applications are

- Oracle Network Manager
- Multiprotocol Interchange
- Oracle Names
- Secure Network Services

Each of these works with SQL*Net to ensure efficient and secure communications between SQL*Net nodes.

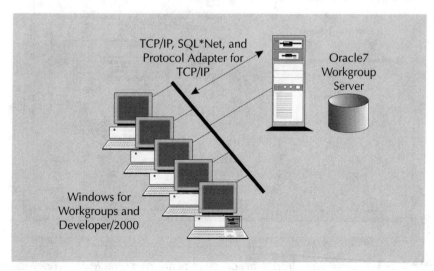

FIGURE 2-2.   *SQL*Net-based solution*

Oracle Network Manager

Oracle Network Manager is used to define and manage components in an Oracle network. The landscape of an Oracle network contains many components that must be cataloged to guarantee secure and reliable data communications. The taxonomy of network components includes domains, protocol communities, nodes, databases, instances, and many more items that define where data and the applications run against them reside. Oracle Network Manager provides the means of cataloging and configuring these items.

As network components are added, removed, or updated, Oracle Network Manager ensures that the resulting network configuration is internally consistent. This means that no data pathways have been inadvertently broken and that each network component's minimum configuration requirements have been met. The ease with which the Oracle Network Manager can relocate a resource is demonstrated in Figure 2-3.

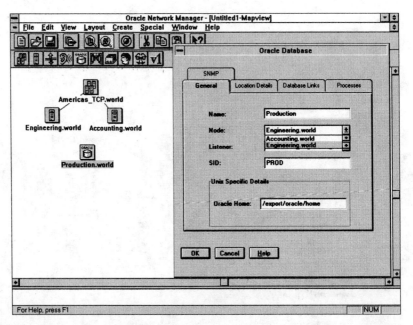

FIGURE 2-3. *Drag and Drop data source relocation in Oracle Network Manager*

Multiprotocol Interchange

In the typical enterprise, different networking protocols are employed to best fulfill each group's needs. This makes it necessary to facilitate communication among differing protocols. At the hardware level, this is done using bridges and multiprotocol routers. At the network application level, SQL*Net performs this using the Oracle Multiprotocol Interchange (MPI).

In an Oracle network, a *community* is a set of nodes using a common network protocol. Using information maintained with the Oracle Network Manager, the MPI ensures seamless communication across communities. In large part, this is achieved using SQL*Net's Transparent Network Substrate (TNS), which is protocol independent. The ability to connect clients and servers in different communities is shown in Figure 2-4.

Oracle Names

Enterprise-level production control demands that load balancing be easily performed. One way to balance network load is to reposition traffic to

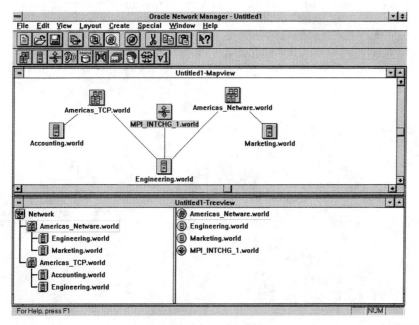

FIGURE 2-4. *Multiprotocol connections using Oracle MPI*

higher-bandwidth pipelines where available. Another way is to vertically scale the processor to provide greater power for server-side processing applications. When such changes are made, databases and clients may need to be relocated. Applications that rely on those databases or are run on those clients need to know where to find their data regardless of where it is located. For example, the service name PRODDB is resolved by Oracle Names to direct the client application to the production database on the engineering server, as shown in Figure 2-5.

Oracle Names is a SQL*Net application that provides the flexible means of identifying resources and their location through universally available database tables and remote-procedure calls (RPCs) that are performed transparently to the user and the application. Additionally, Oracle Names can work in conjunction with operating system naming services, or native naming services, to determine the physical location of database resources on the network.

Secure Network Services

With each additional network component come several additional opportunities to compromise the network. Most network protocols are open to packet sniffing, where network traffic is copied in transit and analyzed without detection. Then there is the problem of authentication, or verifying that a communication session has not been falsified or perhaps captured and retransmitted at a later time. Finally, there is the problem of data modification. (Denial of service is a fourth vulnerability, but as a hardware-mitigated threat, it is not addressed here.)

Fortunately, all three threats against your data may be thwarted using Secure Network Services (SNS). This set of SQL*Net technologies shields your network

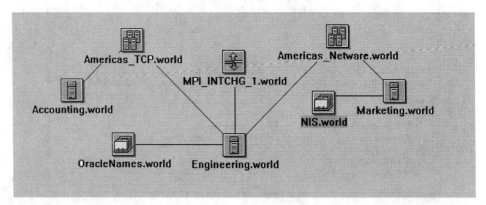

FIGURE 2-5.   *Oracle Names interoperating with native naming services*

traffic from attack. First, by encrypting all network traffic, unauthorized use of data is prevented. Digital signatures ensure authentication of origin. And, finally, checksums ensure data has not been modified after transmission. Each shield may be raised individually or in combination with the others. The mechanisms may also be supported through external security technologies that include biometric authentication and ticket/credential servers such as Kerberos.

SNS operates without regard to the network protocol in use. Even where multiple protocols are connected using the Multiprotocol Interchange (MPI), SNS protects all of your SQL*Net communications. This is because SNS works at the Transparent Network Substrate (TNS) layer, not at the network protocol layer. The shields provided by SNS are shown in use in Figure 2-6.

Simple Network Management Protocol (SNMP)

With the arrival of SQL*Net version 2.2 came support for SNMP. This technology, which has been increasingly used in TCP/IP networks for network component management, is supported in Oracle Network Manager. Additionally, the Oracle7 database also supports SNMP enabling database administrators to tie the database

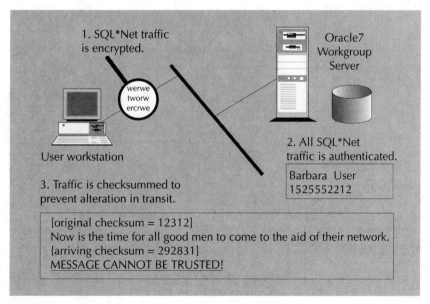

FIGURE 2-6. *SNS roles in a SQL*Net environment*

into enterprise management technologies such as IBM's NetView/6000, HP's OpenView, and SunSoft's Solstice.

Since late 1993, Oracle Corporation has led the development of the Standard Management Information Base (MIB) for relational databases. This means that in addition to monitoring traditional network hardware components, enterprise monitoring of relational database components is now possible. This enables proactive problem resolution, centralized enterprise database activity management, and safe and reliable management of remote resources. Oracle's commitment to SNMP is not limited to the Oracle7 server but is being extended to all Oracle technologies, including Oracle Mobile Agents and the forthcoming Bandwagon technology for large-scale implementation and management of low-maintenance remote sites. The diagram in Figure 2-7 shows how fault monitoring may be centralized using Oracle Enterprise Manager and SNMP technology.

Native Drivers and OCI

Native drivers are middleware products that enable direct access to the target data source. They are built using the application programming interface (API) provided by the data source's manufacturer. The API is usually in the form of a software function library. For example, third-party developers needing to provide native access to Oracle7 use Oracle's API technology, the Oracle Call Interface (OCI), to create such drivers. The OCI function set allows others to write applications that

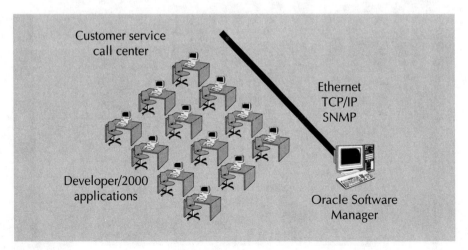

FIGURE 2-7. *Oracle's network component management technologies*

communicate directly with the Oracle7 database through the same functions used to write Oracle's Developer/2000 tools Oracle Forms and Reports.

Native drivers typically offer better performance than generic technologies such as ODBC, which is described in the next section. Oracle provides native drivers to Sybase in Oracle Power Objects (OPO). This allows OPO applications to interact with SQL Server databases as they would with Oracle databases, as shown in Figure 2-8. The only limitations imposed by native drivers are those of the target data source itself.

Open Database Connectivity (ODBC)

In today's open environments, it is critical that the Oracle7 database be accessible from non-Oracle applications. However, native drivers are often not available. To this end, both Oracle and other vendors have developed Open Database Connectivity (ODBC) drivers to the Oracle7 database. ODBC provides non-Oracle access to Oracle7 databases from both the Windows and Macintosh environments. Figure 2-9 shows a Visual Basic application connecting to an Oracle 7 database using the ODBC drivers.

The ODBC API encapsulates the SQL Access Group's Call Level Interface (CLI) specification. This allows an ODBC-compliant application to communicate with a foreign database using a subset of SQL. The application passes ODBC API statements to an ODBC driver. The driver, which is specific to a particular vendor's database, can then either pass the calls as they are to the database engine or convert the ODBC-ese to the vendor's preferred vernacular.

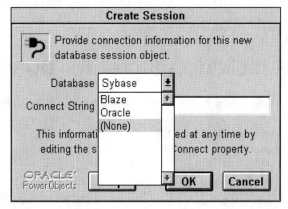

FIGURE 2-8. *OPO access to Blaze, Oracle7, and SQL Server*

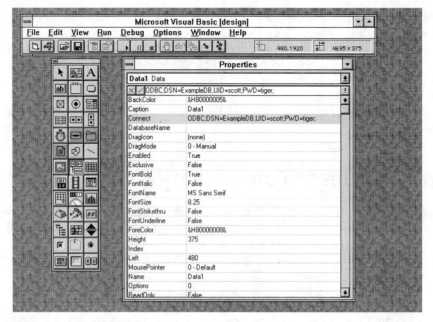

FIGURE 2-9. *ODBC access to Oracle7*

That ODBC generally requires SQL calls to be converted does not necessarily mean decreased performance. All ODBC calls do not have to be translated to native API calls as is often assumed. For example, simple SELECTs may be passed on without translation. Of course, stored procedures and vendor-specific features such as Oracle's NVL and DECODE functions do require conversion/translation, and as such may add to a loss of efficiency where used via ODBC.

Oracle Open Client Adapter for ODBC

Typically, ODBC is used where non-Oracle applications need to communicate with Oracle7 databases. However, there is also the need for Oracle applications, such as those in Developer/2000 and Discoverer/2000, to access non-Oracle7 data sources. In such cases, the Open Client Adapter for ODBC is used. Of course, functionality may be limited because not all Oracle7 features are available from the foreign data source through ODBC.

Oracle Open Client Adapter for ODBC supports the following non-Oracle7 data sources:

- Microsoft SQL Server
- Microsoft Access
- RDB
- Sybase SQL Server and System 10
- Tandem NonStop ODBC Server
- Informix Online

Oracle's Discoverer/2000's data browser can perform heterogeneous data warehouse analysis using the Open Client Adapter to Informix Online, as shown in Figure 2-10.

Open Gateway Technology

To better ensure connectivity to foreign data sources, Oracle developed the Open Gateway Technology. A gateway's role is to properly route communications between disparate schemes. Using the Open Gateway Technology, Oracle and other parties can quickly develop gateways to non-Oracle data. There are two types of gateways—data, or *transparent,* and procedural.

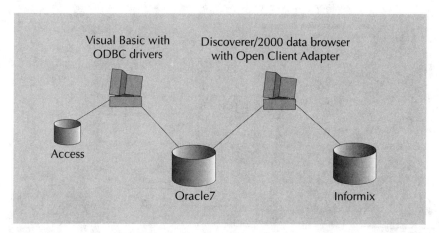

FIGURE 2-10.   *Open Client Adapter utilization*

Transparent Gateways

Oracle developed the Transparent Gateways, which provide a means of exchanging data with a foreign data source as if it were an Oracle7 database. Members of the Transparent Gateway family include

- Transparent Gateway for DB2
- Transparent Gateway for Sybase
- Transparent Gateway for Informix

Transparent Gateways are developed as the market requires. In addition to DB2 for MVS, other platforms for which Transparent Gateways have been developed include DB2 on the AS/400 and RS/6000 platforms, EDA/SQL, and INGRES. Where Oracle does not provide a Transparent Gateway, developers may create their own using the Transparent Gateway toolkit. Such custom gateways enable SQL access to relational or nonrelational data sources. The diagram in Figure 2-11 shows the use of a Transparent Gateway in a heterogeneous database environment.

Procedural Gateways

Sometimes a gateway is required not for data access but for procedural access. For example, server-side applications and remote procedure calls (RPCs) in Oracle7 are

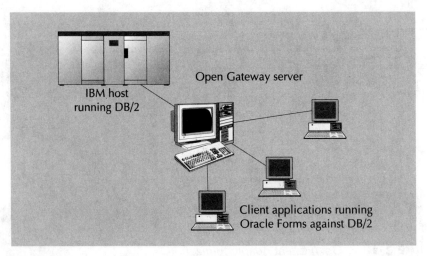

FIGURE 2-11.   *Oracle Open Gateway Technology in use*

written in PL/SQL, Oracle's procedural language for SQL. When applications require RPC access to other technologies, the Procedural Gateway technology provides the means. And, as with the Transparent Gateways, where Oracle has not already provided a Procedural Gateway to a foreign technology, the Procedural Gateway toolkit provides the means for developing a custom procedural gateway. In addition to Transparent Gateway access to a foreign data source, Figure 2-11 shows a Procedural Gateway in use.

Oracle XA Library

A key Oracle7 feature is its ability to provide distributed updates where a non-Oracle7 data source is employed. This is possible because Oracle7 and SQL*Net together provide the features required to manage the components involved in a transaction. This transaction management includes distributed update preparation, execution, and recovery if necessary. In complex online transaction processing (OLTP) architectures, Oracle7 may not be the primary resource manager. In such cases, another application, usually a transaction processing (TP) monitor, may be required to manage the interacting components.

TP monitors are used to efficiently manage the throughput in high-transaction count environments. These typically include order entry and point-of-sale applications where hundreds or even thousands of transactions are simultaneously performed. TP monitors help manage the load of many streams of data through tightly integrated interactions between the data stores, user applications, and the network and computing devices. This interaction is facilitated using the XA libraries.

Oracle's XA library provides the software hooks required to tightly couple Oracle7 applications to X/Open Distributed Transaction Processing (DTP) XA interface-compliant technologies. To use the library, applications are built using Oracle's Call Interface (OCI), the high-performance native application programming interface (API) to the Oracle7 architecture. Such a topology is illustrated in Figure 2-12, where a TP monitor balances the load from many point-of-sale (POS) nodes accessing an Oracle7 Enterprise Server.

Oracle Access Manager

The Open Gateway and Open Client technologies enable access to foreign data sources from Oracle. In order to fully interact with foreign technologies, Oracle has developed the Oracle for MVS Client Solution. The two chief connectivity components of this product are Oracle Access Manager for CICS and Oracle Access Manager for IMS/TM.

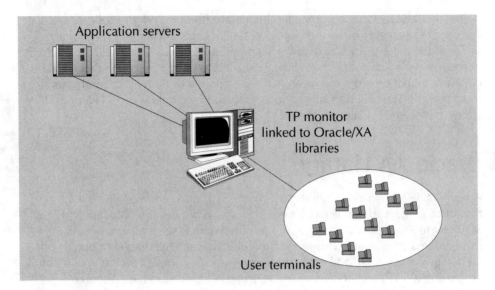

FIGURE 2-12. *The XA library used to interface a TP monitor and Oracle7*

The Access Manager products enable existing CICS or IMS/TM applications to access Oracle7 data. This capability is especially important to facilitate the phased-migration of legacy systems to SQL-based open systems. A legacy CICS application system undergoing right-sizing is shown accessing Oracle7 through the Oracle Access Manager in Figure 2-13.

Oracle Mobile Agents

In an increasingly mobile world, the barriers are often not technological but physical. Geography becomes the limiting factor. To overcome the problems of disconnected users, Oracle developed Mobile Agents, a software applications programming interface (API) for mobile applications. Mobile applications are characterized by support for disconnected use, wireless communications networks, and message-based architectures.

Oracle Mobile Agents (OMA) relies on a Client/Agent/Server processing model to position the high-bandwidth-demand communications paths on the LAN and mitigate effects of the lower-bandwidth wireless network. The agent is the client application's proxy on the destination network side. The agent does work for the client that would be untenable if performed over the slower wireless link but is

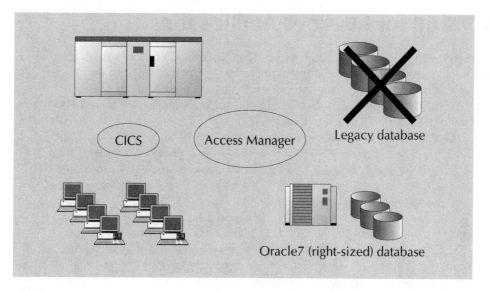

FIGURE 2-13.   *Oracle Access Manager's role in CICS/Oracle7 connectivity*

efficiently processed on the high-speed local area network. An example application of OMA technology is illustrated in Figure 2-14.

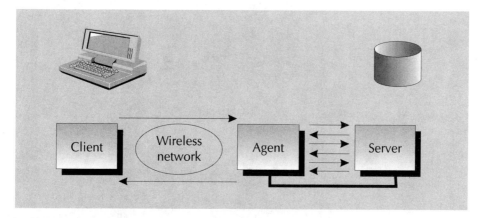

FIGURE 2-14.   *Oracle Mobile Agents technology in the larger Oracle network world*

TCP/IP for Internet Applications

The growth of the Internet has been met by the evolution of Internet-enabled Oracle technologies. As the Internet runs over TCP/IP protocols, so do Oracle's Web technologies. However, this does not mean that other technologies participating in Oracle and Web integration solutions are TCP/IP bound. As is shown in Figure 2-15, once in the Oracle data stream, other pathways may be used.

Oracle's primary Internet applications are PowerBrowser and WebSystem. Each services a different segment of the Web. PowerBrowser offers complete client services including an HTML 3.0-targeted browser and client-side processing via Oracle Basic and Java. PowerBrowser also features a lightweight server and extensive client-side database processing facilities.

WebSystem consists of an HTTP server and a web agent that together offer complete integration with the Oracle7 database via Client/Agent/Server technology. WebSystem technology is also used to Internet-enable Oracle Applications via Oracle Internet Commerce. Oracle Internet Commerce provides a secure and reliable gateway to Oracle Applications data so that, for example, customers may view inventory levels prior to executing orders or check on order status afterward.

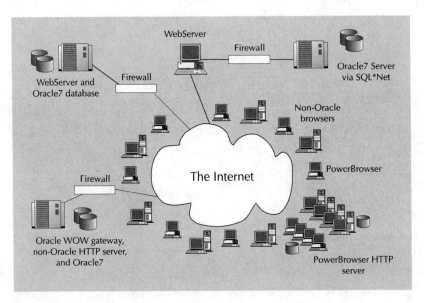

FIGURE 2-15. *Oracle and the Internet*

OpenDOC and OLE

As the role of object- or component-based technologies increases, look to
Microsoft's OLE 2.0 and Apple and IBM's OpenDOC compound document
schemes to become more prominently implemented. Already, products such as
Oracle Objects for OLE (OO4O) and Oracle Power Objects are natively designed
to support object-based communications channels. Compound documents, or
objects, that may contain both data and software provide design-time and run-time
services to applications using them. The management of such objects will prove to
be an increasingly important function as they move from localized entities to
distributed resources.

OO4O is one such example. It provides Microsoft's Visual Basic and C++
sophisticated access methods to Oracle7 for applications written using them.
Instead of relying on ODBC, developers may take advantage of OO4O's visual
development component, provided via an industry standard VBX (Visual Basic
Control), for drag-and-drop development. Figure 2-16 illustrates how the
connection between a Visual Basic application and Oracle7, first shown in Figure
2-9 using ODBC, is easily converted to an object-enabled connection using OO4O.

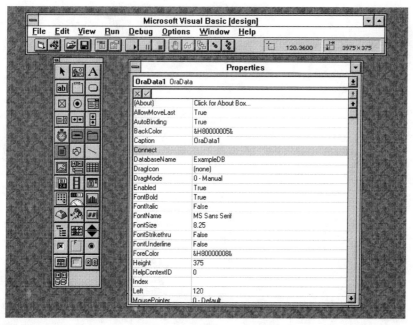

FIGURE 2-16.   *Oracle7 session enabled via Oracle Objects for OLE*

Run-time connectivity is provided in OO4O not through function libraries but through in-process object servers that contain their own logic and storage management components. OO4O can therefore provide complete access to Oracle7 technology, including distributed processing through stored procedures, to all Windows applications that are OLE 2 enabled. In addition to Visual Basic and C++, OLE 2–enabled software includes all Visual Basic for Applications (VBA)– enabled applications, such as Microsoft Excel.

Heterogeneous Networked Environments

Clearly, there are many, many ways in which heterogeneous applications and data sources need to interact in today's architectures. Fortunately, most of the problems traditionally encountered in completing the connections are now accommodated much more simply using Oracle connectivity technologies. This helps in the design of network solutions and also in their management by eliminating interoperability problems and reliably securing communications end to end.

CHAPTER 3

SQL*Net

Intervening network technology should be flexible enough to accept information in whatever format the data source provides it . . . and powerful enough to convey [it] in a format suited to the user's understanding.

—Arno Penzias

SQL*Net V2 is Oracle's primary network application and, generally, the only means of communicating with an Oracle7 server. Even when other connectivity technologies such as Open Data Base Connectivity (ODBC) drivers are employed, SQL*Net is required to complete the connection. It is on top of SQL*Net's technology that distributed updates, end-to-end data encryption, dynamic object name resolution, and most of C. J. Date's distributed database objectives are facilitated in an Oracle environment. In addition, it is SQL*Net that enables connections across disparate network protocol communities. However, all these features are a small fraction of the work SQL*Net performs.

NOTE
As SQL*Net V2 is now the standard, all references to SQL*Net are to version 2, unless otherwise noted.

What Is SQL*Net?

SQL*Net is Oracle's flagship technology for server communications. SQL*Net encompasses a number of technologies and programs, including Oracle Protocol Adapters, Network Manager, MultiProtocol Interchange, SNMP, and Names. Figure 3-1 shows an example of a SQL*Net network that supports two communities, one running TCP/IP over Token Ring and the other running SPX/IPX over Ethernet.

Within SQL*Net's product line are a number of other applications used in management and production support, including LSNRCTL, NETFETCH, and TNSPING. SQL*Net's flexibility and extensibility are largely due to its layered makeup. Each layer communicates only with adjacent layers, similar to the OSI model shown in Chapter 1.

SQL*Net is not a user or presentation application, but a network application. As such, it is not a program a user runs explicitly, but rather a set of software called and used by other Oracle applications, such as database servers and front-end clients. SQL*Net's execution, as well as many of its internal subprograms, is generally transparent to the end user. As such, much of what SQL*Net does goes unheralded.

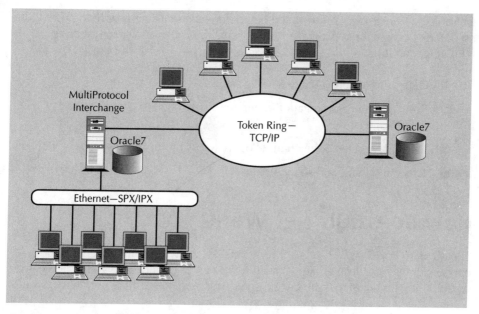

FIGURE 3-1.   *MultiProtocol SQL*Net network*

What Does SQL*Net Do?

As described in Chapter 1, communication in an Oracle environment can involve a single computer, client/server connections, and server/server connections. SQL*Net establishes and maintains connections between the two applications needing to communicate. SQL*Net establishes and maintains connections regardless of differences in the communicants' locations, network protocol communities, computer platforms, operating systems, or practically any other attribute. The applications communicating are generally a client application and a database server, but servers also use SQL*Net to perform distributed queries and updates and to execute server-based application logic on another server.

When an application communicates with the Oracle7 server, it generally performs one function: it supplies a SQL statement and waits for a result set. As described in Chapter 1, there are a relatively small number of SQL statement types that are performed. What makes SQL*Net remarkable is that in addition to performing the relatively simple task of channel control, it does so across disparate technologies. Complicating this are the demands required of a distributed database technology. Remember, a distributed database system must appear to the user to be no different from a local database system. So SQL*Net must also perform the following functions:

- Determine where a database is located
- Resolve data representation differences between the client and server technologies
- Establish and keep the channel open across multiple-network protocols
- Gracefully handle disconnections

How Does SQL*Net Work?

The diagram in Figure 3-2 shows the various layers involved in a client/server connection using SQL*Net. Recall from Chapter 1 that there are varying degrees of distribution of work across the client/server spectrum. Regardless of how the work

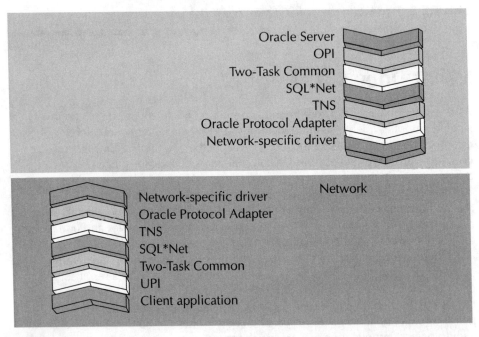

Oracle Server
OPI
Two-Task Common
SQL*Net
TNS
Oracle Protocol Adapter
Network-specific driver

Network

Network-specific driver
Oracle Protocol Adapter
TNS
SQL*Net
Two-Task Common
UPI
Client application

FIGURE 3-2.   *Components of a SQL*Net client/server connection*

is distributed, today's typical strong client provides all of the user presentation technology and much of the raw data manipulation technology, including screen I/O and application navigation. To interact with the database either to establish the connection or exchange data, the user application communicates directly with User Programmatic Interface (UPI).

User Programmatic Interface (UPI)

The UPI is not a product, but is rather the layer expressed by the particular applications programming interface (API) used to develop the client application. The UPI is the necessary interface between the SQL language the server understands and the user application itself. It is accessed through one of several forms:

- A run-time program, such as that used with Oracle Developer/2000's Forms or Reports

- Embedded SQL using one of the Oracle Precompilers, such as Pro*C

- 3GL function calls to the Oracle Call Interface (OCI)

In most cases the UPI was developed using OCI itself, regardless of the method employed.

Why is the UPI necessary? It is not just a matter of saying, "Hey, server! Send over all of the department records." As discussed in Chapter 1, a series of steps must be performed by Oracle to ensure proper interpretation and execution of the SQL statement, beginning with parsing and binding and ending with successful transmission of the result set to the client application. These are all functions that involve the UPI.

The client application must provide a buffer to hold the data set returned from the server. The UPI is responsible for populating this client-application buffer with the return data set. Additionally, the UPI must inform the client application of the status of the call to the server and the number of rows returned, notify the client application of NULL data fields, and handle server disconnections.

In the Oracle Precompilers, a structure called *sqlca*, the SQL communications area, is used to pass status information to the user application from the UPI, including error message text. *Indicator* variables associated with each column are used to flag NULL fields.

Where multiple rows are returned, the orderly processing of these rows must be provided by the UPI as well. It is the UPI that fills up the return data set buffer, and, if more records are returned than the buffer can hold, makes subsequent trips to the server to retrieve, or *fetch*, the remaining rows. Oracle has designed the UPI to efficiently perform such operations. In many cases, the UPI is capable of performing multiple operations in a single exchange with the server.

Two-Task Common

The server and the client are likely to be running on different technology platforms. The client application is likely to be running on an environment optimized for end-user productivity, such as Windows 95. The server, however, is usually best situated on a high-performance operating system such as Unix or MVS. This leads to the possibility of character-set differences such as those between ASCII, commonly used in open systems, and EBCDIC, the standard code set for mainframes. Even where both systems use ASCII, there is the potential problem of bit-orientation. And National Language Support (NLS), with its issue of single-byte versus multibyte character sets, increasingly is a potential problem in distributed systems.

DEFINITION
Bit-orientation: In microprocessor technology, you can order bits from least-significant to most-significant, significance referring to those with the highest magnitude. Big-endian format is where the most significant bits come first; little-endian is the opposite. For more information, see **http://www.cis.ohio-state.edu/htbin/ien/ien137.html**.

DEFINITION
National Language Support (NLS): A standard means of enabling localization, whereby client applications reflect local language conventions, including character set, date, and currency formatting.

Two-Task Common resolves these differences. When the session is first established, and only that time, SQL*Net determines what differences exist, if any, and directs Two-Task Common to intercede throughout the rest of the session and perform only those conversions required.

SQL*Net

SQL*Net per se serves to establish the connection between the client and the server. It passes requests for *connections* and *disconnections* onto and from the Transparent Network Substrate (TNS). In addition to determining the need for Two-Task Common, SQL*Net handles all *data operations* that must be performed. And it also handles certain *exception conditions* that may arise in the course of a session.

Connection Operations

SQL*Net supports two connection operations: connecting to a server and disconnecting from a server. These are referred to as *open* and *close*, respectively. In the open operation, the CONNECT statement is set up using the username, password, and service name specified by the client application. The *service* name is the name that uniquely identifies a database server in a TNS network.

The close operation may be initiated in one of several ways. The first is the *user-initiated* disconnection, in which the client application, or server in the case of server/server communications, has finished its business at the server, and requests disconnection, usually by use of the COMMIT WORK RELEASE or ROLLBACK WORK RELEASE statements.

The next type of close operation occurs when a new database connection is requested without first explicitly closing the extant database connection. In this case, an implicit close is performed before the new connection is attempted. The new database connection need not be to a different database; it just needs a different user name to cause the implicit close.

The third type of close operation happens when an *abnormal connection termination* has occurred in a layer below SQL*Net. In such cases, SQL*Net will likely not be aware of the termination until a subsequent SQL*Net operation is required. At that time, the TNS layer software should recognize the failure condition and instruct SQL*Net to close and release the connection. SQL*Net then alerts the client application of the failure so that it too may handle the situation gracefully.

Beginning with SQL*Net Release 2.1, a fourth type of close condition was provided for. Timer Initiated Disconnect, or *Dead Connection Detection*, handles the case of connections that remain open following the abnormal termination of the client application. When Dead Connection Detection is enabled, a special message is periodically sent from server to client. Should the message fail to successfully reach the client or should the client not respond, the current connection will be closed and the server process, the server end point to the connection, will exit.

NOTE
The server process is not the same as the database server. The server process is the communications point on the database server machine handling incoming connections. More information on server processes is found later in this chapter under the heading "Listener."

Without Dead Connection Detection, resources are wasted and database performance may be severely degraded by unreleased locks on data and the unnecessary servicing of the server process. Also, when the session is released, all uncommitted database transactions are explicitly rolled back by the database server, and locks held by the user, which hold the broken connection, are released.

Data Operations

SQL*Net is capable of four types of data operations. Most common are *synchronous send* and *receive* operations. A message is sent from the client to the server, and a response is awaited from the server to the client. In synchronous send and receive, the receive operation must complete before another send operation is allowed.

With version 2 of SQL*Net came *asynchronous send* and *receive*. In such cases, multiple send operations may be received at the server without intervening receives at the client. Asynchronous send and receive was added to support Oracle7's multi-threaded server (MTS) configuration. This feature is also used in Dead Connection Detection where a receive at the client is required, although it may be in a synchronous send at the time.

Exception Operations

Exceptions are abnormal conditions. SQL*Net performs three types of exception operations. The first two, *connection reset* and *test connection,* are used internally by some SQL*Net applications. Oracle's SQL*Net documentation specifies that these are generally used to resolve network timing issues.

The third exception operation is that of initiating a *break* over the TNS connection. A break is a request to interrupt the current process or connection. Typically, a break is user-initiated when a key is pressed, such as CTRL-C or INTR on the user's keyboard. This is usually done to abort an incorrectly entered query or stop an abnormally long-delayed transaction.

The server is also capable of initiating a break. This typically occurs when the server recognizes that a stream of data originating at the client will fail to process correctly. Rather than letting the data flow continue unabated and then fail, the server sends a break to the client application. Oracle's SQL*Loader utility can create such a condition.

In-Band Breaks   SQL*Net can initiate breaks as in-band or *in stream* messages. This means that the break request is communicated as a TNS message. The receiving application must be set up to handle asynchronous TNS break requests. This is not always the case, as it is up to the application developer, not Oracle, to periodically check for this condition.

Out-of-Band Breaks   SQL*Net can also provide *out-of-band* breaks. In such cases, the break request is transmitted not through TNS but through some other means. Again, however, the receiving software must know how to accommodate this break request and respond appropriately.

Out-of-band breaks are communicated by implementation-specific means. In Unix, when using the Pipe two-task driver (also known as the BEQUEATH driver), the driver indicates an out-of-band break by sending signal SIGCONT to the *oracle* process. Also in Unix, when using the TCP/IP drivers, SIGURG is the signal raised to announce an out-of-band break.

Depending on the protocol in use, the default break mode varies. Primarily because of this, when communicating across multiple protocols using the Oracle MultiProtocol Interchange, only in-band breaks are supported. Additionally, some protocols and operating systems do not support out-of-band breaks.

TIP

Here is a tip straight from Oracle's documentation for the Oracle Protocol Adapter for TCP/IP on Solaris 2. The TCP/IP networking software supports the mechanism utilized by SQL*Net TCP/IP for out-of-band breaks. With SQL*Net V1, the orasrv program is set up to negotiate out-of-band breaks by default. This is also true for the SQL*Net V2 listener process. Depending on how often SQL*Net communication is taking place between a client and server, the improvement in performance when using out-of-band breaks is 0 to 20 percent over using in-band breaks. Some users have seen even bigger improvements.

Transparent Network Substrate (TNS)

The Transparent Network Substrate (TNS) provides a consistent peer-to-peer communications layer functioning over all standard network protocols. Through TNS, network applications such as SQL*Net can operate without regard to the underlying networking technologies. Additionally, TNS provides the necessary infrastructure required to establish and manage sessions across different network protocols.

TIP

In the documentation for SQL*Net Release 2.2, Oracle states, "TNS is the foundation component of all current and planned network products from Oracle. Today, TNS networks connect Oracle clients and servers through SQL*Net V2. In the future, Oracle Corporation will provide additional TNS-based application connectivity tools." This being the case, understanding the role and abilities of TNS will become increasingly important to the Oracle Networking expert.

Network Transparency

SQL*Net performs consistently, irrespective of the presence of an underlying network technology. The presence or absence of a network and of SQL*Net itself is unknown to the application. This is called *network transparency* and is one of Date's 12 objectives for distributed database systems. SQL*Net achieves network transparency through TNS.

Location Transparency

Upon request for connection from the client through SQL*Net, TNS determines the physical location of the service. TNS uses information typically maintained through the Oracle Network Manager application to determine the location of a service. This automatic determination of a database's location fulfills another of Date's ideals, the need for *location transparency*. As described in Chapter 1, the physical location of a database object in Oracle is irrelevant to the application. Synonyms and database links are used to associate database objects, such as tables and views, with service names.

   The location of services may be resolved via a file accessible from the client computer called TNSNAMES.ORA. This is one of the files Oracle Network Manager creates and maintains. TNSNAMES.ORA maps service names to *connection descriptors*. Connection descriptors identify the computer the database server is on and the address for that database's *listener*. The listener is the SQL*Net utility that waits for incoming connection requests at the server and completes the connection to Oracle Programmatic Interface (OPI) at the server end. The following listing shows a simple TNSNAMES.ORA file. The listener program is described later in this chapter. Oracle Network Manager is described in detail in Chapter 5.

```
###############
# Filename......: tnsnames.ora
# Name.........: LOCAL_REGION.world
# Date.........: 29-DEC-95 09:16:12
###############
Oracle_Internet_Server.world =
  (DESCRIPTION =
    (ADDRESS_LIST =
      (ADDRESS =
        (COMMUNITY = TCP.world)
        (PROTOCOL = TCP)
        (Host = OIS)
        (Port = 1526)
      )
    )
    (CONNECT_DATA =
```

```
     (SID = OIS)
     (GLOBAL_NAME = Oracle_Internet_Server.world)
   )
 )
```

Oracle Names   The Oracle Names application may also be used to resolve the location of the service. Oracle Names provides dynamic name resolution through the use of Names servers. Where an environment already has a native naming service, Oracle Native Naming Adapters enable Oracle Names to use them. Native naming services supported include Network Information Services (NIS), Distributed Computing Environment's Cell Directory Service (DCE's CDS), Banyan's StreetTalk, and Novell's NetWare Directory Services (NDS). Oracle Names and Oracle Native Naming Adapters are discussed in detail in Chapter 4.

Protocol, Media, and Topology Independence

TNS offers *protocol, media,* and *topology independence,* where the network protocols in use may differ at all layers, including

- Network protocol, including TCP/IP, SPX/IPX, and LU6.2

- Media, including twisted pair, coaxial cable, and fiber

- Topology, including ring, hub and spoke, and bus

If, in locating the service, TNS determines that it is on a different network protocol, another SQL*Net application, the MultiProtocol Interchange (MPI), is employed. MPI ensures complete heterogeneous networking when using SQL*Net.

If more than one path is available, TNS determines which is most efficient for routing the session, using the cost value entered during MPI setup in Oracle Network Manager. The MultiProtocol Interchange is covered in detail in Chapter 4.

Encryption and Secure Network Services

Another function TNS may perform is that of securing communications between TNS applications. Through the use of Oracle's Secure Network Services (SNS), TNS may establish secure communications on a per-session or permanent basis. The types of security measures available include complete encryption of TNS packet contents to prevent unauthorized viewing; sequenced message digests to prevent unauthorized modification and retransmission of packets; and through Oracle Authentication Adapters, access to sophisticated network security technologies, including Distributed Computing Environment (DCE), Kerberos, SESAME, and SecurID Smart Card. For more information, see the SNS section in Chapter 4, where distributed processing security in general and Secure Network Services in particular are also discussed.

Oracle Protocol Adapters

Oracle Protocol Adapters are protocol-specific network applications that encapsulate TNS packets within the protocols' data areas. Situated between TNS and the network protocol stack, they translate TNS directives into the protocols' own connection requirements. They also perform similar functions in the opposite direction.

Listener

On the server side only, a special application called the *listener* is necessary. This program listens for incoming connection requests. It can handle multiple databases and multiple protocols. It is managed using the LSNRCTL application, described in detail in Chapter 8. Listener configuration is usually performed through Oracle Network Manager.

NOTE
On some platforms, notably DECnet and APPC/LU6.2, the protocols have generic listener applications or other types of connection acceptance software that are able to accept TNS connection requests and process them. Oracle also refers to these as *Native Listeners*.

Incoming connection requests must specify the service with which they seek to establish communication. The listener uses this information to establish a connection to the appropriate *server process* on that machine. The server process is the connection point to the Oracle Server. The Oracle Server may be configured to use *dedicated server* processes or may be in a *multi-threaded server (MTS)* configuration. Each behaves slightly differently from the other, and there are trade-offs in the selection of one over the other. Appropriate method selection is described in Chapter 8.

Dedicated Server Processes
In a *dedicated server* configuration, for each inbound connection, the listener launches a server process that is then dedicated to servicing that connection until it is completed. Upon completion of the session, the server process goes away. This configuration does introduce a processing delay while the server launches and sets up. The diagram in Figure 3-3 shows the steps in the process.

Multi-Threaded Server (MTS)
The listener also may be configured to assign incoming connections to one of a small number of shared server processes that persists beyond the life of the connection. This is in what is called a *multi-threaded server (MTS) configuration*.

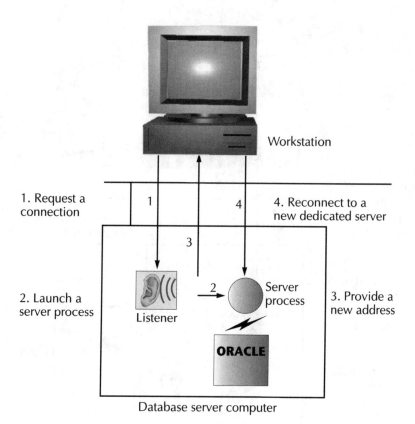

Workstation

1. Request a
connection

1

4

4. Reconnect to a
new dedicated server

3

2. Launch a
server process

2

Server
process

3. Provide a
new address

Listener

ORACLE

Database server computer

FIGURE 3-3.   *Dedicated server processes*

MTS is ideal for circumstances where there are a large number of connections, as it
reduces the server operating system's memory and processing requirements.

MTS relies on a *dispatcher* process. The initial connection to the listener results
in the return of the address of the least-used dispatcher process. The connection to
the listener is then terminated and the client restarts a connection to the dispatcher
process specified. The diagram in Figure 3-4 illustrates this process.

Prespawned Dedicated Server Processes

When configured to use dedicated server processes, each time the listener receives
a connection request, it spawns, or starts, a server process to handle the actual
session. This introduces a small processing delay while the server launches and sets

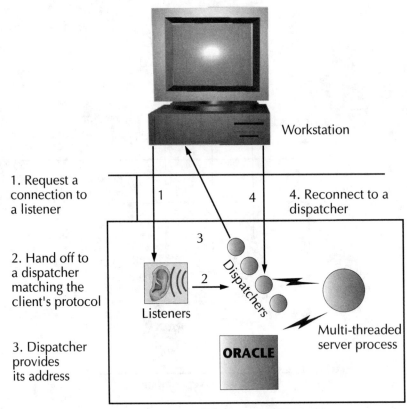

Workstation

1. Request a connection to a listener

1

4

4. Reconnect to a dispatcher

2. Hand off to a dispatcher matching the client's protocol

3

2

Dispatchers

Listeners

Multi-threaded server process

ORACLE

3. Dispatcher provides its address

Database server computer

FIGURE 3-4. *MTS dispatching*

up. To mitigate the effect of this delay, beginning with Release 2.1 of SQL*Net and requiring Oracle7 Server Release 7.1 or later, you may set up the listener to automatically prestart, or *prespawn*, dedicated server processes.

Although not as resource-efficient as the multi-threaded server configuration, prespawned server processes are useful where MTS is unavailable or where dedicated server creation is slow or resource intensive. The diagram in Figure 3-5 shows how prespawned dedicated server processes work. Instead of launching a

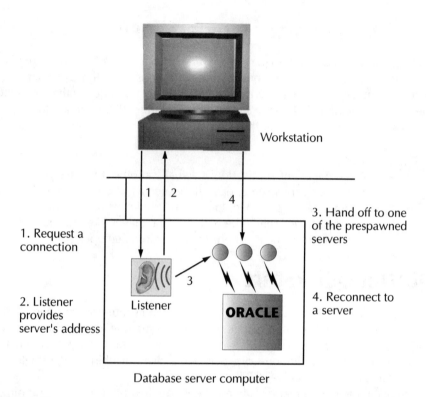

1. Request a connection

2. Listener provides server's address

Listener

ORACLE

Database server computer

Workstation

3. Hand off to one of the prespawned servers

4. Reconnect to a server

FIGURE 3-5.   *Prespawned dedicated server processes*

new dedicated server, control of the initial connection is rerouted to an extant server process. When the session ends, the server process remains available for subsequent connections.

Other Listener Applications

Some protocols, such as NetWare's SPX/IPX, have other supporting listener applications required to support protocol-specific requirements. For example, when using NetWare's SPX/IPX protocol, NTSPXCTL is used to start and stop the server advertising protocol broadcast daemon, and NTISBSDM is used to register and remove names, and to query a bindery. A *bindery* is a NetWare directory service providing name into address translation. These applications are discussed in greater detail in Chapter 8.

Oracle Programmatic Interface (OPI)

The OPI is the server-side analogue to the UPI. For each type of statement the UPI can formulate and send, the OPI must provide a response. It is the layer that directly communicates with the Oracle server, passing to it requests that originated at the client application. When the server responds, the OPI then relays the response back down the layers to the UPI and the client application.

NOTE
When the client application is actually another Oracle server initiating a server/server operation, such as when replication is automatically performed, there is a UPI-like set of code run at the initiating server called the NPI, which behaves like the UPI and performs the same functions for server-initiated operations.

SQL*Net QuickStart

Now that you know all about what SQL*Net does, you should put this knowledge to work. This QuickStart section will get you up and running while the concepts are still fresh in your mind. You will learn how to install and test a very simple but common SQL*Net configuration—one between a client machine and a single Oracle7 database server across TCP/IP.

Assume an Oracle7 server has already been installed on a computer running on the same network and across the same network protocol as the client application. The following examples show how to configure and establish a TCP/IP connection between a Sun Solaris computer running the Oracle7 Enterprise Server and a Dell Intel Pentium computer running Personal Oracle7 for Windows 95.

Confirm Network Availability

These are the most important instructions in this book. Before attempting to use SQL*Net to communicate between two computers, ensure that the two computers can already communicate across the network. Many problems users encounter in setting up distributed database solutions are network-based and not due to SQL*Net difficulties.

Step 1: Confirm That the Server Computer Can Loop Back Across the Network
Verify that the database server computer can communicate with itself with a *loopback test*. Most network protocols provide a means of testing network connections. In TCP/IP, testing is performed by using the program *ping*.

Under TCP/IP, each network device has a unique Internet Protocol (IP) address. Depending on your network configuration, IP addresses may be static or dynamic. A name resolution service such as Domain Name Service (DNS) may be used to determine the IP address of a device using its name. Otherwise, the device addresses and any names or aliases for that device are stored in a public file called *hosts*. In Unix it is located in the /etc directory. Under Windows it is usually in the \WINDOWS directory.

TCP/IP has a special IP address reserved for loopback tests, *127.0.0.1*. This address is used to perform internal checks of the networking software. If such a test fails, then the SQL*Net connection will also fail, as the network software is either not installed or not configured properly on the computer.

Test the connection using the name of the server computer. This ensures that name resolution, at least on the server computer, is working properly. The following test was performed on a Sun SparcStation 5 computer named saraswati.com running Solaris 2.4:

```
# ping saraswati.com
saraswati.com is alive
# _
```

NOTE
On some systems, the ping utility may be inaccessible to nonsupervisory users. In these examples, the super-user, or root, is running the ping utility.

If the previous test failed when using the machine name, try it using the loopback address, 127.0.0.1.

```
# ping 127.0.0.1
127.0.0.1 is alive
# _
```

If the loopback address test was successful, network name resolution is at fault. Check the DNS or hosts file and ensure the name matches the correct IP address for the machine. If subsequent testing still fails, then run the test using the correct IP address for the machine. If this works, alert the network manager to a likely name resolution problem affecting both the loopback address and the machine name.

Step 2: Confirm That the Client Computer Can Loop Back
Follow the instructions in Step 1 on the client computer to ascertain whether the network setup is correct on that end as well. The dialog box here shows the NetManage Chameleon Windows ping utility performing the loopback test.

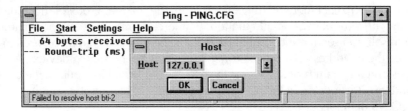

The successful result of such a test is displayed in the resulting dialog box, shown here:

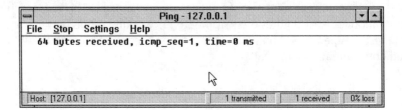

Should the test fail, follow the suggestions for a failed server test in Step 1.

NOTE

In Windows 95 and NT, the native ping utility is a character application, not a windowed application.

Step 3: Confirm That the Client Computer Can Successfully Reach the Server Computer

Use ping to check the client's ability to communicate with the server. If the computers cannot communicate with each other, verify that the network media between them are correctly connected. Another possible source of trouble in TCP/IP networks are routers and other devices used to segment, or *subnet*, networks. Often, messages intended for another computer fail to reach their destination due to network segmentation problems. Contact your network system administrator to correct such problems.

SQL*Net Configuration

Now that basic network connectivity has been confirmed from both the client and server computers, you are ready to produce your SQL*Net configuration files.

TIP
If you are installing a new SQL*Net release 2.3 network, the Dynamic Discovery Option (DDO) of Oracle Names V2, now included with SQL*Net, may be a better solution. See Chapter 4 for more information on Oracle Names and DDO.

There are two ways to create the SQL*Net configuration files. For configuring simple, single-community networks, SQL*Net Easy Configuration is the tool to use. For more complicated network setups where Oracle Names or the MultiProtocol Interchange are involved, the more sophisticated Oracle Network Manager is necessary. All of these products are discussed in detail in Chapters 4 and 5.

CAUTION
You should use only one SQL*Net configuration utility on any single machine. Each utility relies on a different set of files to maintain configuration information necessary to generate the final, distributable *.ora files.

Using SQL*Net Easy Configuration
To further simplify your initial SQL*Net connections, Oracle has developed a simple SQL*Net setup utility, called SQL*Net Easy Configuration. Here is how to set up the SQL*Net configuration files on the client side using this 32-bit application that is available for Windows 95, Windows NT, OS/2, and Power Mac.

CAUTION
Although the SQL*Net *.ora configuration files can be created and updated manually, the risk of creating invalid files, further complicating the connectivity process, is too great to make the manual approach reasonable.

Step 1: Start SQL*Net Easy Configuration   The program is $ORACLE_HOME\BIN\EASYCFG.EXE. In Windows 95 you run it from Start | Programs | Oracle for Windows 95 | SQL*Net Easy Configuration, as shown in Figure 3-6. On Windows NT, the program is found in the Oracle for Windows NT program group. On the Power Mac, the program is in the Oracle: Applications: Networking folder. In OS/2, the program is run through the Oracle Installer.

Step 2: Add a Database Alias   The screen in Figure 3-7 appears when SQL*Net Easy Configuration is launched. The first step is to add a *database alias*. This sets up an alias to the service name for a particular database. To do so, ensure the first radio button "Add Database Alias" is selected. Then click on the OK button.

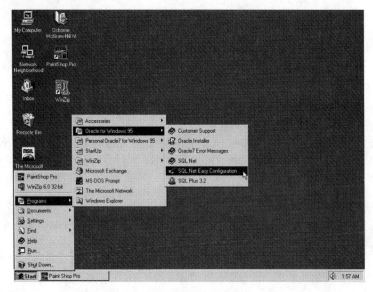

FIGURE 3-6. *Starting SQL*Net Easy Configuration in Windows 95*

Step 3: Choose a Database Alias   The following dialog box appears. Enter the name of the database alias in the text box. For our example, I assigned the alias "OIS." Then click on the OK button, as shown here.

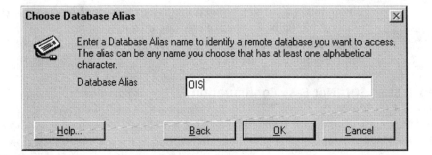

NOTE
You may also press the button labeled "Back" to return to previous dialog boxes and the button labeled "Cancel" to return to the Main dialog box. Additionally, there is a Help button that describes the process and the purpose of each text box entry.

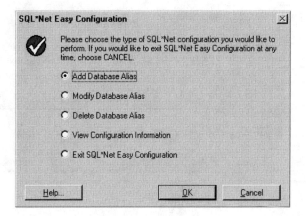

FIGURE 3-7.   *First SQL*Net Easy Configuration dialog box*

Step 4: Choose a Protocol   If you installed more than one Oracle Protocol Adapter on the client, the Choose Protocol dialog box appears. If so, select the appropriate protocol, as shown here. Otherwise, proceed to Step 5.

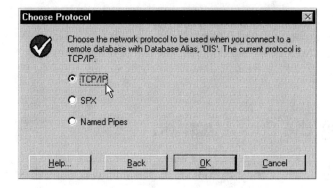

Step 5: Choose the TCP/IP Host Name and Database Instance   Enter the name of the TCP/IP host or the host's IP address in the text box labeled "TCP/IP Host Name." In this example, enter the host name **saraswati.com**. Then enter the SID, which is the name of the database instance for which this alias is being set up. The SID shown here is OIS. Then click on the OK button.

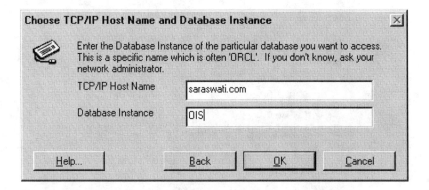

Choose TCP/IP Host Name and Database Instance ☒

Enter the Database Instance of the particular database you want to access. This is a specific name which is often 'ORCL'. If you don't know, ask your network administrator.

TCP/IP Host Name: saraswati.com

Database Instance: OIS

| Help... | | Back | OK | Cancel |

NOTE
The alias and the SID do not have to match, as shown here. However, the service name does have to match the global database name. See Chapter 5 for more information.

Step 6: Confirm Adding Database Alias   The dialog box in Figure 3-8 appears. Verify that the values shown for each attribute are correct. If not, you may press either the Back button to return to previous dialog boxes or the button labeled Cancel to restart the process. If the values are correct, click on the OK button.

Step 7: Exit SQL*Net Easy Configuration   The main dialog box for the SQL*Net Easy Configuration program displays, as shown in Figure 3-9. You may now exit the program, add, modify, delete, or view database aliases. To exit, select the radio button labeled "Exit SQL*Net Easy Configuration" and then press the OK button.

Checking the Configuration

With SQL*Net Release 2.1 and later, Oracle TNSPING is provided. Similar to the TCP/IP ping utility, TNSPING runs on the TNS network application layer. You provide the name of the service and the number of times to ping it. The dialog box in Figure 3-10 shows TNSPING being run.

CAUTION
TNSPING only confirms that the listener has been reached. The database instance is not guaranteed to be up. NetTest, TNSPING's precursor, checked for the database instance, but required a valid user and password to do so, thus mitigating its utility as a purely TNS diagnostic tool.

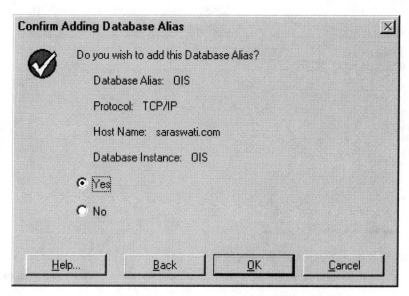

FIGURE 3-8.   *Confirm Adding Database Alias dialog box*

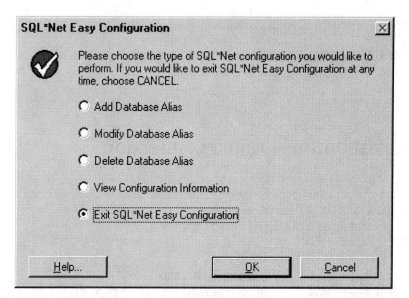

FIGURE 3-9.   *Exiting SQL*Net Easy Configuration*

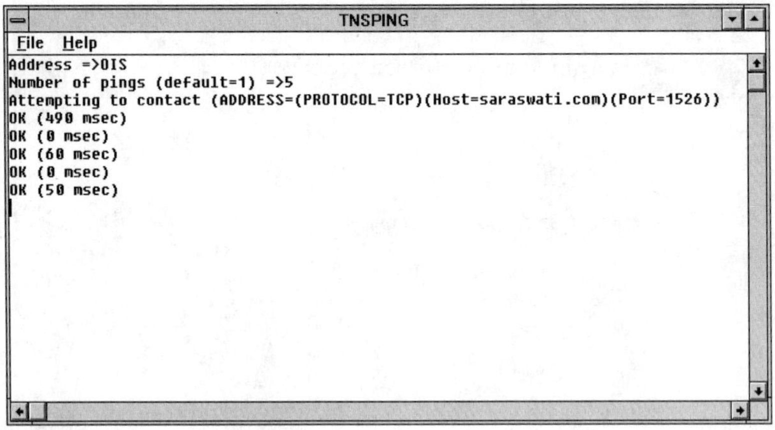

```
─                        TNSPING                    ▼ ▲
 File  Help
Address =>OIS                                           ▲
Number of pings (default=1) =>5
Attempting to contact (ADDRESS=(PROTOCOL=TCP)(Host=saraswati.com)(Port=1526))
OK (490 msec)
OK (0 msec)
OK (60 msec)
OK (0 msec)
OK (50 msec)
                                                        ▼
 ◄ ◄                                                  ► ►
```

FIGURE 3-10.   *TNSPING in process*

Should the test fail, however, one of the following messages is likely to appear. The most likely case is an incorrectly entered service name that results in this message:

TNS-12154: TNS: Could not resolve service name

Another likely cause is that of a listener that has not been started on the database server side. It results in the message shown here.

TNS-12541: TNS: no listener

Troubleshooting a Failed Connection

Log onto the database server machine as an established Oracle user. This user should have the following environment variables properly set: ORACLE_HOME and ORACLE_SID. To do this under Solaris, run the Bourne shell script oraenv, or *coraenv* if running the C shell. Ensure also that the user's PATH includes $ORACLE_HOME/bin.

Step 1: Confirm That the Database Is Started
Using a simple client application such as SQL*Plus, confirm that the database server has been started, is currently running, and is available to be connected to. Connect to the database using any known valid user name and password

combination. The account you use is not relevant; determining if a connection is possible is the goal of this test. Success is confirmed when the "Connected" message is returned. You confirm the database instance is correct by checking the global_name in the database. Here is a transcript of such a test:

```
$ sqlplus scott/tiger
SQL*Plus: Release 3.2.2.0.1 - Production on Thu Jan 04 02:03:30 1996
Copyright (c) Oracle Corporation 1979, 1994.  All rights reserved.

Connected to:
Oracle7 Server Release 7.2.2.3.0 - Production Release
With the distributed, replication and parallel query options
PL/SQL Release 2.2.2.3.0 - Production

SQL> select * from global_name;

GLOBAL_NAME
-------------------------------------------------------------------------
OIS.WORLD

SQL> _
```

If you receive error ORA-01017, "Invalid username or password," check that the name and password combination you entered is correct. SQL*Plus will give you three chances to enter a correct pair.

If you receive error ORA-01034, "ORACLE not available," the database server is not started. Start the Oracle instance. If authorized, use the dbstart shell script to start the instance, as shown here:

```
S dbstart

SQL*DBA: Release 7.2.2.3.0 - Production on Thu Jan  4 21:02:12 1996

Copyright (c) Oracle Corporation 1979, 1994.  All rights reserved.

Oracle7 Server Release 7.2.2.3.0 - Production Release
With the distributed, replication and parallel query options
PL/SQL Release 2.2.2.3.0 - Production

SQLDBA> Connected.
SQLDBA> ORACLE instance started.
Database mounted.
Database opened.
```

```
Total System Global Area        4434160 bytes
               Fixed Size          49760 bytes
            Variable Size        3966608 bytes
         Database Buffers         409600 bytes
             Redo Buffers           8192 bytes
SQLDBA>
SQL*DBA complete.


Database "OIS" warm started.


$ _
```

Step 2: Confirm That the TNS Listener Is Up and Running

The listener is the software component of SQL*Net that responds to requests for connections made across a TNS network. The listener is started using the LSNRCTL command. It is usually located in the ORACLE_HOME/bin directory. To check the status of the listener in Unix, issue the following command:

```
$ lsnrctl status
LSNRCTL for SVR4: Version 2.2.2.0.0 - Production on 03-JAN-96 23:55:28


Copyright (c) Oracle Corporation 1994.  All rights reserved.


Listening on:
(DESCRIPTION=(CONNECT_TIMEOUT=10)(ADDRESS=(PROTOCOL=IPC)(KEY=OIS)))
Listening on:
(DESCRIPTION=(CONNECT_TIMEOUT=10)(ADDRESS=(PROTOCOL=TCP)(Host=saraswati.com))
(Port=1526)))


Connecting to (ADDRESS=(PROTOCOL=IPC)(KEY=OIS))
STATUS of the LISTENER
-------------------------
Alias                   LISTENER
Version                 TNSLSNR for SVR4: Version 2.2.2.0.0 - Production
Start Date              03-JAN-96 23:57:32
Uptime                  0 days 0 hr. 0 min. 0 sec
Trace Level             off
Security                OFF
SNMP                    ON
Listener Parameter File /export/home/oracle/network/admin/listener.ora
Listener Log File       /export/home/oracle/network/log/listener.log
```

```
Services Summary...
   OIS              has 1 service handlers
The command completed successfully
$ _
```

If, instead, the following result appears, the listener has not been started:

```
LSNRCTL for SVR4: Version 2.2.2.0.0 - Production on 03-JAN-96 23:55:28

Copyright (c) Oracle Corporation 1994.  All rights reserved.

TNS-01101: Could not find service name LISTENER
 NNC-00406: name "LISTENER" does not exist
$ _
```

To start the listener process, enter the following command:

```
$ lsnrctl start

LSNRCTL for SVR4: Version 2.2.2.0.0 - Production on 03-JAN-96 23:55:28

Copyright (c) Oracle Corporation 1994.  All rights reserved.

Welcome to LSNRCTL, type "help" for information.


TNSLSNR for SVR4: Version 2.2.2.0.0 - Production
System parameter file is /export/home/oracle/network/admin/listener.ora
Log messages written to /export/home/oracle/network/log/listener.log
Listening on:
(DESCRIPTION=(CONNECT_TIMEOUT=10)(ADDRESS=(PROTOCOL=IPC)(KEY=OIS)))
Listening on:
(DESCRIPTION=(CONNECT_TIMEOUT=10)(ADDRESS=(PROTOCOL=TCP)(Host=saraswati.com)
(Port=1526)))

Connecting to (ADDRESS=(PROTOCOL=IPC)(KEY=OIS))
STATUS of the LISTENER
------------------------
Alias                   LISTENER
Version                 TNSLSNR for SVR4: Version 2.2.2.0.0 - Production
Start Date              03-JAN-96 23:57:32
Uptime                  0 days 0 hr. 0 min. 0 sec
Trace Level             off
```

```
Security                OFF
SNMP                    ON
Listener Parameter File  /export/home/oracle/network/admin/listener.ora
Listener Log File        /export/home/oracle/network/log/listener.log
Services Summary...
  OIS            has 1 service handlers
The command completed successfully
LSNRCTL>
```

If the Oracle environment variable ORACLE_HOME was not set up correctly, the following messages may appear instead:

```
Starting tnslsnr: please wait...

TNSLSNR for SVR4: Version 2.2.2.0.0 - Production
NL-00462: error loading parameter file /var/opt/oracle/listener.ora
 NL-00405: cannot open parameter file
   SNL-00821: nlfncons: file does not exist
     SVR4 Error: 2: No such file or directory
```

To correct this, run the oraenv shell script mentioned previously, and then attempt to start the listener again:

```
$ . oraenv
[OIS]?
$ lsnrctl start
...
```

Step 3: Verify the Database Server TNS Loopback

You may verify that the listener is working at the server by attempting to connect to the server from the server itself. Use SQL*Plus to connect to the database across the TNS network using the service name, as shown here:

```
$ sqlplus scott/tiger@OIS
SQL*Plus: Release 3.2.2.0.1 - Production on Thu Jan 04 02:05:15 1996
Copyright (c) Oracle Corporation 1979, 1994.  All rights reserved.

Connected to:
Oracle7 Server Release 7.2.2.3.0 - Production Release
With the distributed, replication and parallel query options
PL/SQL Release 2.2.2.3.0 - Production

SQL> select * from global_name;
```

```
GLOBAL_NAME
------------------------------------------------------------------------
OIS.WORLD

SQL> _
```

NOTE
You specify the service name on an Oracle application by appending
@service-name to the command, in this case @OIS.

On most Unix systems, you can check network status using the command
netstat. The following example shows how you confirm that you are indeed
communicating across the network and not internally through interprocess
communications (IPC) channels.

```
$ netstat -a    extraneous information has been omitted
...
     *.1526     *.*            0     0     0     0 LISTEN
client.1526   555.121.231.23 11231 0    8760   0 ESTABLISHED
...
```

This indicates that a connection is coming from the client and is indeed connecting
to port 1526, which was specified as the correct listener port for SQL*Net on the
server side.

Using Your New SQL*Net Configuration

It is time to use the SQL*Net configuration. Log onto the remote server using a
client application such as SQL*Plus, shown here:

```
┌─────────────────────────────────────────┐
│ Log On                                   │
│                                          │
│                                          │
│   User Name:    │scott              │    │
│                                          │
│   Password:     │*****              │    │
│                                          │
│   Host String:  │OIS                │    │
│                                          │
│      ┌──────────┐    ┌──────────┐        │
│      │   OK     │    │  Cancel  │        │
│      └──────────┘    └──────────┘        │
└─────────────────────────────────────────┘
```

As shown in Figure 3-11, you should have successfully connected across the TNS network. If not, retrace your steps through the section, "Troubleshooting a Failed Connection."

What More Is There to SQL*Net?

Oracle's other TNS technologies—Oracle Names, the Multiprotocol Adapter, Secure Network Services, and SNMP—are discussed in detail in Chapter 4. Also covered in Chapter 4 is the new Dynamic Discovery Option (DDO), which, in many cases, eliminates the need to create configuration files. For more complicated network configurations, Oracle Network Manager is required. This important application is covered in detail in Chapter 5.

Chapter 6 discusses application connectivity interfaces that provide access to Oracle technology with SQL*Net on the server side. Oracle's Open Gateway technology, which extends SQL*Net's reach to fully embrace mainframe systems, is covered in Chapter 7.

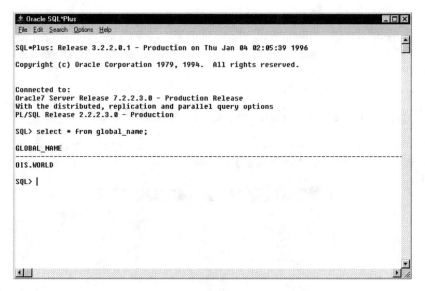

FIGURE 3-11. *Successful SQL*Plus connection*

Information on the differences between SQL*Net versions is found in Chapter 8, including coexistence of SQL*Net V1.x and V2.x components and migration from SQL*Net V1.x to V2.x. Other SQL*Net applications, specific to certain Oracle Protocol Adapters, are also described in Chapter 8.

Chapter 9 is devoted to the Oracle Enterprise Manager, a framework and associated set of tools for management of TNS and non-TNS network components. Thornier Oracle connectivity configuration considerations and troubleshooting are covered in Chapter 10.

CHAPTER 4

TNS Applications: Oracle Names, MPI, SNS, and SNMP

The true value of a network is less about information and more about community.

–Nicholas Negroponte

SQL*Net is Oracle's primary Transparent Network Substrate (TNS) technology application. It provides the means by which distributed database processes communicate. SQL*Net alone, however, cannot bridge a number of the chasms separating network communities—different network protocols, zones of responsibility, and disparate naming schemes. For these problems, Oracle has several other TNS applications that enable SQL*Net to provide for the deployment and management of enterprise-level networks. These applications serve to provide features outlined in Date's 12 Distributed Database Rules, described in Chapter 1. This chapter and the next few cover TNS network component technologies.

The TNS applications discussed in this chapter are

- Oracle Names (ON) for transparent database name resolution

- Oracle Native Naming Adapters for use of native name resolution services

- MultiProtocol Interchange (MPI) for efficient, transparent cross-protocol data communications

- Secure Network Services (SNS) for authentication and encryption services

- Authentication Adapters for seamless incorporation into enterprise security measures

- Simple Network Management Protocol (SNMP) for resource monitoring

- SQL*Net OPEN application programming interface (API) for TNS

TNS Network Components

To better understand what the applications covered in this chapter do, here are definitions of the TNS network components:

- *Node* A computer that is part of a TNS network.

- *Client* An application that contacts network services. It is also the node on which clients are run.

■ *Network service* An application that responds to clients' contacts. Some network services can also initiate contact with other network services.

■ *Database server* An application or node that provides database services. The Oracle7 database server consists of several network services including the listener, server processes, and optional TNS services, such as MPI and SNS, which together enable access to a distributed database.

■ *Server* The node on which network services are run. Often used, confusingly, as a synonym for database server.

■ *Community* A set of nodes that can communicate across the same network protocol.

■ *Connection descriptor* A set of keyword/value pairs that uniquely identifies a network service on a TNS network.

■ *Global database name* The name of a database on a TNS network that uniquely identifies it.

■ *Service name* The name given to a connection descriptor. This is the name used to uniquely identify network services on a TNS network. A database service name must be the same as its global database name.

■ *Alias* An alternative name for a service. Often used to create briefer, easier-to-remember names for use in lieu of the global database name.

Oracle Names

As described in Chapter 3, there is a unique service name associated with each Oracle database. This service name is the same as its global database name. Aliases to each service may be created as well. The means of resolving, or finding and converting, an alias or service name to a physical address should be simple and efficient. This is called *name resolution*. It allows users to use descriptive names rather than physical addresses.

The ease and ubiquity of name resolution directly affects its use. An effective name resolution facility should fulfill the following requirements:

■ Quickly resolve names

■ Support multiple name servers for fault tolerance

■ Centralize management of resource names

■ Support multiple management domains

■ Dynamically respond to physical location changes

Oracle Names meets the requirements of an effective name resolution facility, and as a TNS application, it works without any effort on the part of either the user or the developer.

Resolving Service Names

Service names are resolved transparently, or converted into a physical address by SQL*Net, in one of three ways:

■ By looking it up in the TNSNAMES.ORA file

■ By requesting name resolution of an Oracle Names server (another type of server)

■ By requesting name resolution of an Oracle Native Naming Adapter

Each service name uniquely identifies a single TNS *connection descriptor.* Every endpoint defined for a TNS network has a connection descriptor associated with it. Typically, a connection descriptor identifies a database server process. Some applications, such as the Multiprotocol Interchange, require connection descriptors for each interchange in the TNS network. Also, through the use of the SQL*Net OPEN API, developers may craft their own TNS applications, for which the server side requires a connection descriptor.

Name Space

Starting with SQL*Net V2.1, the global database name of each database is its service name as well. This means that service names must be unique across the entire TNS network. This constraint must be planned for in nontrivial networks. The key to assigning service names in a TNS network is the establishment of a rational name space. The *name space* is the universe of service names from which a naming service such as Oracle Names must determine the connection descriptor for a service. The service name is the key to locating the connection descriptor in the name space.

Most trivial networks use a flat name space; more complex ones, a hierarchical name space. The definitions of the different types of name spaces and the ways in which they differ is the subject of the following sections.

Flat Name Space

A simple TNS network encompasses a flat name space. A *flat name space* consists of simple, single-level names for services. A simple name space is shown in Figure 4-1. In this simple flat name space, the service name PRODDB is used for the production database; DEVDB for the development database; and TESTDB for the system test database.

In nontrivial network configurations, the requirement that service names be unique may be too restrictive. For example, the typical enterprise's information services department has multiple software development groups, each of which may not interact with the other except for sharing the same Oracle network. To enable multiple databases to share the same service name, such as DEVDB, for example, organizational entities called *domains* can be put in place.

Domains

A *domain* is a level in a hierarchy of Oracle network components. By creating a different domain for each development group, each domain can contain service names that are not apparently unique throughout the network. You see, a service name is the concatenation of each domain ending with the service's unique name within that domain. The uniqueness constraint is now met by no two services having the same fully qualified or concatenated name. Additionally, domains aid in the logical segregation of nodes, clients, and services.

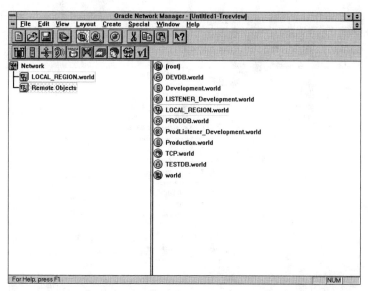

FIGURE 4-1. *A simple TNS name space*

Service names may be resolved without having to use the entire concatenated name. Each node contains the default domain in its SQLNET.ORA file. When a service name is specified, the default domain name is appended if one is not already provided, and the concatenated value is looked up.

Domains do not affect connectivity. Cross-domain communication is no different than interdomain communication. Domains exist to enable easier management of the logical network. The physical network is dependent on *protocol communities,* nodes communicating across the same network protocol, such as TCP/IP or SPX/IPX.

Hierarchical Name Space

Domains are used to create a hierarchical name space. In the case of a TNS network with three nodes, each running production, test, and development databases for each of the marketing, sales, and engineering departments, the solution is to implement a hierarchical name space. The name of the service is then unique because it is the concatenation of the domain name and the service name. Figure 4-2 shows how domain names and hierarchical naming works in practice.

NOTE
Even flat name spaces belong to domains. Although it is generally implied, the flat name space domain is called WORLD.

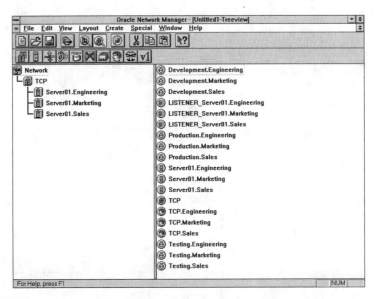

FIGURE 4-2. *A hierarchical name space*

Resolving Service Names

Where Oracle Names is not used, connection descriptors are stored in the
configuration file TNSNAMES.ORA, which contains the addresses of each service
defined through Oracle Network Manager. Without Oracle Names each node
requires access to this file in order to resolve service names. This means that the file
either is copied to each node or is centrally available in shared file storage. In this
example two databases, product development and support, are defined.

```
################
# Filename......: tnsnames.ora
# Node..........: engineering.world
# Date..........: 12-NOV-95 15:12:37
################
proddev.world =
  (DESCRIPTION =
    (ADDRESS_LIST =
      (ADDRESS =
        (COMMUNITY = tcpcomm.world)
        (PROTOCOL = TCP)
        (Host = srvr01)
        (Port = 1526)
      )
    )
    (CONNECT_DATA =
      (SID = PDEV)
      (GLOBAL_NAME = proddev.world)
    )
  )
support.world =
  (DESCRIPTION =
    (ADDRESS_LIST =
      (ADDRESS =
        (COMMUNITY = tcpcomm.world)
        (PROTOCOL = TCP)
        (Host = srvr23)
        (Port = 1526)
      )
    )
    (CONNECT_DATA =
      (SID = PDEV)
      (GLOBAL_NAME = support.world)
    )
  )
```

TNSNAMES.ORA

Each entry in the TNSNAMES.ORA file starts with a service name, such as *proddev.world,* for example. Each service name consists of a description. Each description consists of one or more listeners. Multiple listeners are supported as each node may support more than one network protocol. For each listener, the protocol community, the network protocol, and the host on which the listener runs are provided. Finally, the *connect_data* part of the structure provides the database SID and the global database name.

NOTE
Remember, the service name and global database name are identical for a database connection descriptor. This restriction was introduced with SQL*Net V2.1 to accomodate Oracle Names' automatic creation of a public database link for each database in the TNS network on every Oracle7 database in the network.

This is all well and good for simple environments with few nodes. However, the modern enterprise has greater needs. As databases are added, migrated, expanded, combined, or removed, references to those resources must themselves be altered. Suppose you have 100 users connecting to those various databases. Do you believe it is prudent to undertake the maintenance of 100 TNSNAMES.ORA files? How about 1,000? Not likely. Oracle Names mitigates the effects of resource changes by providing centralized management of resource name resolution. When saving configuration information, you may specify that Oracle Names is to be used. In this case, the configuration information is stored in database tables. Oracle Names servers may then use this information to resolve service names.

CAUTION
One common alternative to Oracle Names is the use of shared TNSNAMES.ORA files placed on file servers. It is important to benchmark the effectiveness of this solution. The net benefit of sharing a few, or even just one, TNSNAMES.ORA files quickly decreases as access latency, the time required to read a file across a network, increases.

Scalability

A single Oracle Names server should probably not be supporting 1,000 users. This could lead to congestion and decreased performance. Oracle Names supports multiple name servers, enabling the load to be distributed. From a single Oracle Network Manager session, the information on multiple Oracle Names servers may be updated. Additionally, the burden of managing the name resolution data may be distributed among multiple administrative regions.

TIP
Oracle recommends that at least two Names servers be available per community. This ensures that operation of TNS network components can survive the failure of one of the Names servers.

Users can create local TNSNAMES.ORA files that provide local aliases to TNS connection descriptors. Local TNSNAMES.ORA files are checked before Oracle Names to resolve addresses. This method does increase connection establishment latency, if employed, but may provide an efficient means of supporting legacy nodes.

Oracle Network Manager

Oracle Network Manager (ONM) simplifies the process of designing and deploying resources on a TNS network. It provides a GUI metaphor with which to develop and maintain your Oracle network. ONM can display and print out logical diagrams of your TNS network and its components in a variety of formats. Oracle Network Manager, shown in Figure 4-3, is described in detail in Chapter 5.

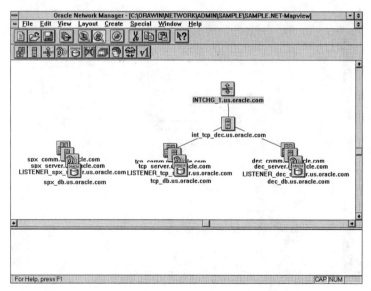

FIGURE 4-3.   *Oracle Network Manager*

CAUTION
ONM V3 only runs under Microsoft Windows. You must take the configuration information ONM creates and distribute it on the target network workstations using NetFetch or make it available through Oracle Names.

Configuring Oracle Names Servers

Oracle Network Manager is used to configure Oracle Names and implement its use in a TNS network. You click and drag the Names server icon into the map view or tree view to add it to the network configuration. The Names server is identified by the following icon:

Once the icon is dropped, a set of tabbed dialog boxes is used to configure the Names server. These values are read when the Names server is started. Figure 4-4 shows the primary tabbed dialog box for Oracle Names servers.

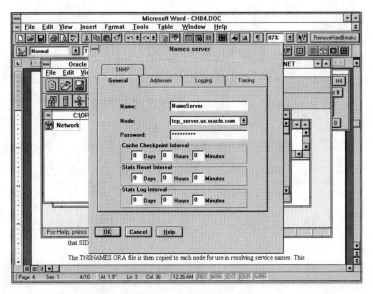

FIGURE 4-4. *Oracle Names server configuration*

General Parameters for Oracle Names
The fields in this tabbed dialog box are as follows:

■ *Name* This is the unique identifier required for every network component. There should be at least two Names servers set up. If one fails or is inaccessible, the other will be used.

■ *Node* This identifies the node on which the Names server resides. In this example, you can see a hierarchical name space is used as the name is in dotted domain format.

■ *Password* If provided, this password is required to start and stop NAMECTL, the name server application.

■ *Cache Checkpoint Interval* This value, specified in days, or hours and minutes, determines how frequently the Names server data cache is written to disk. Should the server crash, this data is used to reconstruct the current names table.

■ *Stats Reset Interval* Oracle Names servers accumulate statistical data. This value specifies how frequently the accumulated data is cleared.

■ *Stats Log Interval* As with the data cache, statistics are written to disk to limit the loss of information should the server crash. This value specifies how frequently this information is written to disk.

The other dialog box tabs and their contents are described in detail in Chapter 8.

Dynamic Discovery Option

Beginning with SQL*Net V2.3, Oracle Names V2 is being bundled in; that is, it is provided as a standard part of SQL*Net. Oracle Names V2 provides the Dynamic Discovery Option (DDO). Most useful where all nodes are running SQL*Net V2.3, DDO provides the following new features:

■ Well-known Names servers

■ Dynamic addition of services to Oracle Names servers

Additionally, the current service replication feature, by which services' information known to one Names server is provided to other Names servers, is extended. With the addition of well-known Names servers, registration with a single well-known Names server is enough to automatically propagate the information to all other Names servers.

NOTE
The term "Dynamic Discovery" is actually a misnomer. Oracle Names V2 does not discover each service. Instead, on starting up, each service notifies a *well-known* Names server of its existence.

Well-Known Names Servers

When using SQL*Net V2.3, each node automatically registers itself with one of up to five well-known Names servers whose addresses are hardcoded into Oracle Names V2. Once a service registers itself with one of these Names servers, the other services are automatically updated by the first Names server contacted. Up to five Names servers may be identified in order to accomodate multiple network protocols and provide fault tolerance. The hardcoded names for each of the Names servers are oranamesrvr1, oranamesrvr2, oranamesrvr3, oranamesrvr4, and oranamesrvr5.

CAUTION
In order to support the Dynamic Discovery Option, each Oracle Names V2 server must run on a node that supports TCP/IP. This is necessary because DDO notification is provided only as a TCP/IP service.

DDO and Domains

DDO obviates the needs for domains. Global database names will continue to be shown in hierarchical format (for example, EMPLOYEE.PAYROLL.ACME) if they were created that way, and the uniqueness of service names will continue to be enforced, but there is no longer a logical domain segmentation of services. All objects are resolvable throughout the entire database network.

Regions

When both DDO and non-DDO nodes exist in a TNS network, two administrative regions are created. *Regions* are administrative groupings of the database network. As the domain naming restrictions are meaningless under DDO, all DDO nodes are under one administrative region, and all non-DDO nodes, generally pre-SQL*Net V2.3, are under another region.

NOTE
DDO is the only difference between Oracle Names V1 and V2. Oracle Names V2 is bundled with SQL*Net V2.3.

NAMESCTL

Names servers, once installed, are network services. As such, they are programs that must be started and stopped and that occasionally may have status information queried and updated. This is accomplished through a control application. The primary Oracle Names control application is called NAMESCTL. It is used to start up Oracle Names servers and to update its names tables. The primary commands accepted by NAMESCTL are listed in Table 4-1. Of those commands, the SET and SHOW commands require a parameter to be provided. The accepted parameters are listed in Table 4-2. Use of NAMESCTL is described in detail in Chapter 8.

Command	Purpose
STARTUP START	Start up a Names server.
RESTART	Restart a Names server.
SHUTDOWN STOP	Stop a Names server.
STATUS	Display the status of the current Names server.
QUIT EXIT	Exit the NAMESCTL utility.
HELP	Display description and syntax of a NAMESCTL command.
FLUSH	Flush all foreign names from the cache.
FLUSH_NAME	Flush an individual name from the foreign data cache.
LOG_STATS	Log the current statistics to the log file.
PING	Attempt to contact another name server. If successful, display the elapsed time to a response. Otherwise, display diagnostic message.
QUERY	Query for the existence or contents of a network object name.
RELOAD	Reload the local region data into the cache.
REPEAT	Perform a name query repeatedly. Specify the number of iterations after the command.
RESET_STATS	Reset the current Names server's statistics to the state they were in at STARTUP.
SET	Set a parameter to a particular value.
SHOW	Display a parameter's current value.

TABLE 4-1.   *NAMECTL Commands*

Parameter	Description
DEFAULT_DOMAIN	Default domain for the NAMESCTL utility.
FORWARDING_ AVAILABLE	Name request forwarding status (on or off).
LOG_STATS_INTERVAL	Frequency with which statistics are logged.
NAMESCTL_TRACE _LEVEL	Level from which NAMESCTL tracing begins.
PASSWORD	Password required to perform for privileged Names server operations such as RESTART and STOP.
REQUESTS_ENABLED	Determines if Names server responds to requests.
RESET_STATS_ INTERVAL	Interval between statistics resetting. Statistics may be reset to zero or to the initial values for a particular Names server.
SERVER	Identifies Names server currently being controlled.
SYSTEM_QUERIES	For current Names server or the NAMESCTL utility. SHOW only.
TRACE_LEVEL	Trace level for the current Names server. SET only.

TABLE 4-2. *NAMECTL Parameters*

Oracle Native Naming Adapters

Oracle Names provides an effective solution to the problem of global name resolution in a TNS network. As excellent as Oracle Names is, however, it provides name resolution only for TNS services. In the modern enterprise, the problem of effective name resolution begins before Oracle technology is even installed. Network managers must have a means of identifying nodes by descriptive names rather than by their physical locations. Many times there is no physical address permanently associated with a node. Addresses are often assigned from a pool dynamically. This means that a file-based address resolution, such as a TCP/IP hosts file, is not possible.

Enterprise Naming Services

The modern enterprise usually has a robust name resolution service in place. Examples of such a service include Sun Microsystems' NIS, Novell's NDS, and the DCE CDS. These native name resolution services are not limited to resolving node addresses from names. They are all capable of storing and resolving any values by keys regardless of the purpose. As such, all can resolve Oracle service names as well. The hook into these services is provided by an Oracle Native Naming Adapter.

Configuring Oracle Native Naming Adapters

As with the other TNS applications, Oracle Network Manager is used to configure the use of Native Naming Adapters. In the Client Profile, in the Naming Services tab dialog in box, you may specify none or all of the Native Naming Adapters shown as available for use. The order is significant because it determines the order in which the name services are contacted. Name resolution begins with the first service and works its way down the list. By default, Oracle Names is the last service contacted.

You can change the order and number of Native Naming Adapters used at any time. The only restrictions are as follows:

- ■ You must not specify a native naming service until it is active; otherwise, not only will requests to the Native Naming Adapter fail, but file-based means such as local TNSNAMES.ORA files will not even be attempted.

- ■ If a Native Naming Adapter is added to an existing TNS network, you must remove all TNSNAMES.ORA files on the network. SQL*Net always consults local TNSNAMES.ORA files before it consults Oracle Names or a Native Naming Adapter. If left, the TNSNAMES.ORA file may quickly get out of sync with the naming service, yielding inconsistent results.

Chapter 8 contains more information on the incorporation of native name services and the Oracle Native Naming Adapters. Consult your operating system for more information on the native naming services themselves; they vary by manufacturer and target platform.

NOTE
Unlike Oracle Names, Native Naming Adapters are not bundled with SQL*Net V2.3.

■ MultiProtocol Interchange

The modern enterprise rarely relies on a single network protocol. To communicate across protocols generally requires software and hardware to encapsulate and extract packets of one protocol from another. Oracle provides a better, transparent means of communicating across protocols with the MultiProtocol Interchange

(MPI). Through TNS, MPI enables internetwork data communications with multiple path route optimization and with no developer or user intervention required.

As with Oracle Names, the Multiprotocol Interchange configuration is maintained through Oracle Network Manager. Through ONM, you specify where the interchanges intervene, which of several interchanges a client should default to, and other parameters the MPI uses to optimize TNS network routing.

Configuring Interchanges

Interchanges are configured through Oracle's Network Manager. As with other TNS network components, an MPI interchange is inserted into the configuration by dragging its icon into the tree or map view. The MPI Interchange icon looks like this:

Once the icon is dropped, a set of tabbed dialog boxes are used to configure the interchange. Figure 4-5 shows the primary tabbed dialog box for an MPI interchange.

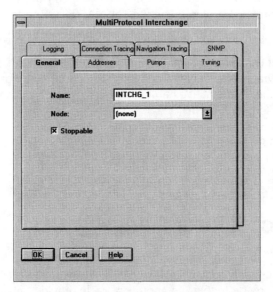

FIGURE 4-5. *Multiprotocol Interchange configuration*

General Parameters of Oracle Interchange

The fields in this tabbed dialog box are as follows:

- *Name* This is the unique identifier required for every network component.

- *Node* This is the node on which the interchange is located.

- *Stoppable* This indicates whether the interchange is remotely stoppable. As it may completely disrupt communication across network communities, it may not be desirable to allow shutdown of the interchange.

Two Values Used in Connection Routing

Two key values entered into ONM for use by the MPI include the community cost value and preferred connection managers, which are discussed in the next two sections. Optimal connection routing is determined from among multiple paths using these values.

Community Cost Value   Central to MPI is the concept of communities. As stated earlier, a community is a set of nodes that can communicate across the same network protocol. MPI facilitates communication between different communities through the use of *interchanges* located on nodes that run more than one network protocol. Each network segment between one node and another is called a *hop*. TNS design permits communication between nodes regardless of the number of interchange hops required. As there may be multiple paths to a service, MPI's configuration takes into account a user-defined cost for that segment. This is called the *community cost value.*

Preferred Connection Managers   Additionally, the concept of preferred connection managers is used to enable network designers to distribute network database traffic. Where multiple MPI interchanges are employed, each node has at least two *preferred connection managers* identified with itself. These are the interchanges selected to manage that node's connections by default. This provides for interchange congestion management.

Data Pumps

Interchanges function much like the SQL*Net Multithreaded Server. An interchange's listener and data pumps, which together form the Connection Manager, are similar to the listener and server process on the multithreaded server. The interchange navigator functions like the SQL*Net dispatcher. As with the SQL*Net listener, the Connection Manager's listener detects the connection request. The navigator then determines which *data pump,* or proxy, for the client initiating the TNS connection, should complete the connection. If one is not available, the Connection Manager launches one. Otherwise, an existing data pump is selected. This behavior is actually more like the dedicated server process in SQL*Net. And, as with SQL*Net multithreaded server dispatchers, the data pumps are specific to a single network protocol.

The selected data pump address is passed back to the listener, and the data pump is notified of the impending client connection. One of two handoffs then occurs. The Connection Manager may instruct the client to reconnect to the selected data pump. This is called a *redirect*. Otherwise, the Connection Manager may hand off, or *bequeath*, its current connection from the client to the pump.

INTCTL

INTCTL is the primary MultiProtocol Interchange application. Similar to SQL*Net's listener control and Oracle Names' NAMECTL, INTCTL can be command-line driven or operated interactively. Using commands such as START, STOP, and STATUS, the network manager can alter the behavior of network database session routing. Additionally, more specific options such as INTERCHANGE, NAVIGATOR, and CMANAGER can be used to alter the behavior of a specific MPI component.

Chapter 8 contains more information on the implementation of MPI.

Secure Network Services

Even when your network is completely internal to your enterprise, you are still required to take reasonable steps to secure your data. Data security means providing for the following:

- Hardware and software failure recovery

- Interception and theft of data

- In-transit modification of data

- Identity falsification

- Reuse of old data

As global internetworking grows, so does the likelihood that your network is vulnerable. It only takes one machine with a modem to compromise what is otherwise an isolated network. The problem, then, is to close up the points where security is most likely to be breached, across the media and at media interfaces.

Secure Network Services (SNS) solves this problem by providing the following features without intervention and with little overhead:

- *Checksumming* To ensure no message modification has taken place
- *Encryption* To ensure the message cannot be read by anyone other than the intended recipient
- *Message digest* To ensure the current message is not a previous message being retransmitted or mimicked

SNS works transparently among SQL*Net applications. Where a connection is established, SNS negotiates connection parameters. Non-SNS nodes may be blocked or may function without SNS protection as needed.

Configuring SNS Parameters

Oracle Network Manager is used to configure Oracle Secure Network Services and implement its use in a TNS network. The client profile contains SNS parameters. Automatically created for each community, additional client profiles may be dropped into the map view or tree view to add it to the network configuration. The client profile is identified by the following icon:

Once the icon is dropped, a set of tabbed dialog boxes is used to configure the client. These values are read each time the client establishes a new TNS connection server.

Client Profile Encryption Parameters for SNS
Figure 4-6 shows the primary tabbed Client Profiles dialog box. The fields in this tabbed dialog are as follows:

- *Level* This specifies whether the encryption scheme highlighted in the selected column is "Accepted," "Requested," "Required," or "Refused."
- *Selected* This identifies the encryption scheme for which the level is being set.
- *Available* This identifies the encryption schemes available to the client.

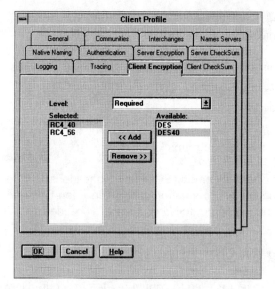

FIGURE 4-6. *Client Profile Encryption configuration*

Server Profile Checksumming Parameters for SNS

Similar tabs exist for the server-side requirements of the client configuration for SNS. Figure 4-7 shows the tabbed dialog box for server checksumming.

The fields in this tabbed dialog box are as follows:

- *Level* This specifies whether the checksumming scheme highlighted in the selected column is "Accepted," "Requested," "Required," or "Refused."

- *Selected* This identifies the checksumming scheme for which the level is being set.

- *Available* This identifies the checksumming schemes available to server processes.

Despite its sophisticated capabilities, SNS is a very simple technology to implement, with little user configuration required. What remains to be told about configuring SNS are a few other client and server profile dialog box tabs described in detail in Chapter 8.

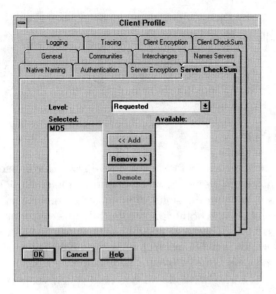

FIGURE 4-7. *Server profile client checksumming configuration*

NOTE
Secure Network Services V2 requires SQL*Net V2.2 or higher and Oracle7 release 7.2 or higher. Interaction between SNS V2 and a prior SNS version limits SNS functionality to that of the earlier release.

Oracle Authentication Adapters

Beginning with Secure Network Services V2, Oracle TNS networks can employ Oracle Authentication Adapters to seamlessly integrate with other enterprise security platforms. This enables secure integration in single sign-on environments through the use of the following external technologies:

- *CYBERSafe* for Kerberos-based centralized authentication and single sign on

- *SmartCard* for smart-card–based dynamic challenge/response authentication

Additional Authentication Adapters will be added as they become certified. Anticipated technologies include biometric sensing devices and associated software interfaces.

General information on incorporating Oracle Authentication Adapters, as well as information specific to those highlighted here, is discussed in Chapter 8.

Oracle SNMP

The Simple Network Management Protocol (SNMP) was developed to manage resources, called *managed elements*, on a network. Oracle SNMP enables resource managers to monitor the status of managed elements, alter the behavior of managed elements, and be notified automatically of exceptional conditions at managed elements. Most importantly, because the SNMP standard is a key component to enterprise network management, the needs of Oracle managers are better in line with network management capabilities when using Oracle SNMP.

Many popular enterprise network management systems support SNMP. These include the following:

- Hewlett-Packard OpenView
- Novell NetWare Management System
- SunSoft SunNet Manager
- IBM NetView/6000

Message Information Base

Central to SNMP is the concept of a management information base (MIB). It is a hierarchical structure containing control parameters and status values for a node. The MIB conveys to the SNMP management software the capabilities of the managed element, with regard to response and notification of conditions.

Originally, SNMP was for managing network components such as hosts, bridges, hubs, and routers. Because each node runs a master agent and because each managed element can also run a subagent, SNMP can be extended to include management of significant software applications such as relational databases and other multiuser server technologies such as the Oracle Media Server.

Oracle has been a leader in the development of software MIBs. The company sponsored the development of the RDBMS MIB (RFC 1697). Additional MIBs are available for Oracle's SQL*Net Listener Control utility, the MPI Interchange Control utility, Oracle Names, and the Oracle Media Server.

Configuring SNMP Parameters

Oracle Network Manager is used to configure Oracle SNMP and implement its use in a TNS network. Each Oracle SNMP-aware application contains a tabbed dialog box for its SNMP parameter maintenance. Figure 4-8 shows the SNMP dialog box for Oracle Names.

SNMP Parameters for Oracle Names

The fields in the SNMP tabbed dialog box are as follows:

- *SNMP Visible*   This specifies whether the SNMP agent is visible or merely collecting data.

- *Service Index*   SNMP MIBs are designed as hierarchies. This is the number identifying the item at its level. For example, if the MIB has three levels, this item might be 121.2.5.

- *Contact Information*   This is the standard means of providing response information to the Master SNMP application. When a condition is alerted, this contact information specifies the responsible party for that SNMP agent.

Chapter 8 provides more information on the implementation and use of Oracle SNMP.

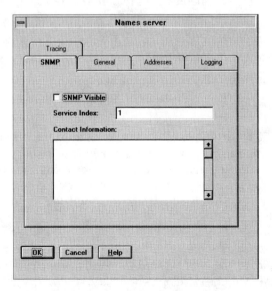

FIGURE 4-8.   *Oracle Names SNMP configuration*

SQL*Net OPEN

Open technology has been key to Oracle's success. In keeping with this principle, Oracle provides access to TNS through the SQL*Net OPEN application program interface (API). By using the API, developers may write applications that exploit the many benefits provided by Oracle's TNS technology. These benefits include transparent access to nodes across disparate network protocols and end-to-end secure communications when the Multiprotocol Interchange and Secure Network Services are in place. Use of the SQL*Net OPEN API is not limited to database applications.

Developing SQL*Net OPEN Applications

Applications using the API are typically written in pairs consisting of a client program and a server program. Server applications are launched by the listener much as are database server processes. This means that server applications must run on platforms on which the listener has been installed.

You merely configure the LISTENER.ORA file to handle your server application as it would handle a database server. As with other Oracle client applications, client applications written to the SQL*Net OPEN API do not require any configuration files.

The SQL*Net OPEN API enables users to perform the following actions:

- Establish a SQL*Net connection handle

- Send data to a connection handle

- Receive data from a connection handle

- Shut down a connection

Currently, the SQL*Net OPEN API is written for implementation through programs written in C. Sample makefiles are provided with the API, which must be modified to use the correct library and header file locations for your system.

The required header file for applications that use the API is *tnsapi.h*. It is typically found in the $ORACLE_HOME/network/include directory under Unix and by default in the directory \ORAWIN\NETWORK\INCLUDE on Windows systems.

The libraries for the API contain "TNSAPI" as part of the filename. For example, under Unix, the API library is named $ORACLE_HOME/lib/libtnsapi.a. Windows implentations require two files—TNSAPI.DLL, the dynamic link library used at runtime, and TNSAPI.LIB, the development library.

The typical SQL*Net OPEN API application performs synchronous sends and receives. This is to ensure that each send has been properly handled. It is possible to set up applications that simulate asynchronous send and receive behavior; however, as with in-band and out-of-band breaks, explained in Chapter 3, it is up to the developer to support such a feature.

CAUTION
SQL*Net OPEN is in beta through SQL*Net V2.3.2. Until it goes into production with SQL*Net V2.3.3, changes may continue to be made to the API. At that time, SQL*Net OPEN will likely contain expanded functionality. Refer to the Release Notes for SQL*Net V2.3.3 for more information.

SQL*Net OPEN API Functions

The SQL*Net OPEN API operations are performed through functions. A successful function results in a zero return value. Nonzero return values are the SQL*Net OPEN API error numbers. The SQL*Net OPEN API error numbers are described later in this chapter. The following sections describe each API function and its syntax.

TNSOPEN( )
The function TNSOPEN() is used to establish a SQL*Net connection handle. It does not establish the actual connection. SQL*Net considers connections to be made when a send function has been mated successfully with a corresponding receive function, described in the section "TNSRECV()." TNSOPEN() must always be called before any other API function. The syntax for TNSOPEN() is as follows:

```
int tnsopen(handlep, name)
void **handlep;
const char *name;
```

TNSOPEN() populates the structure pointed to by *handlep*. You must have previously allocated space for the handle to which *handlep* points. The structure pointed to by *handlep* is defined in the include file *tnsapi.h*. When writing a client application, the second parameter, *name*, must be set to the service name of its server application peer. When TNSOPEN() is called from a server application, the *name* parameter must be NULL. An API server application is called from the server process to which the listener handed off the request; therefore no service name is required.

TNSSEND( )
TNSSEND() is used to send data to a SQL*Net connection handle. The connection handle must first have been established with a TNSOPEN() call. In a client

application, this is the second API call performed after TNSOPEN(). On a server application, TNSSEND() may not be called until after an initial TNSRECV() has been performed. The syntax for TNSSEND() is as follows:

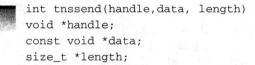

```
int tnssend(handle,data, length)
void *handle;
const void *data;
size_t *length;
```

TNSSEND() uses information in the structure pointed to by *handlep* to establish the connection. The data referred to by the pointer is in the second parameter. Finally, when calling TNSSEND(), the third parameter *points to*, but does not contain, the length of the data pointed to by the second parameter. You generally use the SIZEOF() function to set this value. On completion, the third parameter contains the number of bytes successfully sent.

TNSRECV( )
The function TNSRECV() is used to receive data sent from an established SQL*Net connection; it must always be called after TNSOPEN() in a server application. The syntax for TNSRECV() is as follows:

```
int tnsrecv(handle, data, length)
void *handle;
void *data;
size_t *length;
```

TNSRECV() uses information in the structure pointed to by *handlep* to manage the connection. The data received is stored in the previously allocated buffer pointed to by the second parameter. The third parameter *points to*, but does not contain, the size of the data buffer pointed to by the second parameter. On completion, the third parameter contains the number of bytes successfully received.

NOTE
The server application is automatically launched by the SQL*Net listener. Because multiple copies of your application may be simultaneously active, you must provide for shared access to data structures and devices.

TNSCLOSE( )
The function TNSCLOSE() is used to terminate a SQL*Net connection. The syntax for TNSCLOSE() is as follows:

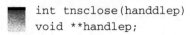

```
int tnsclose(handdlep)
void **handlep;
```

Upon successful completion, the connection is closed and resources allocated to the connection are released.

SQL*Net OPEN API Errors

SQL*Net OPEN API functions return zero on successful completion. Failed API function calls return an error number. The API error numbers begin at 20000. The following table shows API errors and their descriptions:

Error Number	Description
20002	The underlying "send" command failed in TNSSEND()
20003	The underlying "receive" command failed in TNSRECV()
20004	The operation is invalid as the server
20005	The operation is invalid as the client
20006	The connection should be initialized by calling TNSOPEN()
20007	The server failed in inheriting the connection from the listener
20008	The server failed in accepting the connection request from the client
20009	A null handle was passed into the call
20010	An invalid operation was passed into the call
20011	A malloc failed in a TNS API call
20012	The API function failed in NL (network layer) initialization
20013	The service name is too long
20014	The client connect request failed
20015	The server failed to listen for the connect request
20016	The server failed to answer the connect request
20017	The API function failed to resolve the service name
20020	A TNS error occurred

SQL*Net OPEN Sample Applications

The SQL*Net OPEN API comes with two sample client/server applications to demonstrate the use of the technology. The first sample application is a simple implementation of a finger utility. As with the common TCP/IP utility after which it is named, finger provides information about who is logged into the server computer. Unlike the TCP/IP finger, this application can function across network protocols. In addition, if Secure Network Services is in place, all of the traffic between the client and server is secured. Client versions of the program are provided for both Solaris and Windows NT. The server program is provided for use on a Unix server.

Also provided is a TNS implementation of the Trivial File Transport Protocol (TFTP). A more sophisticated application than finger, which is basically query and response, TFTP copies files from one node to the other. This application's samples come with client and server programs written for use on a Unix platform.

Conclusion

Clearly, the TNS architecture affords Oracle extensive modularity. The fact that the SQL*Net OPEN API is readily available should encourage further adoption of the TNS layer for enterprise distributed database computing. Finally, the bundling of much of the TNS application features described here, including the new Dynamic Discovery Option with the new Oracle Universal Server, ensures that Oracle is the most broadly applicable distributed database technology available.

In Chapter 5 you will learn how to configure TNS applications using the Oracle Network Manager. Look to the information in Chapter 8 to help you determine which features of the TNS applications to incorporate as you design and deploy your TNS network. Chapter 10 highlights ways in which both TNS and SNMP technologies enable the effective management of your Oracle network components.

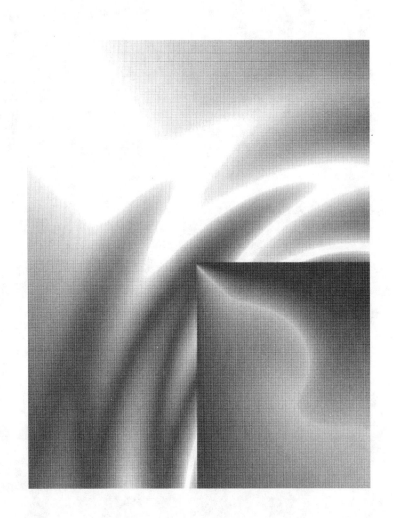

CHAPTER 5

Oracle Network Manager

A picture is worth a thousand words.

—Anonymous

Unlike the single-protocol example used in the SQL*Net QuickStart section of Chapter 3, most Oracle networks are nontrivial, consisting of multiple database servers and network protocols. As an enterprise's needs change, the resources supporting it must be repurposed. Such sophisticated network change management requires a reliable means of tracking resources. To this end, Oracle has developed its most effective means of managing the design and deployment of a Transparent Network Substrate (TNS) network, Oracle Network Manager (ONM).

Oracle Network Manager enables the data network architect to visualize the layout of the network, prior to implementing it, through a visual design metaphor. Another benefit of ONM is that the management of configuration files is automated, preventing propogation of errors as they are copied throughout the network.

NOTE
When using Oracle Names' Dynamic Discovery Option, most configuration needs are met automatically. However, when you need to set specific parameters or manage nodes outside of DDO-controlled regions, Oracle Network Manager performs these changes.

Somewhat misnamed, Oracle Network Manager is not a network monitoring tool; Oracle's network resource monitor is the Oracle Enterprise Manager, which is covered in detail in Chapter 9. Instead, Oracle Network Manager and its associated utilities—NetPrint, NetFetch, and NetConv—serve to make the design and deployment of a TNS network, as well as management of its configuration files, painless.

TIP
Although Oracle Network Manager is not a production control tool, it can be used to launch the Listener Control utility, the Interchange Control utility, the Oracle Names Control utility, and Oracle Server Manager, which in turn provide real-time resource management.

Oracle Network Manager

Oracle Network Manager is a Windows-based tool used to create, modify, validate, and distribute TNS configuration files. Unlike the SQL*Net Easy Configuration utility shown in Chapter 3, most Oracle networks must contend with multiple servers, multiple databases, and multiple network protocols. Oracle Network Manager can walk you through the process of creating the configuration files, ensuring that required configuration data is entered only once and is properly propagated throughout the network. ONM can then display the network graph, as shown in Figure 5-1. This helps visually confirm that the configuration files successfully reflect the desired network. Additionally, Oracle Network Manager, along with Oracle Names and the NetFetch utility, may be used to retrieve and distribute this information across other TNS nodes.

CAUTION

It bears repeating that Oracle Network Manager only runs under Microsoft Windows. The tools are provided to distribute the network configuration information to other nodes on the network. However, you must have a computer running Windows from which to manage the configuration information and generate the configuration files.

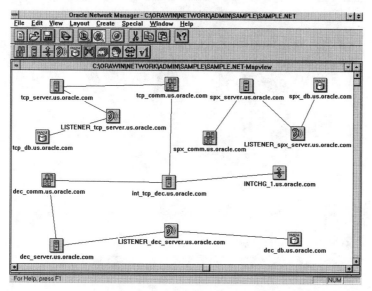

FIGURE 5-1. *Oracle Network Manager displaying an existing configuration*

In Chapter 3, you saw how simple it was to configure a connection between an Oracle7 server and a client workstation. This was done using the SQL*Net Easy Configuration utility. Most of the work was performed by following dialog box prompts. Although it was a simple means of configuring the client end of a connection, it is inadequate for full network configuration.

Oracle Network Manager provides a GUI metaphor enabling you to visually develop and maintain your Oracle network by dragging and dropping network components. Oracle Network Manager can even superimpose your configuration on an image, for example, a map allowing for a view of components logically and geographically, as shown in Figure 5-2.

Network Configuration Files

Something you did not see in Chapter 3 were the network configuration files that resulted from the use of SQL*Net Easy Configuration. In a TNS network, there may be seven of these, all with the extension .ora, as shown in Table 5-1.

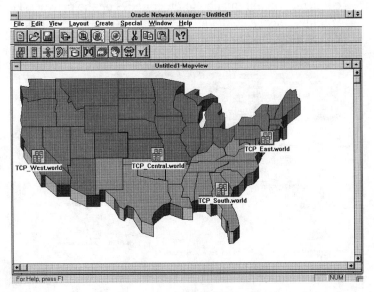

FIGURE 5-2. *Network configuration superimposed on an image*

Filename	Description
SQLNET.ORA	Contains node-specific SQL*Net configuration information
TNSNAMES.ORA	Contains service names and descriptions accessible to that node
PROTOCOL.ORA	Used to store node-specific parameters for certain network protocols
LISTENER.ORA	Contains SQL*Net listener parameters for that node
INTCHG.ORA	Contains Multiprotocol Interchange (MPI) parameters
TNSNAV.ORA	Contains MPI navigation information for clients
TNSNET.ORA	Contains community/interchange information for use by the MPI

TABLE 5-1. *TNS Configuration Files*

NOTE
PROTOCOL.ORA is exceptional in that it is not created by Oracle Network Manager. Also, while more general in purpose, the database instance configuration file INIT.ORA may also contain parameters that affect network behavior. These are discussed in detail in Chapter 8.

The SQL*Net Easy Configuration Tool only created the required client side file, TNSNAMES.ORA. It is presumed that only the client requires configuration. Even on a platform such as Windows95, where Personal Oracle7 has a listener, configuration must be performed from Network Manager and the files migrated.

CAUTION
Although the .ora files may successfully be modified manually, this is strongly discouraged. First of all, the configuration information used by Oracle Network Manager is stored in a specially formatted .net file. Changes made manually to the .ora files are not reflected in the .net file. Also, it is too easy to make mistakes in the formatting of the .ora files.

File or Database Storage?

You may store the network configuration information in the database or in a file. There are trade-offs associated with each choice. If you store the information in the database, it may be accessible from other nodes. If you store it in a file, it may not be. But if you store it in the database, you need to have the database up and accessible to work with the configuration. File-based configurations can be stored on removable medium and transported. Where nodes are on different operating systems, however, the files may not be easily exchanged. As you see, it can become a chicken-and-egg problem.

NOTE
File or database storage refers only to the network configuration information. This is not the same as retrieving TNS information from Oracle Names. This is only for the configuration information used by Oracle Network Manager, not the .ora product of its use.

Storing the Configuration in the Database

If you wish to store the network configuration information in the database, the scripts shown in Table 5-2 must be run to create the Resource Object Store (ROS) common database objects and the Network Manager database objects that hold network configuration data. The scripts must be run from a database administrator account such as SYSTEM. A tool such as SQL*Plus or SQL*DBA can be used to run the scripts. Once created, access to the objects may be granted to other users.

ROSBILD.SQL	Creates the Resource Object Store (ROS) common database objects
ROSGRNT.SQL	Grants access to common objects
ROSRVKE.SQL	Revokes access to common objects
NMCBILD.SQL	Creates the Network Manager database objects
NMCGRNT.SQL	Grants access to Network Manager database objects
NMCRVKE.SQL	Revokes access to Network Manager database objects
ROSDROP.SQL	Drops common objects
NMCDROP.SQL	Drops Network Manager objects
NMCUPDT.SQL	Updates previous versions of the Network Manager objects
ROSUPDT.SQL	Updates the ROS database object contents

TABLE 5-2.   *Resource Object Store (ROS) Database Object Scripts*

The Oracle NetPrint Utility

Oracle Network Manager uses a visual metaphor to display configurations. The NetPrint utility provides a means of viewing the network configuration as descriptive text. Upon retrieval, this text is displayed on the screen. Additionally, the contents may be printed or saved to a file. The window in Figure 5-3 is displaying part of the contents of the OIS network configuration.

CAUTION
NetPrint is released in sync with Network Manager. NetPrint can only display and print network definitions created with the corresponding version of Network Manager. If necessary, use the NetConv utility to bring the network definition up to the proper version format.

Using NetPrint

NetPrint is a very simple utility. On startup, a dialog box appears in which you specify the source of the network configuration, File or Database, as shown in the next illustration. If you are using a file-based configuration, you provide the name of the file using the standard Windows Open dialog box.

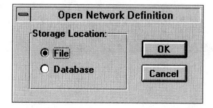

The Oracle NetConv Utility

Oracle Network Manager V3 brought a number of innovations to the tool. Additionally, it changed the format of the files used to maintain each network definition. To bring previously developed network definition files, it is necessary to first convert them using the NetConv utility. Invocation of the NetConv utility is shown in Figure 5-4.

CAUTION
As with NetPrint, NetConv is released in sync with Network Manager. NetConv updates only network definitions created with a previous version of Network Manager.

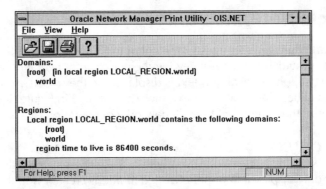

FIGURE 5-3. *NetPrint display*

The Oracle NetFetch Utility

Configuration files are generally maintained centrally. Where database access to the configuration data is not available, the configuration files must be generated and then transported to each node where they are required. However, especially

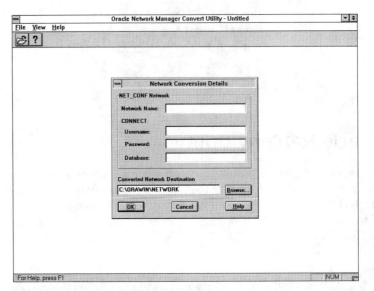

FIGURE 5-4. *The NetConv utility*

where multiple protocols are involved, there may be no means of exchanging files—except SQL*Net. The Oracle Network Manager NetFetch utility uses SQL*Net alone to transfer configuration file information between two machines on a TNS network. An example of NetFetch in use is shown in Figure 5-5.

QuickStart for Oracle Network Manager

Before you begin, you should decide several things:

- Do you want to store the information in a configuration file or the database?

- Will you be supporting multiple protocols?

- Do you want to use flat naming space or hierarchical with domains?

- Will you include SQL*Net V2 nodes in your network?

- Do you want to use Oracle Names?

TIP
Consider using a configuration file first and then converting to Oracle Names unless you are setting up the Names server first or can run Names off the first machine set up until the production Names servers are up. Doing this prevents problems should the Names server become unavailable.

```
┌──────────────────────────────────────────────────────────────┐
│ ═  Oracle Network Manager Fetch Utility - OIS.NET    ▼│▲│
│ File   View   Help                                             │
│ ┌──┐┌──┐                                                       │
│ │📂││ ?│                                                       │
│ └──┘└──┘                                                       │
│        ┌────────────────────────────────────────┐            │
│        │ ═│          Export Details               │            │
│        │ Export files for:  │OIS.world          │±││            │
│        │ Export Directory:                        │            │
│        │ │C:\ORAWIN\NETWORK          │  ┌────────┐│            │
│        │                              │  │Browse...││            │
│        │ ☐ Export with Oracle Name    └────────┘│            │
│        │  ┌──────┐  ┌────────┐  ┌────────┐       │            │
│        │  │ OK   │  │ Cancel │  │  Help  │       │            │
│        │  └──────┘  └────────┘  └────────┘       │            │
│        └────────────────────────────────────────┘            │
│ For Help, press F1                        │NUM│              │
└──────────────────────────────────────────────────────────────┘
```

FIGURE 5-5.   *The NetFetch utility*

When you first start ONM, it presumes you are modifying an existing network. ONM will prompt for file or database storage. The dialog box in Figure 5-6 shows the initial Oracle Network Manager display.

ONM Walk-Through Feature

As we are creating a new network configuration, select File and press the OK Button. The File Open dialog appears, prompting for the location of the configuration files to open. Close this window. We are going to create a new configuration. From the menu, select File | New.

Oracle Network Manager can walk you through the proper configuration of your network. You will use this feature to ensure no items are left out. Click on Yes when the following prompt appears.

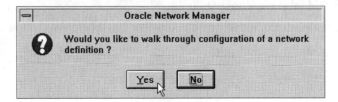

Configuring a Flat-Hierarchy, Single-Protocol Network

The dialog box in the following illustration appears. Specify a flat, single-protocol network. In this example, we indicate it is a TCP/IP protocol and the configuration is retrieved from files.

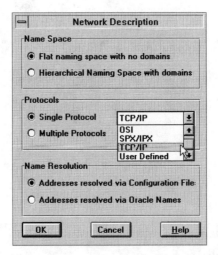

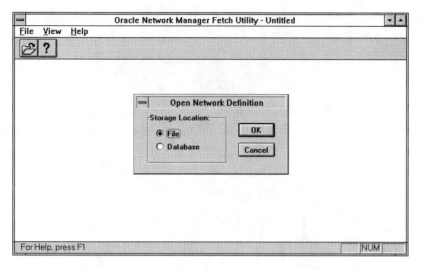

FIGURE 5-6.   *File or Database storage*

Once completed, Oracle Network Manager's walk-through feature prepares you for the next dialog box, as shown here:

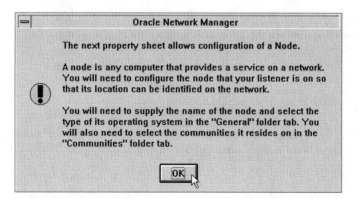

Defining Your First Node

To define your first node, generally the computer on which the first database will reside, you must provide the name, the domain, and the type of server. Figure 5-7 shows the dialog box properly populated.

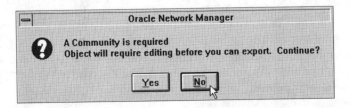

FIGURE 5-7. *Defining a node*

You must then identify the protocol community to which this node belongs. Remember that a community is a group of nodes sharing a common network protocol. Select the Community tab at the top to enter this information.

NOTE
If you accidentally pressed the OK button, Oracle Network Manager's walk-through feature will prevent you from continuing. It will display the following two warning dialog boxes in succession.

The dialog box will appear as in Figure 5-8. You need only press the Add button to have the TCP/IP community added to the node's list. Later, when multiple protocols are introduced, additional communities will be shown.

Node addition is complete. Click on No in the dialog box, as illustrated here:

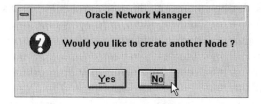

Node configuration is not yet complete. You are merely stating that you do not wish to add additional nodes at this time.

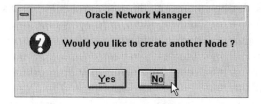

FIGURE 5-8.   *Communities tab in Node dialog box*

CAUTION

The property sheets are shown as tabbed-dialog boxes. Whenever a dialog box is up, until you save the contents to memory by clicking OK, canceling from any of the tabbed sections results in the changes made in any of the other tabbed sections within that dialog box reverting to their previous values. However, until you Save or Save as..., which writes the information to either the database or configuration file, the data is retained in memory only. It is not saved to disk for any network properties until an explicit save is performed. So save and save often!

Listener Configuration

Once again, the walk-through software will notify you of the next step, listener configuration. As shown in Figure 5-9, you should accept the default configuration provided. It is not enough to complete this tab alone; you must provide at least one listener address. In TCP/IP, this address is in the form of a port number. At the Service Address tab, press the Create button and then click on OK to accept, as shown in Figure 5-10.

Note that the listener has been created before the database. This is because the listener is capable of supporting multiple databases and therefore may precede the

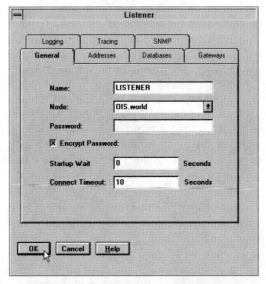

FIGURE 5-9.   *Default listener configuration acceptance*

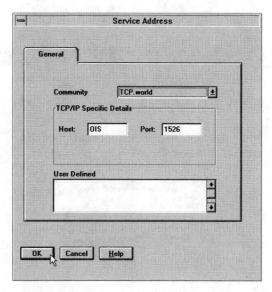

FIGURE 5-10. *Service Address tab in Listener dialog box*

database's existence. The walk-through will require a database, however, before the configuration is minimally complete and validated.

Create Database
As with previous steps, you are not actually creating the database. Rather, you are creating the configuration information that matches the database that is or will be there. The dialog box in Figure 5-11 shows the elements that must be provided: the service name, the node, the database SID, and the value for Oracle Home.

Once created, you are prompted for another listener. Click on No.

Configuration Validation and Generation
You may now save network configuration and generate the network configuration files. Click on OK and Yes in the following dialog boxes, respectively.

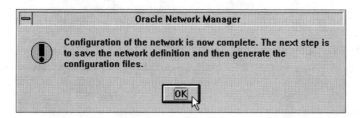

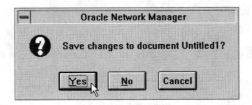

You must then specify the destination of the network configuration itself in the Save Network Definition dialog box shown in this illustration.

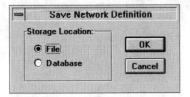

Your configuration walk-through is now complete.

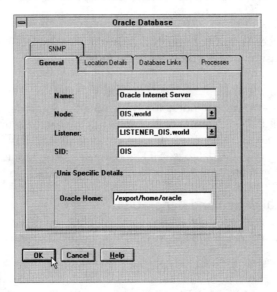

FIGURE 5-11. *Database creation tab in Listener dialog box*

Views of the Network

The Tree view of the network configuration is displayed as shown in Figure 5-12.

As you see, there is also a Mapview window. You should reposition your windows as shown in Figure 5-13 to see both. As you change the highlighted element in the left pane of tree view, the right pane will change to reflect that portion of the network hierarchy.

In Map view, you first see the network components you have configured in the bottom pane as shown in this illustration.

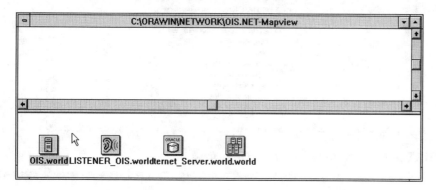

If you click and drag on the server as shown here,

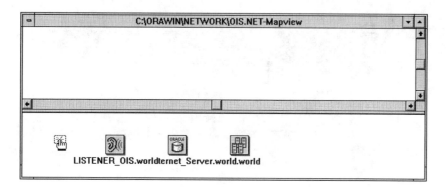

you see the community dragged up with it. Every element in the network hierarchy will pull up the levels above it if they are not already in the top pane.

When done, all of the elements for the network configuration you just created will appear as in Figure 5-14.

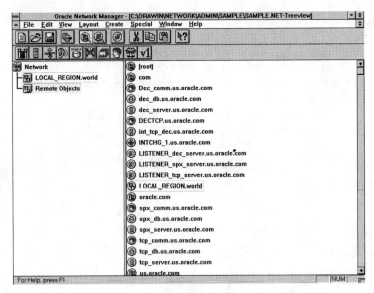

FIGURE 5-12.   *Network display in tree view*

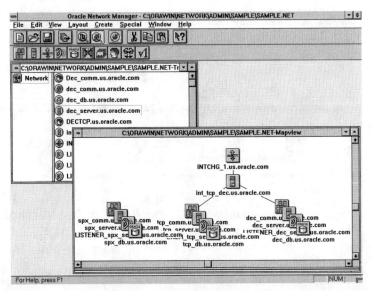

FIGURE 5-13.   *Treeview and Mapview windows*

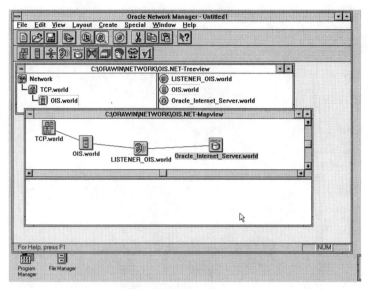

FIGURE 5-14. *Map view, showing all elements in top pane*

Advanced Network Management

The intention of this chapter was to familiarize you with Oracle Network Manager. So far, you have only been shown the basics of using it. Chapter 8 features more sophisticated examples of Oracle Network Manager's capabilities, as well as in-depth coverage of the more important aspects of TNS network design.

CHAPTER 6

Application Interfaces

. . .[U]tility is success.

—Thomas Edison

To be considered viable in the marketplace, Oracle products must be able to connect to non-Oracle7 data sources. Likewise, access to Oracle7 must be facilitated from other relevant non-Oracle applications. Without these two qualifications, Oracle technology would not have become the total solution source it now is. Both Oracle's Open Gateway technology and the Open Client Adapter for ODBC provide general solutions to this problem for Oracle-sourced connections. With them, Oracle servers and clients can establish connections to non-Oracle technology. However, those two technologies only solve some of the possible connectivity problems.

The primary connectivity technology used with Oracle products is SQL*Net. It ensures reliable connections between Oracle's products and supports Oracle's advanced features, including distributed updates, protocol transparency, and location transparency. However, SQL*Net connects only those applications developed that use Oracle's own applications programming interface (API) and that communicate across Oracle's Transparent Network Substrate (TNS).

The access methods described in this chapter are all external to SQL*Net. SQL*Net may complete the connection on the Oracle technology end, such as when using ODBC to access a remote database. However, SQL*Net is not the primary enabling technology. This connectivity between different types of applications is called *heterogeneous access.*

Heterogeneous Access Needs

There are several forms of heterogeneous access. The first is *heterogeneous data access,* such as when an Oracle application needs to communicate with a non-Oracle7 data source. The second is *heterogeneous procedural access,* such as when a non-Oracle application needs to perform Oracle7 procedures written in PL/SQL. These different forms of heterogeneous access each bridge a particular gap between technologies, but also may magnify differences between the technologies. The examples in Table 6-1 illustrate some of the different forms of heterogeneous access.

Client Application	Server Application
Forms 4.5	Access
Powerbuilder	Oracle7 Workgroup Server
Visual Basic	Oracle7 PL/SQL stored procedure
Data conversion utility	Oracle7 and Progress databases

TABLE 6-1. *Oracle/Non-Oracle Connectivity Examples*

Oracle Bridging Technologies

Access to Oracle7 from non-Oracle applications is provided by several Oracle products:

- Oracle Call Interface (OCI)
- Oracle Precompilers (Pro*C, Pro*ADA, Pro*COBOL, etc.)
- Oracle SQL*Module
- Open Database Connectivity (ODBC) drivers
- Oracle Objects for OLE (OO4O)

Access to non-Oracle7 data sources is provided by the following products:

- Oracle Open Gateway Technology
- Oracle Open Client Adapter for ODBC
- Native drivers

Each product and its appropriate application will be described in this chapter. First, however, a discussion of heterogeneous communications issues is necessary.

Heterogeneous Communications Considerations

When connecting incompatible technologies, it is important to consider trade-offs that may need to be made. The following distributed processing pitfalls may be encountered:

■ *Lack of features*   Server-side processing functions such as Oracle's stored procedures are likely to be nonexistent, as are SQL extensions such as the DECODE function.

■ *Less extensive features*   Data types may differ in variety, length, and granularity; mixed data-type operations may also differ in results or may be disallowed entirely.

■ *Throughput limitations*   With each additional intervening technology comes increased latency; that is, each layer slows down throughput.

■ *Distributed processing*   Two-phase commit may not be possible with foreign data sources.

■ *Database structure limitations*   Features such as synonyms and sequences may have to be worked around when using other technologies.

■ *Client-side PL/SQL*   Where allowed, PL/SQL procedures may need to be modified to accommodate limitations in foreign data sources.

Keep these considerations in mind as you read the following sections on heterogeneous access. Limitations in technologies will be highlighted where appropriate.

Access to Non-Oracle7 Databases

Oracle applications may need to connect non-Oracle7 data sources either as their primary connection or to provide simultaneous connections between the two (or more) heterogeneous technologies. Examples of this include Oracle Power Objects' ability to simultaneously connect to Oracle7 and SQL Server. Regardless of the data source, the syntax used is identical. Of course, the data source may limit which syntax may successfully be used at run time. For example, database synonyms are not available under SQL Server.

Native Drivers

Data source flexibility may be achieved using native drivers. For example, Oracle Power Objects (OPO) is designed to accommodate data source differences at run time using native drivers. When connecting to Oracle7, OPO uses SQL*Net, Oracle's native network transport. When connecting to SQL Server, OPO uses the DBLIB API. And when connecting to Blaze, its local data store, OPO uses its native drivers for Blaze.

In order to use native drivers, however, OPO's developers had to write code that called each of the native drivers' APIs appropriately. Each data source accommodated required additional coding. Developers choosing to use native drivers trade off decreased development simplicity for the increased performance native drivers provide. For the developer using OPO, however, this complexity is hidden. The OPO developer uses a single interface, OPO itself, regardless of the data source.

ODBC

A different approach, the open database connectivity standard, ODBC, is taken when the tool developer wishes to avoid the use of native drivers. ODBC works by providing a generic API. The benefit of the ODBC scheme is that a technology-specific driver need only be written once. And applications need only be written to the ODBC specification, not to proprietary database APIs. There may be a loss of performance compared to leaner proprietary solutions in many cases, but this may be acceptable in light of the ease of use provided.

The ODBC-enabled application communicates directly with a standard ODBC function layer. This layer then communicates with the appropriate driver for the data source in use. This driver is usually developed using the data source's native API. Rather than translating between a foreign technology and the native API, the driver need only know about ODBC. The following listing, taken from an ODBC log, shows the function calls made to perform a SQL INSERT.

```
SQLAllocStmt(hdbc382F0000, phstmt2A7F0000);
SQLGetFunctions(hdbc382F0000, 69, pfExists);
SQLPrepare(hstmt2A7F0000, "INSERT INTO S2ODTMAP VALUES( 56, 'INT', 'NUMBER' )", 58);
SQLExecute(hstmt2A7F0000);
SQLFreeStmt(hstmt2A7F0000, 1);
```

Regardless of the data source, the application would always perform the functions shown in the listing. The database-specific driver performs the necessary conversion of syntactical differences and error handling.

Using the Open Client Adapter for ODBC, Oracle applications such as Developer/2000's Forms, Reports, and Graphics can perform their functions against non-Oracle7 databases for which ODBC drivers have been developed.

Access to Oracle7 Data from a Non-Oracle Application

Applications developed with non-Oracle technology may use external bridging technologies to communicate with the Oracle7 database. This is the case when using Oracle Objects for OLE (OO4O) to communicate with Oracle7 databases from Visual Basic or C++. Such connections may be achieved using either Oracle technology, such as OO4O, or a combination of technologies, such as ODBC drivers for Oracle7. The Oracle7 ODBC Setup dialog box in Figure 6-1 is used to create an ODBC connection to an Oracle7 database. Once created, a Visual Basic application can then communicate with Oracle7 as if it were an Access database. ODBC is an option to consider when upsizing from low-end databases to Oracle7.

Access to Oracle7 Stored Procedures from a Non-Oracle Application

Applications that need to execute Oracle7 stored procedures from non-Oracle clients require technology such as OCI or one of the Oracle precompilers to pass the procedure call and facilitate the return of the resulting data set. Database triggers are an exception, however, as they are performed at the server and are not explicitly called from client applications.

Additionally, to make software development more flexible, Oracle's SQL*Module permits the management of database procedures that are separate from the applications that use them. Using ANSI standard Module development language, 3GL applications may be created that perform stored procedures but require neither the use of embedded SQL (as do the precompilers), nor API calls (as

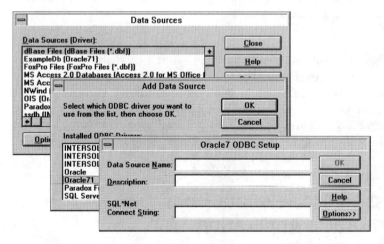

FIGURE 6-1. *Setting up ODBC access to Oracle7 databases*

does OCI). The following listing shows an example of Module code taken from SQL*Module's demonstration code.

```
MODULE        demomod
LANGUAGE      C
AUTHORIZATION modtest

DECLARE GET_STUDENTS_CURS CURSOR FOR
    SELECT last_name, first_name, mi, id, status, major, advisor_id
        FROM students
PROCEDURE open_get_students_curs (
        SQLCODE);
    OPEN GET_STUDENTS_CURS;
PROCEDURE close_get_students_curs (
        SQLCODE);
    CLOSE GET_STUDENTS_CURS;
```

Access to Non-Oracle7 Procedures from an Oracle Application

There is much existing legacy software containing business rules that must be enforced. To successfully coexist, Oracle applications may need to perform functions available only through such software. The most common method is through user exits. A *user exit* is a set of code external to the application itself, usually written in C using the Pro*C precompiler, or with OCI. The Oracle run time, Oracle Forms, for example, is then relinked with the external function to provide access from within Forms itself using the USER_EXIT procedure.

Another method is available through the Open Client Adapter for ODBC. Developer/2000 users can access databases through ODBC and execute a non-Oracle7 stored procedure by using the DO_SQL statement.

NOTE

Unlike Oracle7 stored procedures, stored procedures executed on non-Oracle7 databases can only use input parameters and foreign stored procedures cannot return values. That is, foreign stored procedures cannot behave as functions.

Oracle also has developed procedural gateway technology, which facilitates foreign code execution through PL/SQL's procedural syntax. Oracle's Open Gateway technology, which encompasses both transparent and procedural gateways, is covered in detail in Chapter 7.

Heterogeneous Access Means

To review, communicating with an incompatible data source can be done through the following methods:

- An application-specific solution built using a third-generation language such as C or COBOL
- An intermediate conversion technology such as ODBC
- A component-based technology such as OLE or OpenDOC
- A gateway that provides a bridge to a foreign platform
- A native, or heterogeneous-link-specific, driver

TIP
When running most bridging applications, supporting code is often found in dynamically loaded libraries. For example, under Windows, OCI and ODBC applications must call in routines from various dynamic link library (DLL) files. If these files are in a shared location not on the executing machine, performance degradation may occur as a result of network latency in retrieving code from the DLLs.

The following sections will address Oracle's non-SQL*Net connectivity products and how they fulfill various heterogeneous access needs.

Oracle Call Interface (OCI)

Native Oracle software is written using an application programming interface (API) called the Oracle Call Interface (OCI). It is a series of platform-independent routines that facilitate communication with the Oracle7 database engine. With each release of the Oracle7 database, OCI libraries are updated to ensure that both Oracle's and third-party developers can write 3GL applications that access Oracle7. In order to provide access from other technologies, developers can "roll their own" bridging software using OCI and the foreign data source's API.

TIP
OCI applications should be relinked whenever the database kernel is upgraded. Ideally, the OCI application should be completely recompiled and regression tested to ensure there are no unforeseen side effects related to the database upgrade.

OCI provides access to remote Oracle7 databases also, because it communicates with SQL*Net directly. As such, the developer can use any valid Oracle7 connect string and ensure connectivity regardless of whether SQL*Net is used. Most of Oracle's own products are written using OCI extensively.

The code snippet shown in the following listing performs the connection to the Oracle7 database and opens a cursor. It is somewhat abstruse, relying on calls by reference and returned values for success determination. But what OCI lacks in clarity of purpose, it makes up for in sheer performance. The critical CGI component of Oracle's WOW Gateway is written using OCI for this reason, as well as for portability.

```
if (orlon(&lda, hda, username, -1, password, -1, 0))
    {
        err_report(&lda);
        exit(EXIT_FAILURE);
    }
    printf("Connected to ORACLE as %s\n", username);

    if (oopen(&cda1, &lda, (text *) 0, -1, -1, (text *) 0, -1))
    {
        err_report(&cda1);
        do_exit(EXIT_FAILURE);
    }
```

Development life cycle issues, including adaptability and maintainability, generally call for solutions developed using the Oracle precompiler technology, described in the next section. But where the absolutely tightest code is required, there is no substitute for OCI-based solutions.

TIP
Array processing allows more records to be sent per fetch. OCI programs can perform multiple record reads in a single call by using the OFEN call.

Oracle Precompilers

OCI application development requires that database access be performed by populating data structures and calling processing routines and then extracting returned values and result codes from other data structures. This can be a daunting task if flexible SQL statement execution is required. To this end, Oracle developed high-level language precompilers that couple the performance benefits of 3GL programming with the flexibility of embedded SQL statements. Each precompiler is named after the language it supports. The C precompiler is called Pro*C, the COBOL precompiler is Pro*COBOL, Ada's is Pro*Ada, and so on.

The precompiler converts all of the 3GL code's embedded SQL statements into a compilable format by encapsulating all the EXEC SQL statements and sections into structures and function calls. Structures such as SQLCA and SQLDA are provided to verify the status of statement execution—for example, the number of rows returned by a SELECT statement—and to alter the behavior of statements such as the number of rows physically retrieved at a time. Finally, the use of indicator variables enable the developer to check for NULL and truncated values. Where necessary, the precompiler library code converts between Oracle7's and the 3GL's native datatypes.

The Oracle precompilers allow developers to embed SQL statements that are passed to the Oracle7 engine at run time, obviating the need to develop complex SQL query-handling routines. Of course, to take advantage of pre-prepared SQL statements, the flexibility is provided to merely pass parameters of known types at run time to pre-bound SQL statements, which results in much better performance. The Pro*C code shown in the following listing illustrates the more palatable syntax of embedded SQL.

```
EXEC SQL INCLUDE sqlca;
EXEC SQL INCLUDE sqlda;
EXEC SQL BEGIN DECLARE SECTION;
   VARCHAR LOGIN[20];
EXEC SQL END DECLARE SECTION;
   .
   .
   .
   strcpy(LOGIN.arr, "scott/tiger ");
   LOGIN.len = strlen(LOGIN.arr);
   EXEC SQL CONNECT :LOGIN;
   EXEC SQL SELECT afctemp_sq.NEXTVAL INTO :USERNAME;
   if (sqlca.sqlcode != SQL_OK) sqlerror();
```

TIP
Like OCI, the Oracle precompilers facilitate array processing for improved performance. In Pro*C, if the host variable or variables are an array, a single EXEC SQL INSERT will result in multiple records being inserted into the table. Likewise, non-singleton SQL SELECTs may be set to return multiple records by using the PL/SQL FETCH statement.

Oracle SQL*Module

Oracle's SQL*Module gives third-party applications the ability to call stored procedures without the need to use embedded SQL or native API code such as OCI. At compile time, SQL modules are part of the code that gets linked. This enables changes in the 3GL code to be distinct from database procedure changes and vice versa. The code in the following listing is roughly equivalent to that shown earlier for Pro*C. Notice the difference in syntax and sparseness of code.

```
PROCEDURE connect1 (SQLCODE, :mod10   char(8));
CONNECT TO 'inst1_alias' USER 'scott' USING :mod10;
```

The next listing shows how the SQL*Module code is implemented using standard C routines and calling syntax. This code is not part of the stored procedure but is Module code used to initiate the connection to the database. Note the absence of embedded SQL and abstruse OCI calls.

```
connect1(&sc, mod10);
    if (!sc)
        printf("Successful connect\n");
else printf("Connect failed, sqlcode = %ld\n", sc);
```

To call a PL/SQL stored procedure, it must first be declared using the WITH INTERFACE clause. This results in the generation of stub code providing the appropriate prototypes for the call to the stored procedure. SQL*Module handles the actual communication layer between the 3GL application and the stored procedure. All that is required is that the variable through which the interface will communicate be declared and that one of them be named *sqlcode.*

The following shows an example of C code used to iteratively retrieve records using a C function called fetch_from_cursor(). The actual logic is hidden from the C function. It only serves to fetch a single value at a time. The *sc* variable is used to check the sqlcode value. This is equivalent to the SQLCA.SQLCODE value in the precompilers.

```
for (;;)
{
    fetch_from_cursor(&sc, cp, name);
    if (sc)
        break;
    name[10]=0;
    printf("Successful fetch, value = %s\n", name);
}
```

Native Drivers

Much as Oracle provides OCI, other vendors develop native drivers to their own technologies. By using these native drivers, usually in the form of APIs, Oracle developers can use either OCI or an Oracle precompiler to develop a bridge between the technologies. Native drivers also form part of the technology used in ODBC drivers.

As mentioned before, an example of this bridging is found in Oracle Power Objects, which contains native drivers to Oracle7, Blaze, and SQL Server. By combining both Oracle's OCI and the DBLIB API for SQL Server, Power Objects developers have high-performance access to both Oracle and non-Oracle data sources simultaneously. The dialog box in Figure 6-2 shows how the developer can select from different data sources using native drivers.

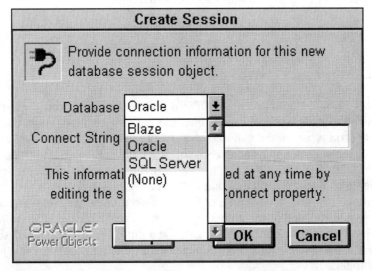

FIGURE 6-2. *Data source selection in Oracle Power Objects*

NOTE
In addition to the native drivers, much as SQL*Net is required to communicate with Oracle7, other technologies require their own network communications technologies. In the case of Microsoft's version of SQL Server, the SQL Server Client for Windows is required. To access Sybase's version of SQL Server, their Open Client/C for PC/MS Windows is required.

Open Database Connectivity (ODBC)

The open database connectivity standard, ODBC, is a procedural interface to relational databases. This enables the development of back-end drivers that, when coupled with standard ODBC front-end technology, provide flexible data source capability to applications. ODBC drivers are provided as part of Oracle's Workgroup/2000 offerings, including the Oracle Workgroup Server and Personal Oracle7.

NOTE
Oracle ODBC 1.11 drivers are 16-bit technology. These have been developed by Oracle and others for use with the Oracle7 database. Oracle itself will not be producing 32-bit drivers for use in Windows NT and Windows 95; instead, it has licensed the rights to develop future Oracle ODBC drivers to Intersolv. 32-bit drivers have 2.x version numbers, indicating that they are ODBC version 2.x drivers.

ODBC and SQL*Net
ODBC drivers have an open technology component and a platform-specific component. In Oracle's case, its ODBC drivers are dependent on SQL*Net and also require the ORA71WIN.DLL file for supporting functions.

Quick Start for Windows ODBC
Prior to using an ODBC connection, you must set up database, and possibly user, information for each data source to which you will be connecting. To administer ODBC, select ODBC Administration from the Control Panel dialog or from the Oracle7 ODBC program group. The dialog box in Figure 6-3 is then displayed. All ODBC status and setup information is stored in the ODBC.INI file usually located in the main Windows directory.

ODBC Administrator   From the ODBC Administrator you can set up each connection you will use. Additionally, you can delete or modify an existing connection. The Drivers button is for adding or deleting drivers as opposed to

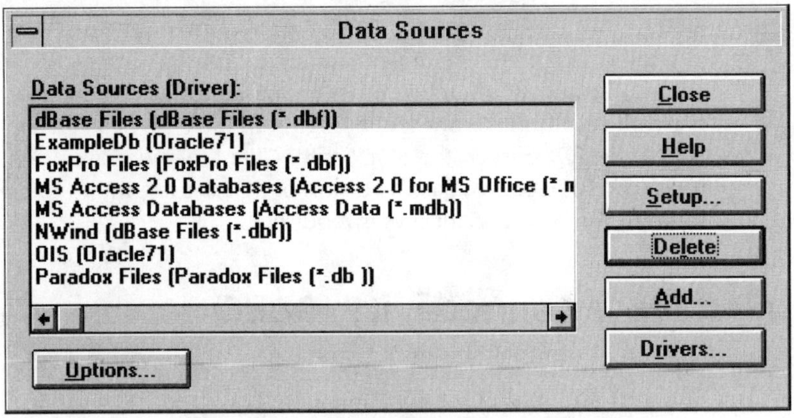

FIGURE 6-3. *ODBC Administrator main dialog, Data Sources*

connections. Pressing the Help button from this dialog results in the ODBC Administrator help screens, not driver-specific help information.

Adding an Oracle7 ODBC Connection Suppose you need to set up a connection to an Oracle7 Enterprise Server for use with a Visual Basic application. From the ODBC Administrator dialog box, perform the following steps:

1. Press the Add button to add a new data source. The dialog box shown in Figure 6-4 is then displayed.

2. Select Oracle71. The Oracle data source is from the original Microsoft driver set and is limited to Oracle V6 databases using SQL*Net V1. Press the OK button. The following dialog box is then displayed.

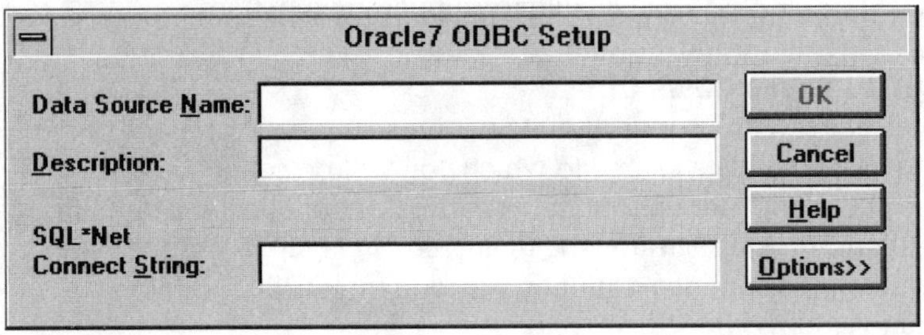

3. In the Data Source Name field shown above, you enter the name used to identify this data source within applications using ODBC. For example, the Oracle Objects for OLE Visual Basic examples expect the scott/tiger, or EMP/DEPT, sample user and his tables to be called EmployeeDb. In the Data Source Name field, then, you enter EmployeeDb.

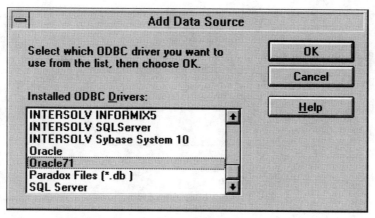

FIGURE 6-4. *Add Data Source dialog box*

4. In the Description field you may enter any description. It is solely for informational purposes.

5. In the SQL*Net Connect String field, enter the appropriate SQL*Net connect string for the Oracle7 server you wish to connect to using this ODBC connection. For example, to connect to Personal Oracle7, use 2: as the connect string. To connect to a database instance called PROD across TCP/IP using SQL*Net V1, you may use a connection such as T:srvr1:PROD. For SQL*Net V2 connections, simply use the service name that you set up using Oracle Network Manager or manually in version 2.0. For example, the same PROD instance on srvr1 may simply be referred to as PROD under SQL*Net V2.

6. You do not need to press the Options button unless you require special code translations to take place. Refer to your driver documentation for more information on such implementation-specific features.

7. In Visual Basic, you can then specify the data source using either of the following syntax examples:

```
"DSN=EmployeeDb;UID=SCOTT;PWD=TIGER", or
DatabaseName$="EmployeeDb"
Connect$="scott/tiger"
```

8. An example of the Informix driver dialog is shown in Figure 6-5. Note the additional items that may be specified. Each vendor will provide a different set of features that are accessible either through the Add Connection dialog box or programmatically.

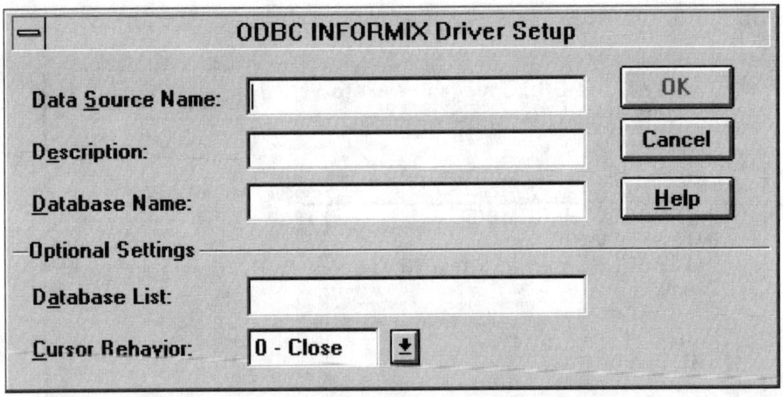

FIGURE 6-5. *Informix ODBC Driver Add Connection dialog box*

Oracle7 ODBC Driver Caveats To ensure you are using the latest driver, you may view information on each driver from the Drivers dialog by pressing the About button. The highlighted driver's information is then displayed. Figures 6-6 and 6-7 show how this is done.

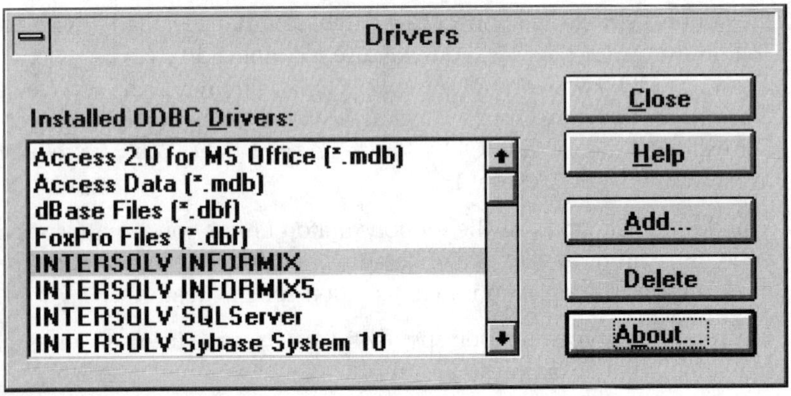

FIGURE 6-6. *Locating driver information using the About button in the Drivers dialog box*

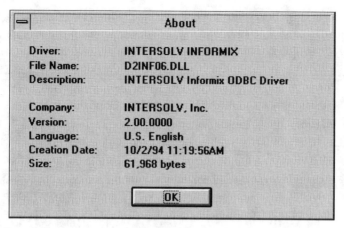

FIGURE 6-7. *Informix driver information dialog box*

The driver information for the Intersolv Oracle7 driver for Oracle7 release 7.1 is shown in Figure 6-8.

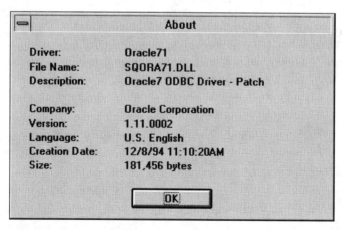

FIGURE 6-8. *Oracle7 release 7.1 driver information dialog box*

You may troubleshoot ODBC connections using the ODBC tracing facility. To get to the dialog box shown here, press the Options button from the ODBC Administrator dialog.

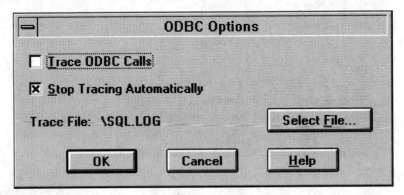

The contents of the log file will be shown as ODBC functions. The following listing is an example of a failed connection to a SQL Server database from Oracle Data Browser using Open Client for ODBC.

```
SQLAllocEnv(phenv3DFF0000);
SQLAllocConnect(henv3DFF0000, phdbc3F2F0000);
SQLDriverConnect(hdbc3F2F0000, hwnd462C, "UID=HUGO;PWD=********;", -3,
szConnStrOut, 255, pcbConnStrOut, 3);
SQLError(henv3DFF0000, hdbc3F2F0000, hstmt00000000, szSqlState,
        pfNativeError, szErrorMsg, 511, pcbErrorMsg);
```

CHAPTER 7

Transparent Gateways and Other Open System Integration Technologies

The reports of my death have been greatly exaggerated.

—*Mark Twain*

Before the late 1980s, the vast majority of enterprise information resided on monolithic platforms: mainframes. With the development of increasingly more reliable client/server technologies, there came a call to "downsize," or migrate from mainframes to lower-end technologies. These technologies were considered less expensive and more flexible. They also lent themselves well to reconfiguration and redeployment as enterprise needs changed. Or so it was thought.

From the late 1980s to now, the term "right-size," also borrowed from corporate restructuring, has been used to include both downsizing and the attendant migration to these workgroup technologies from low-end desktop applications. With all of this sizing, you'd think the mainframe was dead, right? Wrong. What has happened is a reevaluation of the role "big iron" plays in today's network-dominated environments. The mainframe is alive and well, in fact, prospering, as its horsepower is better harnessed.

In addition to the repositioning of monolithic computer systems, heterogeneous data access has become an information systems fact of life. No longer are single-vendor solutions the norm or the ideal. An ideal technology is one that enables its incorporation with foreign technologies, especially those developed before it. This is a key point. Many technologies now provide pathways for linking to other technologies; it is the legacy technology, which was developed sometime in the past and often lacks substantial documentation, with which the developer must grapple to extract key data. Such needs and the way Oracle's technologies fulfill them are the focus of this chapter.

Oracle has developed various technologies that serve to enable access to legacy technologies and foreign data sources. Some of these were discussed in detail in Chapter 6. What differentiates the solutions in this chapter is that they use intermediate technology, gateways of one sort or another, to do one of two things:

■ Enable non-Oracle7 data stores to look like Oracle7 data objects

or

■ Make an Oracle7 database resemble a non-Oracle7 data store.

The image in Figure 7-1 shows several examples of gateways in use. At the top of the picture is a typical mainframe running several legacy database technologies, including DB/2 and IMS, and utilizing VSAM files. There is also an AS/400 system

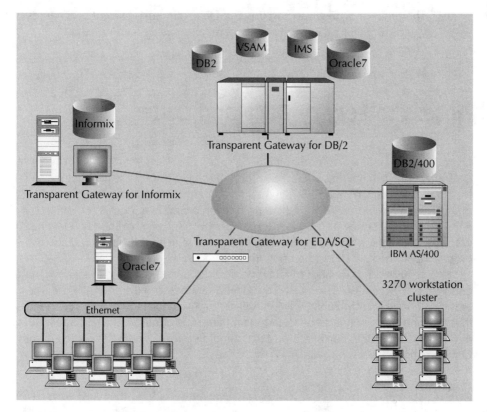

FIGURE 7-1. *Oracle Gateway Technologies in a mixed legacy/open systems environment*

running DB2/400. You also have a small Informix database server, an Oracle7 workgroup, and a 3270 workstation cluster. The technologies covered in this chapter permit the following scenarios:

- The 3270 workstation cluster can enter orders into the mainframe, although a key database has been migrated from DB/2 on the mainframe to the Oracle7 workgroup database. This is made possible through the Oracle Client Solution for MVS.

- Until it is migrated to Oracle7, the Informix resident data can be accessed from Oracle applications as if it were on Oracle, using the Transparent Gateway for Informix.

■ The Oracle7 workgroup can use PL/SQL to run host-resident procedures against the DB/2 database on the mainframe, using the Procedural Gateway for APPC.

Access to Legacy Data and Code

The role of the mainframe evolved to where it was used to provide robust centralized processing in a completely controlled environment. The key was centralization. The result was concentration of data and software in a single location. This concentration hindered tactical changes in information-processing initiatives. To develop a new application or even a simple query screen often required committee review and impact assessment. But you had no choice, since that was where the data was. With the emergence of true distributed database processing in the late 1980s, you now have choices.

Oracle provides a number of technologies that open up access to legacy data and systems. Oracle has partitioned these technologies into three sets by the role they fulfill, as shown in Table 7-1. In addition to serving legacy data access needs, these technologies may also be used to facilitate incorporation of non-Oracle7 data into distributed processing needs and to promote easier migration to Oracle7 from other technologies.

Open Gateway Technology

Oracle's Open Gateway Technology helps foster contemporary information services (IS) strategies of compartmentalization and group enablement. Each

Open Gateways	Enable access to legacy data and procedures
Transaction Integration	Enable participation in transaction-processing events
Migration Technologies	Enable migration of legacy systems to open systems

TABLE 7-1. *Oracle's Three Sets of Legacy/Open Systems Integration Technologies*

technology provides a bridge to a particular data source or procedural entry point. Oracle's Open Gateway Technology consists of the following components:

- Transparent Gateways
- Procedural Gateways
- Open Gateway Toolkits

The Transparent Gateways are available for key legacy technologies, including DB/2, and for technologies traditionally positioned against Oracle, including Informix and Sybase. A Procedural Gateway is currently available for IBM's Systems Network Architectures' (SNA) Advanced Peer-to-Peer Communications (APPC) technology. And, for situations for which a gateway has not yet been developed, Oracle's Open Gateway Toolkits provide all of the elements needed to craft a custom solution.

NOTE
A fully functional gateway, custom developed, may be indistinguishable from a prewritten one. The significant draw is that a custom gateway need only provide the services required and no more. Additionally, the gateway kit may be used to add features not normally provided by the predeveloped gateways, such as optimized external interfaces to specialized devices.

Oracle Transparent Gateways

Oracle's Transparent Gateways (TG) replaces Oracle's previous technology, SQL*Connect. A key difference between the two technologies is that the TGs are built on Oracle7 technology. So what does a TG do? Simply stated, an Oracle Transparent Gateway provides access to non-Oracle7 data as if it were an Oracle7 data object. Access to the gateway is not limited to Oracle applications alone, but is open to any application that can normally access Oracle7 databases.

Key Oracle7 features provided by the Transparent Gateways include the following:

- Technology transparency (hence the name), including SQL dialect independence, object name mapping, operating system and network independence, and automatic data type conversion

- Full support for SQL*Net technologies, including Secure Network Services, Multi-Protocol Interchange, and Oracle Names

- Distributed processing, including distributed updates, participation in distributed updates, and remote join performance

- PL/SQL server application processing

The typical Transparent Gateway solution places both the Transparent Gateway Technology and the foreign data source on the same platform. An Oracle7 database is required to provide the transaction and object resolution services. SQL*Net is the technology used to communicate between the clients and the databases. It is SQL*Net's participation that facilitates many of the desirable features of a Transparent Gateway solution, including distributed updates and protocol independence. The diagram in Figure 7-2 shows an example using the Transparent Gateway for SQL/400. This setup is also appropriate for the Transparent Gateway for DB/2.

NOTE
Oracle supports three different vendors' implementations of TCP/IP for MVS: IBM's TCP/IP for MVS 2.2.1, Interlink's SNS/TCPaccess 2.0 and 1.1, and Gulf Computers KNET 5.0 and 4.0.2.

It must be understood that you do not need to map the foreign data to Oracle7 space. That is, the Oracle7 schema does not keep track of the foreign database schema. It is purely dynamic access. No maintenance of the Transparent Gateway is required to utilize it.

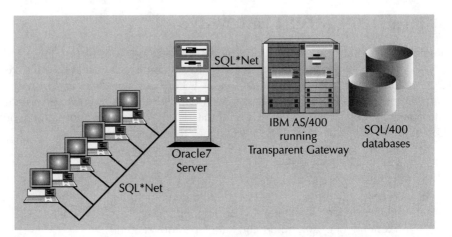

FIGURE 7-2. *Typical configuration for Transparent Gateway solution*

DB2	DB2/400	RDB
EDA/SQL	IBM DRDA	SESAM (Beta)
Informix	INGRES	UDS (Beta)
RMS	Sybase	RDMS (Beta)
Teradata	Turbo Image	

TABLE 7-2.   *Transparent Gateway Platforms*

Table 7-2 shows the non-Oracle technologies for which Transparent Gateways are currently available. Most of the Transparent Gateways are at release level 3.1, although some versions of release 3.0 are still in production. Regardless, all existing versions of release 3.0 are still supported.

TIP
Want to know what Oracle products and release levels are in production? SupportLink on CompuServe carries a file in the Client Relations library containing all platforms and products released to manufacturing. See Chapter 15 for details on SupportLink and accessing the CompuServe forum.

Transparent Gateway for EDA/SQL

Despite the number of platforms supported by Transparent Gateways, they don't seem to add up to the over 30 sources Oracle indicates they support. Why is that? It is because a large number of them are provided through Oracle's and Information Builders' Transparent Gateway for Enterprise Data Access (EDA)/SQL. This product bears special mention because it provides a general solution often appropriate for IBM platforms where a Transparent Gateway is not already provided. Oracle's Transparent Gateway for EDA/SQL (TG4EDA) is available from both Information Builders, EDA/SQL's developer, and Oracle. EDA/SQL itself supports over 60 data sources, although some restrictions may exist when used with TG4EDA. Some of TG4EDA's key technologies are shown in Table 7-3.

An important feature of EDA/SQL is its ability to communicate with nonrelational data stores such as file-based VSAM, ISAM, and QSAM. EDA/SQL provides mapping facilities that enable these technologies to be accessed as if they were part of relational tables. Equally compelling is EDA/SQL's ability to do so for flat files, indexed files, and hierarchical and network databases.

VSAM	IMS	ADABAS
CA-IDMS/DB	CA-Datacom/DB	TOTAL
CA-IDMS/R	Model 204	QSAM
Infoman	System 2000	SAP
SUPRA	ISAM	FOCUS

TABLE 7-3. *Foreign Data Sources Available Through EDA/SQL*

Sequential Files   The simplest form of managing information on computers is storing data in *sequential* or *flat files*. These are files that do not have any imposed structure but, rather, are used by programs that have the format of the file coded into them. To read them, each program must start at the beginning and read through the file sequentially until the information sought is found.

Each program is responsible for managing access and changes to the file. Generally, concurrent access by multiple updating applications is not possible. Also, inserting new data except at the end of the file is generally not possible without rewriting the entire file. Likewise, deleting records generally requires rewriting as well.

Today, most newly implemented sequential files are used only to store simple configuration data. However, a wealth of data, particularly on legacy systems, is stored in flat files. TG4EDA makes it possible to interact with some of these files as if they were databases. In order to do this, TG4EDA requires configuration information identifying each file's format.

Indexed Files   Slightly more sophisticated implementations of flat files are *indexed files*. These allow faster dynamic access to records based on key values. However, the program interacting with the indexed file still needs to know the file's structure. Also, the addition and deletion of records must still be handled by each program. Some concurrent access may be possible, since discrete record access and therefore record locking is possible.

Hierarchical Databases   The breakthrough in multiuser data access came with the development of the *hierarchical database* management system. It managed multiple users, multiple files, indexing, and record and space management. This meant that each application did not need to perform these tasks for itself.

Predating the relational database, hierarchical databases store information through subcategorization, or hierarchies. This means that to work with a record, you start at the top of the hierarchy and work your way down, refining your search until you find the record or records you seek.

Hierarchical databases require more storage than relational databases due to duplication of information. However, by keeping related information close together, hierarchical databases make up for storage profligacy with processing efficiency. The most common hierarchical database today is IMS.

Network Databases Less commonly used are network databases, a more general case of hierarchical databases in which each component may contain a link to another component. These tend to contain recursive relationships. The canonical example of a network database is the bill-of-materials. Each item in a bill-of-materials may itself consist of other items. The earliest network database, developed by IBM, was called BOMP, for Bill of Materials Processor. The most common network database technology in use today is CA/IDMS-DB.

Relational Databases Relational databases store information in relations, or rows. Relational databases are a relatively new technology. In return for a simpler design, they require more CPU cycles to combine data effectively. The key concept of the relational database design is the one-to-many relationship. Theoretically, ideal relational database designs eliminate duplication through a process called *normalization.* Oracle is the most widely used relational database management system.

Caveats
The following issues must be considered when using an Oracle Transparent Gateway.

- The Transparent Gateway Technologies do not always support writing to remote data stores, as in the case of the Transparent Gateway for EDA/SQL. Check with the documentation for your particular gateway.

TIP
In such circumstances, look to Oracle's other integration technologies such as those in the two sections "Transaction Integration Technology" and "Migration Technologies" for the appropriate solution.

- Only one foreign data source is permitted to participate in distributed updates.

- When a foreign data source accessed via the Transparent Gateway participates in a distributed update, it is that foreign data source that becomes the controlling *commit point.*

NOTE
Oracle7 distributed updates are based on a two-phase commit (2PC) strategy to reliably commit transactions. The first phase is called the Prepare phase, in which a single server is granted the role of commit point. The success or failure of the commit point determines whether the other servers participating in the distributed update are instructed to commit or roll back their transactions. As the non-Oracle7 database is not intimately tied to the Oracle7 technology, it is presumed to be the odd man out, hence its role as commit point.

Oracle Procedural Gateways

Oracle's Transparent Gateways make non-Oracle7 data sources behave like Oracle7 databases. In the same manner, Oracle's Procedural Gateways permit Oracle procedures to be written using PL/SQL, which can call procedures on the host systems. In effect, this is a Remote Procedure Call (RPC) technology. The effect of this is to provide mainframe programmability from Oracle7 database servers, where the host transactions monitors, such as CICS, CA-IDMS/DC, and IMS/TM, are in control of the Oracle7-originated transaction.

How is this accomplished? Oracle's Procedural Gateway for APPC provides the technology. APPC is IBM's Advanced Peer-to-Peer Communications standard within the broader Systems Network Architecture (SNA). APPC provides single-technology entry into multiple-host hardware, operating system, transaction monitor, and application systems. Because APPC communicates at the network layer through SNA's LU6.2 protocol, high-throughput transaction processing is available without resorting to custom development using the Oracle XA Libraries.

The Oracle Procedural Gateway for APPC supports the following technologies:

- CICS on MVS, AS/400, AIX, OS/2, and DOS/VSE operating systems

- IMS/TM, IDMS/DC, and APPC/MVS on MVS systems

A sample of the data sources that can be simultaneously accessed includes

ADABAS	Model 204
CA-IDMS	SQL/DS
Datacom/DB	TOTAL
DB2	VSAM
IMS	

Transaction Integration Technology

Oracle's gateway technologies address Oracle access to non-Oracle resources. What about the need to access Oracle7 data from non-Oracle technologies? Oracle has such technology in the Oracle for MVS Client Solution, which provides Access Managers for CICS and IMS/TM, Oracle Precompilers, SQL*Net, and the SQL*Loader and SQL*Plus utilities. Using these technologies, CICS and IMS/TM applications have complete access to remote Oracle7 data, not just that residing within the mainframe's legacy data stores. Such applications may continue to fully participate in distributed processing and even transaction-processing (TP) monitored transactions.

Access Manager for CICS and Access Manager for IMS/TM

This technology provides the ability for host-based applications running under either CICS or IMS/TM to access Oracle7 data, including participating in distributed transactions, under the watchful eye of the appropriate transaction monitor. Unlike in the Transparent Gateway Technologies, the Oracle7 server does not provide the transaction management facilities.

Oracle Precompilers for COBOL, C, and PL/I

Additionally, the Oracle for MVS Client package comes with Oracle Precompiler technology. This enables the creation of native host applications with embedded Oracle SQL statements. Such applications can interact with both host-based and Oracle7 databases. Additionally, the applications may be executed under CICS, IMS/TM, batch, and TSO.

Oracle SQL*Loader

SQL*Loader is Oracle's standard utility application for loading data from external files into Oracle7 database tables. It can accommodate a wide variety of element and record formats, filter data based on external and derived criteria, and provide parallel and optimized, pre-sorted data loading if desired. Used in combination with Oracle's transaction-based technologies, SQL*Loader facilitates the population of other data stores from host-extracted data dumps.

Migration Technologies

The final need met by Oracle's technologies is for migration technology and services required to "rightsize." This is accomplished with all of the above technologies and may also include the assistance of Oracle Services personnel to provide valuable expertise in the migration from legacy technology to open systems. An additional set of products, Oracle's SQL*Loader, Distributed Relational

Database Architecture (DRDA) Server, and VSAM Transparency technology, may be put to use as is appropriate.

The DRDA Server is an Oracle application that utilizes IBM's DRDA technology to facilitate continued access to data after it has been migrated from an IBM DRDA data source to Oracle7. This extends the life of the DRDA application until a more appropriate open solution is crafted. And, rather than throwing a switch and praying the entire migrated system hangs together, DRDA Server enables a more considered, staged migration off of the IBM platform and onto a more flexible, distributed open system.

Under development at the time this book went to press, the VSAM Transparency technology was created to ease the migration from legacy application systems to open technologies. VSAM is IBM's Virtual Storage Access Method, probably the most widely used repository of data in the IBM world. Unfortunately, unlike Oracle applications where there is often an orderly apples-and-apples connection between data elements and their data store, VSAM data sets and the applications that interact with them rarely follow such wise conventions. As a result, the migration from VSAM data storage to any contemporary relational database technology often requires largely customized strategies and practices.

VSAM Transparency can ease this transition by providing Oracle7 data storage and mapping VSAM application requests to Oracle7 data accesses. This means that unmodified applications run against the VSAM Transparency technology seamlessly. This aids in a more timely and structured migration.

NOTE
DRDA Server and VSAM Transparency are transitional technologies. It is not desirable to continue use of these products in production environments. Oracle7 relational database technology accomplishes much more for less effort.

To recap, the migration technologies fulfill the following needs. SQL*Loader enables efficient loading of Oracle7 database tables from files containing exported data usually on a one-time basis. Oracle's DRDA Server enables access to Oracle7 data storage transparently from DRDA applications. And VSAM Transparency enables access to Oracle7 tables mimicking VSAM files.

The Open Road

Due to the size of the investment in monolithic technologies, it is not possible to offer a particular magic bullet to the problem of open systems migration. As you are deciding on the path to take, consider the following issues and the options they leave.

- Do you need to provide access to Oracle7 data from non-Oracle applications? You need Oracle for MVS Client solution or the XA/Libraries if in an XA TP environment.

- Do you need to update legacy data? If so, you may be unable to use the Transparent Gateways on some platforms such as EDA/SQL, but you can always rely on the Procedural Gateways or Oracle for MVS Client solution to do so.

- Do you need to participate in monitored transactions? Use Oracle for MVS Client Solution, XA Libraries, or DRDA Server, as appropriate.

- Do you need to provide access to decision-support systems or high-transaction count systems? Oracle for MVS Client solution and XA Libraries are the way to go.

- Do you have the resources to run the technology on its required platform (e.g., Transparent Gateway for DRDA must run on the mainframe)? If not, migrate or use a transitional technology such as DRDA Server or VSAM Transparency.

TIP
Oracle continues to provide additional paths to open systems. For more timely information, contact Oracle and request "Mainframes and Open Systems Computing in a Distributed Enterprise," an Oracle White Paper. Ask for Part number A22585. Another good source is each of the Product Overviews on Open Gateway Technologies.

CHAPTER 8

TNS Network Design and Deployment

When a limitation is reached, [redefine space] so that it can accommodate the new need.

—Stanley Davis

O nce an organization appreciates the value of its data and considers it a corporate resource, you can begin to craft a strategy for turning data into something better: *knowledge capital.* Much of the responsibility will fall on those who create and those who consume data. The job of the Oracle connectivity subject matter expert is to ensure that access to data is met within the parameters set by your customers.

As stated previously, the only way to get to a remote Oracle7 server is through Transparent Network Substrate (TNS) technology. TNS is employed even when ODBC or native drivers are used. The preceding chapters have also informed you of the primary Oracle connectivity technologies available to your enterprise. There is certainly no lack of solutions for serving data to your users. What is not certain is how to craft the optimum architecture.

In this chapter you will learn how to determine the design goals of your Oracle connectivity architecture, craft a flexible solution, and then implement it to deliver the levels of service required by your customer base.

Architecting Oracle Connectivity

It is appropriate to look at your Oracle network design process as that of architecting a structure—in this case, your Oracle connectivity framework. Like the traditional architect, the Oracle connectivity architect works in several stages, shown in Table 8-1.

Community Involvement

The steps in Table 8-1 will be used in the following sections to describe the process you should employ to architect an Oracle solution. Of course, this process is not performed in isolation but with the cooperation of the other communities. While it may seem as if some members will lack sufficient understanding of the issues to

Oracle Connectivity Architect

Planning

Design

Installation and implementation

Maintenance

Support

TABLE 8-1. *Stages in Architecting Oracle Connectivity*

provide worthwhile input, an inclusive process is likely to yield information that may make the difference between final acceptance and rejection. These communities include

■ User community representatives

■ Database administrators

■ Software developers

■ Telecommunications architects

■ End-user support

The following sections illustrate the roles and responsibilities of each community's representatives.

User Community Representatives

An information services department exists for only one reason: to enable effective user access to information by crafting data processing systems. Therefore, nothing that has an impact on information delivery or data access should occur without the end-user community playing a role in determining if their needs will be met.

It is the responsibility of the user community representatives to understand the role data processing and information access plays in their respective segments of the organization. They will be expected to provide end-user perspectives on issues such as single sign-on, performance perceptions, and other human factor preferences. Most importantly, they must be able to convey the directions in which their groups are headed and how information will play a role. This will help the technologists better plan for future requirements.

Database Administrators
In Oracle7, there are many places where the division between server functions and network functions are blurred. For example, global names and database links are database objects. Likewise, TNS session data is found in the V$SESSION virtual table, which is solely managed by the Oracle7 engine. The database administrators are expected to advocate data management requirements and provide anecdotal insight into operational data issues. Their input is critical in determining replication considerations and for estimating volume and other metrics.

Software Developers
There are many options for achieving Oracle7 connectivity—many more when you add non-Oracle connectivity needs. The software development staff will be keenly interested in the means to which they will be limited. From ODBC to Objects for OLE to 3GL solutions, the realm of possibilities must be constrained in a manner that does not prevent necessary operations from being performed. The primary role the developers play is validating the architecture's efficacy with an eye to coding considerations—both from a procedural and a performance point of view.

Telecommunications Architects
As stated at the beginning of the chapter, it is likely that the Oracle TNS infrastructure will be deployed across an extant physical network. This means that those truly responsible for the enterprise network are in the best position to provide insight into media restrictions and topology considerations. The telecom architects are expected to inform the other communities' members of directions in the enterprise technology and provide a preview of the corporate network topology plan.

Telecommunications and Software End-User Support
Much as the end-users are your true customers, not the developers or the DBAs, the support staff is your true right hand. The Help Desk is likely to be the first to deal with problems arising from either inappropriate implementations or insufficient training. Not certain how support becomes involved in TNS issues? Here is an example. Users call in because they are unable to switch between applications while waiting for a query to complete. Application problem? Not necessarily. It could be trouble with a blocking operation in SQL*Net. Other roles of the support personnel include advocating usability features related to end-user support and recovery processes. These may include integration with enterprise help desk management applications.

Planning Your TNS Network

Once the team has been assembled, you may begin to plan your TNS network. Planning is the first stage in architecting a solution. Planning consists of two major phases: present status assessment and determining design goals. The *present status assessment* is intended to start the responsible parties off on the same page. *Determining design goals* helps ensure the goal is a shared vision understood by all involved. Carefully consider the need to perform these steps. Additional effort expended in these early phases will yield far more than the time saved by skipping them ever can.

Present Status Assessment

Before you can consider where you want to be, you must know where you are. A present status assessment will provide you with the datum or benchmark from which to measure your progress to your goal. Information on the following elements should be compiled in the present status assessment.

- Existing applications and systems
- Critical processing flows
- Workgroup layouts and interactions
- Anticipated future applications and systems

The following sections describe the reason for capturing each characteristic and aspects related to the Oracle network design.

Existing Software Applications
Many times, extant technology will constrain deployment of improved technology. The reasons for this include unreasonable replacement costs for the legacy technology, stable operational costs for legacy systems, and the preference for a known solution versus a perhaps better but unknown one. The planned Oracle network must accommodate these legacy systems. You need to know what loads they currently place on the infrastructure and use this information to extrapolate the effects on a new technology.

Critical Processing Flows
Where does the data go? You should document the data flows that are likely to continue regardless of the Oracle connectivity implementation. You must focus on the physical movement of packets and the attendant loads placed both in terms of bandwidth and timeliness. Especially consider the needs of critical or time-sensitive

operations that may impede backups and other preventative maintenance operations typically performed after hours.

The following critical operations are typical of those that should be tracked and documented:

- Electronic Data Interchange (EDI) functions

- Transaction Processing (TP) Monitor processing

- Data Replication operations

- Trans-network Backup and Data Consolidation operations

Workgroup Layouts and Interactions

Collaborative operations ranging from file sharing to messaging systems and other forms of groupware will affect the peaks and valleys of the network's load and operational requirements. More importantly, workgroups generally express a natural order of operation. You should expect extant workgroup flows to continue with similar interactions if they are to be part of the architected solution. Such workgroups may naturally translate into SQL*Net domains with their attendant management as a group.

Anticipated Future Applications and Systems

Complete the present status assessment with the inclusion of applications planned for deployment regardless of the final Oracle connectivity solution employed. Remember, it is important that everyone providing input into the Oracle network design know the status quo. Equally important is understanding the existing plan for technology deployment. As this information is compiled, specify when each new application will be ported to the new Oracle network. This will likely affect the order in which configurations are generated and deployed, especially when adding or changing the supported SQL*Net versions.

Design Goals

With any design project, your goal should be clearly defined. There is probably not a single goal to your network architecture but several—not necessarily complementary—goals to be met. Your organizational structure may even present multiple units whose data access goals are in opposition. For example, the data entry staff is concerned with heads-down processing speed; the analysis group is concerned with massive ad hoc data processing operations. Some will see ease of management as their primary need, some will stress performance, and others flexibility.

Again, the Oracle connectivity expert is *unlikely* to also be the party responsible for controlling the most critical component in the enterprise network, the communications media. Therefore, issues regarding the general physical network and available network protocols are considered closed. However, the determination of which of several protocols available on a particular segment should be employed is certainly the province of the Oracle connectivity expert.

First things first. Determine the customer needs requested of your TNS network design. The following section describes what aspects should be considered, each a need that must be met.

Customer's Needs

The needs with which a traditional structural architect is typically concerned include the following:

- Aesthetic appeal
- Reasonable construction requirements
- Natural flow
- Extensibility
- Security
- Reasonable maintenance requirements
- Flexibility
- Reliability
- Comfort

These needs, or their analogues, also exist in the creation of an Oracle network architecture—except for the first item, an appropriate metric for gauging the aesthetic appeal of an Oracle network not yet having been agreed on! The following sections amplify each need and what you must consider to meet it in the context of an Oracle connectivity infrastructure. Consider this your requirements assessment.

Reasonable Construction Requirements   The *cost* of erecting your framework should neither severely disrupt operations nor exceed the return on the investment over an agreed-upon period of time.

Natural Flow   The appropriate architecture should have a *natural flow*. The number of interfaces or components required to complete connections should be minimal and consistent. When a natural flow has been expressed, it is generally much easier to extend the architecture.

Extensibility   An important part of capacity planning is the ability to *extend* a solution to accommodate utilization growth—and decline—efficiently and without much additional effort. A significant factor in extending an architecture is the ease with which an extension is repeatable. Ideally, any one extension should be readily duplicated. For example, once an architecture extension to include a new workgroup configuration has been completed, that same extension should be repeatable. Oracle Network Manager supports this process with Client profiles.

Security   Certainly it is necessary to ensure that an integral and monitored structure is created. It is often more important to employ a security policy than it is to erect barriers. This is one of the two hallmarks of proper risk management: *maintaining data integrity.* Oracle Network Manager helps you design and maintain proper Oracle network security policy. Secure Network Services provides facilities for erecting and maintaining such a security barrier.

Reasonable Maintenance Requirements   Too often disregarded is the need to mitigate ongoing costs. The return on investment must consider the operational costs, of which maintenance is typically the highest. A variety of Oracle7 tools, including the 32-bit Navigator and Oracle Enterprise Manager, help ensure the enforcement of a maintenance policy with automated monitoring and recovery technology.

Flexibility   With the speed of change in business practices, it is critical to implement a solution that will accommodate, as can best be determined, future changes in utilization. You must not employ solutions that are rigid without factoring in the true future cost of altering utilization. Generally, Oracle7's many scalability options help ensure that *flexibility* is not a problem.

Reliability   The other hallmark of risk management is *reliability.* The assurance that the infrastructure will perform in a known, consistent manner is necessary to monitor deviations from the norm. Do not confuse *error-free* operation with *reliable* operation. For example, a connection to a remote database may always succeed. However, if it has been configured with equal community costs for two networks of significantly varying throughput characteristics, users will be unable to rely on consistent times to completion. Such unreliability does not instill comfort.

Comfort   Although subjective, *comfort* plays a large role in acceptance of a solution. Remember, restrictions your developers place on applications because of underlying architectural constraints may eventually lead to user dissatisfaction.

Additionally, if there is no clarity in the architecture, a low rumble of uncertainty will continue among all of those extending, maintaining, and using the architecture.

There Are No Technological "Needs"

We speak of customer needs but not of technological needs. Why? Because a technological solution responds only to objective necessities, not subject preferences. The correct solution does not settle here and there. Even when the optimal solution is not implemented, the one that is should consist only of that which is minimally required for it to be employed. Otherwise, you are employing another problem's solution. Should you still want to implement this other problem's solution, make certain you know what the problem is. The reason for this mindset is *verification*. You can only verify that the solution is appropriate by comparing it to the problem set, point for point. Otherwise, you risk adding points of failure that are easily missed by their not having a corresponding reason for inclusion.

Customer Requirements

Substantial customer requirements, on the other hand, can be counted on. The list of specific requirements customers may impose on your Oracle connectivity infrastructure include the following:

- Throughput levels (as measured in transactions or bytes per unit of time)
- Volume (as measured in bytes accessible or processed)
- Specific processing windows in time
- Accommodation of very large databases (VLDB), very many databases (VMDB), and very many users (VMU)
- Accommodation of connections to legacy systems
- Object serving (e.g., CORBA and OLE automation)
- Accommodation of ancillary channel loads (e.g., data capture bursts or metrics dumps)
- High availability (both fault-tolerance and around-the-clock access to data)
- Distributed processing (including distributed updates and client/server operations)
- Single sign-on (or centralized password management)
- Specific network protocols (on specific segments)
- Global access to resources
- Automated Network Management (including SNMP support)

- Extended enterprise technologies

- Mobility; wireless access

- Internet and multimedia services

- Real-time audio/video (for conferencing and news) and instructional audio/video

- Image/document management

- Replication conflict management (centralized or not; automated or not)

- Concurrent application development, testing, and deployment requirements

- Nonproduction instances (including development and several test instances)

- Replication of stored procedures, packages, and perhaps DDL

- Source code control (vis-à-vis automatic recompilation of stored procedures)

- Prototyping, benchmarking, and performance tuning

- Routing where no routing was previously available

- Security needs including node isolation, role management, external interfaces, and multilevel security (MLS)

Designing Your TNS Network

Now that you have compiled information on the load your TNS network design must bear, it is time to design it. First, get a lot of paper and a pencil. You will want to visualize and experiment with the logical placement of nodes. Remember, a picture is worth a thousand words.

TIP
Better yet, get a good network design program. It is likely that you will want to maintain information on your assets. When planning a new TNS is a good time to start. A network design application may already be employed in your organization. If so, get a hold of it and learn how to use it.

Physical Design

It is likely that you will be crafting a solution for supporting your TNS network over an existing physical infrastructure. If so, begin with the network diagram for all affected components. Keep in mind that the more detailed a picture you start with, the better off you will be in the long run. Then determine answers to the following questions.

Is More Than One Network Protocol Supported on the Network?

If more than one network protocol will be supported, you need to determine which protocols will be employed for TNS communication. Each protocol employed will require at least one SQL*Net community. Also, if a node can support more than one protocol, you must decide whether to support multiple Oracle Protocol Adapters on the node.

Will Nodes on Disparate Protocols Need to Communicate with Each Other?

If a connection needs to be established between nodes on different network protocols, such as between an SPX/IPX node and a TCP/IP node, you should employ the Oracle MultiProtocol Interchange (MPI). If you run the MPI, you need to decide whether to do so on a node performing other functions such as running an Oracle7 server. Such decisions are dependent on hardware capabilities and network throughput.

Will You Employ the Oracle Names Release 2.0 Dynamic Discovery Option (DDO)?

DDO is only possible with nodes running SQL*Net release 2.3. Nodes running earlier SQL*Net releases will not belong to the SQL*Net region within which DDO is employed. Also, you must run TCP/IP for DDO to work. DDO relies on well-known ports for address resolution.

TIP

Although a router or IP domain name server may not strike you as a vital consideration in the logical design of the TNS network, it may be. When using a native naming service such as TCP/IP's Domain Naming Service (DNS), you may encounter a penalty if a query is required to resolve a node name stored in a connection descriptor in your SQL*Net configuration file. If you are using static addresses for your servers, and performance is of utmost importance, you can trade operational performance time for maintenance time by storing only the IP address of a node in the connection descriptor rather than the domain name. Although it will require greater maintenance effort, connection establishment time is saved for each first connection to a node.

Techniques

As you work through the various Oracle technology choices to be made, consider the following forms of performance and manageability enhancement. Some concern themselves with how the system is structured, others with the distribution of data. In any case, these techniques may serve to greatly improve the ease of access to data and the simplicity of making changes to your Oracle connectivity infrastructure. The techniques described in the following sections include Optimal Flexible Architecture (OFA) and Segmentation.

Optimal Flexible Architecture

First proposed in 1991 by Cary V. Millsap, Director of Oracle's System Performance Group, a part of the Oracle Services Advanced Technologies group, the Optimal Flexible Architecture (OFA) standard is the recommended scheme for configuring complex Oracle installations. OFA requires some forethought prior to implementation, but it is time well spent. When in place, OFA-compliant sites are easily extensible. In fact, OFA is such a proven success that most of Oracle's ports now install themselves according to OFA principles.

OFA predominantly concerns itself with employing a directory and configuration structure that can support multiple releases of the Oracle7 server on a single node. This is what makes OFA an attractive standard to embrace. The ability to support multiple releases simultaneously will significantly ease the burden put on the database administrator when migrations take place and multiple releases are in place. This feature will aid during any multiple upgrade cycles and reconfigurations required when moving to a new version of the Oracle7 and SQL*Net. Also, employing OFA enables easier duplication of Oracle data files from one machine to the next should this form of partitioning be desired.

TIP
Comprehensive information on OFA is found in "The OFA Standard—Oracle7 for Open Systems," Millsap, Oracle Corporation, September 24, 1995. You can download it from the Oracle Developer Programme web site or order from Alliances Marketing. The Adobe portable display format (PDF) file is numbered 30432.PDF.

Segmentation

An effective means of improving access to data is to segment groups of users. There are two primary forms of segmentation: physical (network) and logical (data). Physical segmentation may take the form of node groupings such as *subnets*. Subnets reduce the amount of network overhead by enabling smaller trips. Also, the fact that there are fewer users on a network segment vying for bandwidth improves performance overall.

Partitioning

Logical segmentation is also advocated. Database access should often be limited to those requiring only certain tables or sets of data in tables. This form of segmentation is called *partitioning*. Entire databases may be limited or just access to certain elements.

Replication

Segmentation is a technique. The processes that make segmentation particularly useful are replication and listener load balancing. Both replication and listener load balancing provide restricted access to certain physical objects to distinct sets of users, allowing you to level across your infrastructure. This aids in increasing reliability with regard to access expectations.

Implementation

The following are some of the migration considerations created by the status quo ante.

NOTE
Whenever the Oracle7 release or the SQL*Net release is changed, you should always recompile any user-developed 3GL applications, including those created with any of the Oracle Precompilers such as Pro*C and applications using SQL*Module. Doing so will ensure that the libraries used to access the server and TNS applications are the same as those used to create them.

Existing SQL*Net Release 2.0 Nodes

There was a change in the format of configuration files after SQL*Net release 2.0. Although the nodes are compatible with SQL*Net release 2.1 and later, you must either update the configuration files or install a later release of SQL*Net. If you chose not to upgrade your configuration files for use with Oracle Network Manager release 3.1, you will not be able to participate in several SQL*Net features that were later introduced. These features are

- Listener load balancing
- The Dynamic Discovery option (DDO) of Oracle Names release 2.0
- Encrypted passwords in LISTENER.ORA

To update the configuration files for use with Oracle Network Manager release 3.1, run the NETCONV program.

Existing ODBC Drivers (Possibly Out of Date or Limited)

Do not presume that because Open Database Connectivity Drivers are already in place that it will be simple to establish a connection to an Oracle7 server. Two factors, discussed in more detail in the ODBC section in Chapter 6, affect your ability to use ODBC to connect to Oracle:

- *Driver availability*—Drivers change with the version of SQL*Net supported; additionally, each driver is installed once per data source. Once you have installed the new SQL*Net release 2.x, you must alter or re-create the data source sets to ensure they use the latest SQL*Net code base.

- *ODBC conformance*—Certain features are only found in Level 2 ODBC drivers; both Level 1 and Level 2 drivers to the same technology may exist in a system. When creating data sources, ensure the driver level is correct. In Windows you can verify the vendor and release through the About box the button opens.

NOTE
Oracle's own drivers, also found in Microsoft's ODBC pack, conform to Level 1 specifications. Other vendors' drivers, such as the Intersolv ODBC Driver Pack included with the Oracle Open Client Adapter for ODBC, conform to Level 2.

Wide Area Network Dispersal

In a distributed database system, especially one in which multiple servers function autonomously as specified by Date's rule, there should exist a single shared time frame. The source must be agreed upon, maintained, and understood by all. Otherwise, inconsistencies created by the use of the SYSDATE() and other local time-stamp functions may result in differing values for the same point in time. Recovery of failed replications, database resynchronization, and other either time-stamped or time-sensitive operations, are subject to improper performance if a single time frame is not shared. This is especially a problem where wide area networks (WANs) are employed to connect geographically dispersed servers.

CHAPTER 9

Oracle Connectivity
Troubleshooting

What we have here is failure to communicate.

—Strother Martin

Despite your best efforts at ensuring trouble-free communication across your Oracle connectivity infrastructure, problems will arise occasionally. It is important that you work to implement appropriate procedures for swift and sustainable problem resolution. One of the key means of doing this is employing enterprise management technology to continually monitor conditions and automate problem resolution. Oracle Enterprise Manager does this quite well. It is covered in Chapter 10. However, many organizations may either not employ such means or choose not to do so for the more mundane problems, which are often simple enough to resolve as they occur.

Fortunately, most problem conditions may be resolved with a single, simple change. With SQL*Net, for example, the likeliest problems are improperly formatted configuration files, typographic errors in the names or addresses of services and nodes, and incomplete installations. This chapter will guide you in employing key best practices for solving problems. Most are nonspecific techniques, applicable to most problem states regardless of the technologies involved.

TIP
Nothing is more humbling than toiling for hours attempting to resolve a problem only to realize the solution was right in front of you all along. Well, perhaps one thing is this: toiling for hours only because you didn't bother to check and discover that the answer was right there in the manual. So, remember: RTFM—Read The Fine Manual! That said, make certain you avail yourself of the many fine sources of reliable Oracle information outlined in Chapter 15. Don't reinvent the wheel, learn from others' mistakes.

Problem Resolution Policy

It is necessary to educate your staff and your users on the appropriate policy to follow when problems occur. Much of this policy will be directed by your standard Help Desk procedures. Where it is not, however, you can do much to ensure you collect the information you need to mitigate the effects of the problem state when it again arises, which it probably will. The following sections will describe useful techniques to employ in the pursuit of effectively error-free operation.

Documentation

There is an adage in the legal profession: "If it isn't written down, it never happened." In many ways this is very true of problem resolution. The single most important thing you can do to improve your enterprise's problem resolution capabilities is to document. Always log problem conditions and their solutions. There are three key reasons for doing this. First, this information will enable you to measure performance and, through analysis, determine where systemic problems lie. Second, you will save time and effort by eliminating the need to re-resolve the typical, recurring problem state. Finally, this information can guide the direction of your training programs, enabling you to focus on areas where the greatest return will be achieved.

Logging Problems

As is often the case, the exact means you employ to log problems is far less important than inculcating the logging practice. At the very least, the following steps should be followed.

1. *Note the symptoms.* Try to include all available metrics or objective measurements such as response timings and records counts to aid in diagnosing the problem.

2. *Note the conditions under which the problem arises.* These conditions should place the problem in an absolute framework, such as "always around 2:00 A.M.," or in a relative framework, such as "after steps a, b, and c have been completed."

3. *Note the conditions under which the problem does not arise.* Known workarounds are helpful in focusing your attention on intersecting elements.

 TIP
Remember, the first time an instance of a particular type of problem is encountered, document first! Regardless of how trivial the problem is, you are documenting it for several reasons including ensuring that new team members are able to learn from your experience.

Documenting Solutions

Once the problem has been resolved, you must document the resolution so that there is a lasting benefit to the exercise.

1. Document the successful alteration.

2. Go back to the original problem documentation. Was any one symptom clearly associated with the problem set? If so, note this as the primary symptom for the solution set.

Clearly, we have skipped the steps on actually resolving the problem. Why? Because it is most important that you log your work. It cannot be overstressed that only with proper measurement and analysis can a process be refined and determined to be robust. That said, it is appropriate to now turn our attention to the actual process of resolving problems.

Proactive Measures

Clearly, you avoid problems by planning for them. There are three primary steps you should take to ensure trouble-free operation. Think of them as the analogues of the shampoo instructions "lather-rinse-repeat." The three proactive steps you should take are

- Think before you design.
- Plan before you implement.
- Test before you deploy to production (repeat this step several times).

In practice, despite best efforts at implementing the most reliable of solutions, problems will occur. Therefore, the following means should be employed to ensure that they are detected early on, preferably before they become problems.

Make certain to note leading indicators of trouble. Leading indicators are the changes in state or thresholds exceeded that indicate impending trouble. You generally detect leading indicators in the following three forms, each of which is described later in this chapter:

- Logging and Audit Trail
- Tracing
- Polling

As you collect sufficient information to determine a leading indicator, put this information back into your monitoring technology, such as Oracle Enterprise Manager. In this manner you quickly ameliorate developing problem conditions and are prepared to effectively resolve those you cannot avoid.

Logging

Logging is an automatic function that is specified at the SQL*Net or ODBC level. In the case of ODBC, as described in Chapter 6, logging is enabled using the DEBUG facility. With SQL*Net, errors are always logged. In the Windows and OS/2 environments, the log files are stored in the ORACLE_HOME hierarchy under the NETWORK\LOG subdirectory. Separate log files are maintained for SQL*Net and for each of the other TNS applications in, for example, SQLNET.LOG and LISTENER.LOG, respectively.

Logging falls under the control of the Logging Facility of SQL*Net. The output of the Logging Facility is easily read and requires no special processing to interpret. The location of the log files is analogous to that of the configuration information that controls logging that, following the previous example, is stored in SQLNET.ORA and LISTENER.ORA, respectively. The configuration files are typically found in the NETWORK\ADMIN subdirectory under ORACLE_HOME.

Error Stack The log file displays its information in a format called the *error stack*. The error stack shows a snapshot of the state of the various software layers. The log file contains consistent state information by performing the following functions:

■ Appending error data to the log file when the event occurs.

NOTE
Logging cannot be disabled for the client, server, listener, and Names Server. This ensures that all errors are recorded. The MultiProtocol Interchange Navigator and Connection Manager may have their logging disabled. When enabled, connection statistics will be collected. The Navigator may optionally log additional information for process or audit control of operations.

■ Logging all connection request data from a client and from most listener control commands.

■ You set logging parameters using Oracle Network Manager, thus ensuring the log file can only be replaced or erased by an administrator. If desired, client log files, stored at each node, can be deleted by the user whose application created them.

CAUTION
In general, these files should not be deleted by users for two reasons: a program using them may still be actively logging, and persistent enterprise-wide determination of problem states may be hindered. Central control of log files should be maintained where possible.

Here is an example of a SQLNET.LOG file from Oracle's SQL*Net release 2.3 documentation.

```
*******************************************************************
Fatal OSN connect error 12533, connecting to:
  (DESCRIPTION=(CONNECT_DATA=(SID=trace)(CID=(PROGRAM=)(HOST=lala)
     (USER=ginger)))(ADDRESS_LIST=(ADDRESS=(PROTOCOL=ipc)
     (KEY=bad_port))(ADDRESS=(PROTOCOL=tcp)(HOST=lala)(POT=1521))))

   VERSION INFORMATION:
     TNS for SunOS: Version 2.0.14.0.0 - Developer's Release
     Oracle Bequeath NT Protocol Adapter for SunOS: Version
     2.0.14.0.0 - Developer's Release
     Unix Domain Socket IPC NT Protocol Adaptor for SunOS: Version
     2.0.14.0.0 - Developer's Release
     TCP/IP NT Protocol Adapter for SunOS: Version 2.0.14.0.0 -
     Developer's Release
   Time: 07-MAY-96 17:38:50
   Tracing to file: /home/ginger/trace_admin.trc
   Tns error struct:
     nr err code: 12206
     TNS-12206: TNS:received a TNS error while doing navigation
     ns main err code: 12533
     TNS-12533: TNS:illegal ADDRESS parameters
     ns secondary err code: 12560
     nt main err code: 503
     TNS-00503: Illegal ADDRESS parameters
     nt secondary err code: 0
     nt OS err code: 0
```

In this case, the problem was caused by a typographical error. The identifier for the parameter PORT in the connection descriptor was misspelled "POT."

Audit Trail   The *audit trail utility* is a feature that began shipping with SQL*Net release 2.3. Audit Trail enables improved utilization of data stored in the listener log file. It takes the data and analyzes its contents, rendering usage statistics in new and more informative ways. The Audit Trail output format is such that it can be easily incorporated into management reports. It yields information such as database access by domain.

Tracing

Tracing is a process that is explicitly activated through a configuration parameter. The Trace Facility produces the trace output. Unlike the log files, trace files contain complete, ongoing details of the connection between the listener and the client. Timing and node information are stored, with complete details on the purpose of the operation including data and SQL operations performed.

Tracing is usually activated for the resolution of a specific problem for which the log file is inconclusive. Tracing is typically not active for very long, as it generates a lot of data that in itself will slow down performance. Also, unlike the log file, trace files require an application to properly interpret. The location of the trace output is generally the NETWORK\TRACE subdirectory under ORACLE_HOME. Each TNS application will create a file with the extension TRC, such as LISTENER.TRC for the SQL*Net listener application.

Here is the same example condition from before, this time from the Trace Facility's point of view:

```
--- TRACE CONFIGURATION INFORMATION FOLLOWS ---
New trace stream is "/private1/oracle/trace_user.trc"
New trace level is 4
--- TRACE CONFIGURATION INFORMATION ENDS ---

--- PARAMETER SOURCE INFORMATION FOLLOWS ---
Attempted load of system pfile source
/private1/oracle/network/admin/sqlnet.ora
Parameter source was not loaded
Error stack follows:
NL-00405: cannot open parameter file

Attempted load of local pfile source /home/ginger/.sqlnet.ora
Parameter source loaded successfully

 -> PARAMETER TABLE LOAD RESULTS FOLLOW <-
Some parameters may not have been loaded
See dump for parameters that loaded OK
 -> PARAMETER TABLE HAS THE FOLLOWING CONTENTS <-
  TRACE_DIRECTORY_CLIENT = /private1/oracle
  trace_level_client = USER
  TRACE_FILE_CLIENT = trace_user
--- PARAMETER SOURCE INFORMATION ENDS ---

--- LOG CONFIGURATION INFORMATION FOLLOWS ---
Attempted open of log stream "/tmp_mnt/home/ginger/sqlnet.log"
Successful stream open
--- LOG CONFIGURATION INFORMATION ENDS ---

Unable to get data from navigation file tnsnav.ora
```

```
local names file is /home/ginger/.tnsnames.ora
system names file is /etc/tnsnames.ora
-<ERROR>- failure, error stack follows
-<ERROR>- NL-00427: bad list
-<ERROR>-   NOTE: FILE CONTAINS ERRORS, SOME NAMES MAY BE MISSING


Calling address:
(DESCRIPTION=(CONNECT_DATA=(SID=trace)(CID=(PROGRAM=)(HOST=lala)
(USER=ginger)))(ADDRESS_LIST=(ADDRESS=(PROTOCOL=ipc)(KEY=bad_port))
(ADDRESS=(PROTOCOL=tcp)(HOST=lala)(POT=1521))))
Getting local community information
Looking for local addresses setup by nrigla
No addresses in the preferred address list
TNSNAV.ORA is not present. No local communities entry.
Getting local address information
Address list being processed...
No community information so all addresses are "local"
Resolving address to use to call destination or next hop
Processing address list...
No community entries so iterate over address list
This is a local community access
Got routable address information
Making call with following address information:
(DESCRIPTION=(EMPTY=0)(ADDRESS=(PROTOCOL=ipc)(KEY=bad_port)))
Calling with outgoing connect data
(DESCRIPTION=(CONNECT_DATA=(SID=trace)(CID=(PROGRAM=)(HOST=lala)
(USER=ginger)))(ADDRESS_LIST=(ADDRESS=(PROTOCOL=tcp)(HOST=lala)
(POT=1521))))
(DESCRIPTION=(EMPTY=0)(ADDRESS=(PROTOCOL=ipc)(KEY=bad_port)))
KEY = bad_port
connecting...
opening transport...
-<ERROR>- sd=8, op=1, resnt[0]=511, resnt[1]=2, resnt[2]=0
-<ERROR>- unable to open transport
-<ERROR>- nsres: id=0, op=1, ns=12541, ns2=12560; nt[0]=511,
nt[1]=2, nt[2]=0
connect attempt failed
Call failed...
Call made to destination
Processing address list so continuing
Getting local community information
Looking for local addresses setup by nrigla
No addresses in the preferred address list
```

```
TNSNAV.ORA is not present. No local communities entry.
Getting local address information
Address list being processed...
No community information so all addresses are "local"
Resolving address to use to call destination or next hop
Processing address list...
No community entries so iterate over address list
This is a local community access
Got routable address information
Making call with following address information:
(DESCRIPTION=(EMPTY=0)(ADDRESS=(PROTOCOL=tcp)(HOST=lala)(POT=1521)))
Calling with outgoing connect data
(DESCRIPTION=(CONNECT_DATA=(SID=trace)(CID=(PROGRAM=)(HOST=lala)(USER
=ginger)))(ADDRESS_LIST=(ADDRESS=(PROTOCOL=tcp)(HOST=lala)(POT=1521))))
(DESCRIPTION=(EMPTY=0)(ADDRESS=(PROTOCOL=tcp)(HOST=lala)(POT=1521)))

-<FATAL?>- failed to recognize: POT

-<ERROR>- nsres: id=0, op=13, ns=12533, ns2=12560; nt[0]=503,
nt[1]=0, nt[2]=0
Call failed...
Exiting NRICALL with following termination result -1
-<ERROR>-  error from nricall
-<ERROR>-    nr err code: 12206
-<ERROR>-    ns main err code: 12533
-<ERROR>-    ns (2)  err code: 12560
-<ERROR>-    nt main err code: 503
-<ERROR>-    nt (2)  err code: 0
-<ERROR>-    nt OS   err code: 0
-<ERROR>- Couldn't connect, returning 12533
```

SQL*DBA, Server Manager, and Navigator   All of these tools provide real-time access to the information saved by the trace facility. Check the documentation for each one on the specifics of activating tracing and setting the collection intervals.

Polling

With Oracle SNMP, you can establish SNMP subagents for your managed nodes. An application such as Oracle Enterprise Manager will periodically poll the master agent for each managed node and compile information on the state of each component. This data will help you formulate the baseline characteristics for your Oracle network. More information can be found in Chapter 4, for SNMP, and in Chapter 10, for Oracle Enterprise Manager.

Reactive (or Ad Hoc) Measures

Many problems cannot be prevented until they happen. The lack of rigor that goes into the design and implementation of most systems will ensure that unanticipated sets of circumstances exist that will evince problem states. Therefore, you should plan to encounter unexpected error states and resolve them as they occur (ad hoc).

You plan for effective reactive problem resolution by employing the following functions:

■ Knowing and wisely employing your tools

■ Employing a consistent problem resolution process

Tools

Remember the adage about only having a hammer and everything resembling a nail? Well, here is a recap of the tools you have at your disposal:

■ Log files

■ Trace files

■ Audit Trail utility output

■ Oracle error message numbers

TIP

New to SQL*Net release 2.3 are these two utilities: Client Status Monitor and Trace Route Utility. The first lets you manage the data in the SQLNET.ORA file without having to resort to an editor. Additionally, it enables remote access to the file from a controlling node, a feature missing from Oracle Network Manager. The second, Trace Route, only works with SQL*Net release 2.3 nodes. It functions similarly to the TCP/IP trace route utility in that it returns the name and order of all nodes traversed in reaching a destination. Should a connection fail, the last connection established identifies the forward failure point of the error condition.

Problem Solving Strategy

Once you have logged the problem conditions, attend to formulating a plan of attack. Like any good diagnostician, recall Occam's Razor: Do not multiply entities needlessly. Simply stated, this means you should not create a complicated explanation for an unknown condition if a simple one is sufficient to explain it. For example, when you go to a doctor presenting certain symptoms, the doctor does not presume you have a rare ailment; instead, the likeliest problem is presumed and the simplest, most efficacious solution is employed. The simplest solution to a problem is likely to be the appropriate one.

The following steps should consistently lead to successful problem resolution practices.

1. Note the likeliest causes of the problem condition.

2. Determine what alterations will likely evoke a successful resolution.

3. Order your alteration candidates in order of confidence.

4. Perform each alteration one at a time and always from the same base problem state unless a previous one has yielded significant improvement.

5. When altering the state of an element to see if it resolves the problem state, only alter a single attribute at a time.

Troubleshooting Connectivity Problems

When a connectivity problem arises, after documenting the initial problem state, check the following first:

- Is the node itself operating properly? Resolve non-Oracle problems first!

- Is the network media active? Ensure the connection works at the network level.

- Is the database active? Test locally with SQL*Plus or SQL*DBA.

- Is the listener to the database active? Test with TNSPING or NETTEST.

Products

Chapter 3 details the installation and debugging of SQL*Net. However, here are a few more conditions and their possible solutions on a product-by-product basis.

ODBC Drivers

ODBC drivers are employed to connect to non-Oracle databases using the Oracle Open Client Adapter for ODBC, or to connect to Oracle7 databases from non-Oracle applications. When connecting to a remote Oracle7 database, SQL*Net is employed; likewise, it is employed when using the two-task driver for a local connection. When using Personal Oracle7 or Oracle Lite, SQL*Net is not required. In the case of Personal Oracle7, the Required Support Files (RSFs) must also previously have been installed.

In addition to Oracle, a number of third-party vendors including the following have ODBC technology both for access to Oracle7 and from Oracle applications:

- Visigenic
- Intersolv
- OpenLink

Conformance Level

A significant performance benefit may be derived by employing ODBC Level 2 drivers. ODBC drivers are rated by conformance level, which may be either 1 or 2. The specification indicates the relative level of conformance to the complete ODBC specification. Oracle's own ODBC drivers are Level 1 compliant.

TIP

Oracle's Open Client Adapter for ODBC comes with Intersolv's Level 2 compliant drivers and manager for a 30-day trial. These offer superior performance and more extensive data source sets than the default sets from Oracle and Microsoft. Open Client Adapter for ODBC comes bundled with Oracle Discoverer/2000. You may also contact Intersolv directly to acquire them.

Performance Problems

Ensure that user expectations are managed when employing ODBC technology. Although ODBC is not innately inferior, the flexibility of a nonspecific database interface comes at the cost of technology-specific performance enhancements. Problems related to ODBC performance are generally implementation-specific. Ensure that appropriate blocking of records is being performed for optimum throughput.

Error Messages

When using ODBC drivers, you will be provided with error messages from several sources:

- The ODBC driver
- The database management system
- The ODBC driver manager

Each generates error messages in an indentifiable format. The following sections explain how to determine the source of the error message and what steps to next take.

ODBC Driver Error Messages   When the ODBC driver provides an error message, it will be in the following format:

```
[vendor] [ODBC_component] message
```

"ODBC_component" is the component in which the error occurred and "message" describes the error condition as reported by the component. The usefulness of the message is based solely on the quality of the message provided by the ODBC driver vendor. Here is an example of an error message from Intersolv's ODBC driver for Oracle7:

```
[INTERSOLV] [ODBC Oracle7 driver] Login incorrect.
```

To determine the appropriate solution, check the last ODBC call your application made for possible problems or contact your ODBC application vendor. Determining the last ODBC call is performed with the DEBUG feature of ODBC. Information on employing DEBUG in ODBC is in Chapter 6.

Database Management System Error Messages   Recall, if employing Open Client Adapter for ODBC, the data source is likely not to be an Oracle7 server. It may even be a flat file. These messages will be in the following format:

```
[vendor] [ODBC_component] [data_source] message
```

Here is an example of an error message from a Microsoft Access database:

```
[MICROSOFT] [ODBC Access driver] [Access] Error 94: Invalid use of NULL
```

ODBC Driver Manager Error Messages   The driver manager is the dynamic link library (DLL) that establishes the connection to the ODBC driver, submits queries to the driver, and hands the result sets back to the calling application. Driver manager errors are provided in the following format:

```
[vendor] [ODBC DLL] message
```

The vendor will be the originator of the driver manager software. Typically it is Microsoft, Oracle, or Intersolv. In some cases it will be the hardware vendor such as Apple or Sun. An example of an error from the Oracle driver manager will look like this:

```
[Oracle] [ODBC DLL] Driver does not support this function
```

Open Client Adapter for ODBC

Most of the problems that arise from use of the Open Client Adapter for ODBC (OCA/ODBC) are presented by the ODBC drivers. However, as there are many areas in which an application developed using Developer/2000 technology may inadvertently use Oracle7-specific operations, you should be aware of the following suggestions Oracle makes regarding the successful use of OCA/ODBC.

TIP

Always check the Release Notes for the specific OCA/ODBC target database accessed. Each varies with regard to features supported. The Release Notes are your likeliest source of solutions for OCA/ODBC problems.

Generic Restrictions

This section contains the generic restrictions Oracle indicates apply to each Developer/2000 application when running with Oracle Open Client Adapter.

Case Sensitivity   Oracle automatically converts the names of all database objects to uppercase. Some databases, such as SQL Server, however, are case sensitive. If possible, install the target database to be case insensitive.

Scalar Functions   One of the defining characteristics of Oracle7 technology is the set of user-extendable scalar functions that can be employed in SQL statements. These include TO_CHAR() and DECODE(). PL/SQL is responsible for parsing the Oracle7-specific scalar functions. Therefore, functions such as USER that may be employed to determine connectivity issues will not work with non-Oracle databases. SQL functions common to both Oracle7 and non-Oracle databases will function as expected.

Data Dictionary Objects   There are Oracle-specific views, especially the virtual objects, that do not exist in non-Oracle databases. This is an issue when attempting to employ techniques requiring checking the V$SESSION object, for example.

Locking   Applications cannot always perform locking on foreign database objects. For example, to lock an Access table, the user must specify the appropriate locking mode in the ODBC setup panel when establishing the ODBC data source. Locking modes in the Developer/2000 application have no effect on many of the foreign databases.

NOWAIT Clause for Locks   Performance may be significantly affected when the NOWAIT clause, appended to SELECT statements, is not supported by non-Oracle7 databases. NOWAIT enables call-specific pessimistic blocking to be employed. Without it, the application will behave as if it is in *delayed locking mode,* also called *optimistic locking mode.* The application will wait to lock the corresponding row in the database until the transaction is about to be committed. With this setting, the record is locked only while the transaction is being posted to the database, not while the operator is editing the record.

   If another user has a lock and the application is consequently unable to obtain a lock, the application will query the user as to whether a reattempt should be made. The operator, through the lock dialog box, can click on "Yes" and wait for the lock, or terminate the locking procedure by pressing CTRL-C (or its equivalent as determined by Oracle Terminal).

CAUTION
Be very aware of the impact this has on noninteractive applications. When the lock dialog cannot be employed, the application may hang or abend depending on the implementation.

SELECT FOR UPDATE   If you are using a driver that does not support the FOR UPDATE in SELECT statements, set the Locking Mode property to Delayed and override (nullify) any default On-Lock triggers.

COMMIT/ROLLBACK   Unlike Oracle, other databases may only support one cursor per connection, as does SQL Server. Because each cursor has an individual connection, committing a master-detail block application requires coordinating the various cursors and may lead to significant performance hits. This is especially the case when two-phase commits are required. If possible, select a driver to the target database that does support this feature.

LONG Columns   Some databases do not permit LONG data to be fetched in blocks. This may severely degrade performance if a complete transmission and reception of a LONG data item must be completed before other operations may continue. Likewise, some databases prohibit the fetching of more than one LONG column per query, requiring modification of code.

Additionally, incremental offset-based fetching of LONG field data is not supported by ODBC. The ODBC specification permits only sequential fetching of data. Therefore, if only a known segment of LONG data is required, the entire LONG element still must be retrieved.

DDL Statements   The Transaction option is turned on for some drivers in OCA/ODBC. When on, the usage of the DDL statements in the following table may be restricted.

CREATE DATABASE	CREATE TABLE
CREATE INDEX	CREATE VIEW
All DROP statements	SELECT INTO
GRANT	REVOKE
ALTER DATABASE	TRUNCATE TABLE
UPDATE STATISTICS	RECONFIGURE
LOAD DATABASE	LOAD TRANSACTION
DISK INIT	

When issuing DDL statements, such as through the FORMS_DDL built-in, you must not issue any subsequent DML statements until you commit or roll back your transaction.

CAUTION
It is useful to enable logging and tracing to debug connections to foreign data sources. Most of these options, however, are dynamically set using DDL. For that reason, heed the considerations in this last item.

Multiple Inserts in a PL/SQL Block   You will detect what appears to be a connection failure if you try multiple inserts in a PL/SQL block. Should multiple insert statements refer to the same database page for the table in a PL/SQL block, the application will deadlock. This is because the ODBC driver executes the insert statements through separate connections, each of which locks the other out. (This is related to the item above on a single cursor per connection.)

Oracle Objects for OLE (OO4O)

The following error conditions and resolutions are most common when diagnosing problems in solutions employing OO4O.

OLE Initialization and OLE Automation Errors

As OO4O relies on dynamic link libraries (DLLs) that may already be on your Windows system, you should ensure that the installation process was properly performed. Determine if any of the OLE DLLs, listed here, are duplicated on your system. If so, use the Properties function in Windows File Manager to check the version number of the DLLs. Check the numbers against those indicated in the Release Notes that accompanied your version of OO4O.

TIP

If you are using Visual Basic 3.0, be aware that it does not include the OLE file TYPELIB.DLL. This is a common problem and one you should check first.

Missing or Incorrect OLE Files   If you are missing the Microsoft OLE 2.0 runtime files or if you find the files but they are out of date or of a previous release, you should rerun the OO4O installation process. Select the option entitled "Microsoft OLE 2.0 Libraries" only. This will install only the correct OLE files and will not require you to go through the entire installation process. The files Microsoft requires for OLE2 are shown in the following table.

COMPOBJ.DLL	OLE2.DLL
OLE2.REG	OLE2CONV.DLL
OLE2DISP.DLL	OLE2NLS.DLL
OLE2PROX.DLL	STDOLE.TLB
STORAGE.DLL	TYPELIB.DLL

Registration Database Missing OLE2 Data   Whenever OLE components are employed, the Windows registration database must be updated. Should there be a problem during installation, OLE data may end up incompletely registered. To correct this condition, run the program REGEDIT.EXE from Program Manager or File Manager. Select the option Merge Registration File... as shown here:

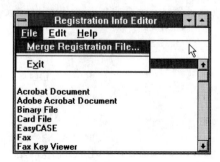

The registration file you should select for merging is called OLE2.REG. It is typically found in the directory in which Windows was installed in the System subdirectory below it. For example, here it is shown in the most likely location, C:\WINDOWS\SYSTEM.

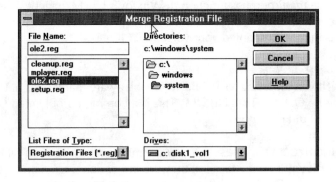

Missing or Incorrect OO4O Files

As with the Microsoft OLE2 data, OO4O's own files may not have been installed. As with the OLE2 libraries, you may install just the OO4O files by running OO4O setup again. Select the option entitled "Oracle Objects Server" to install it alone.

Registration Database Missing OO4O Information

OO4O objects may not have been completely registered in the Windows registration database. As with the OLE2 objects, run the REGEDIT.EXE program and merge information from a file. In the case of the OO4O objects, select the file ORAIPSRV.REG, typically found in the same location as the OLE2.REG file.

Redistributable Files

When running an OO4O application, there should be one and only one copy each of the files ORAIPSRV.DLL, ORAIPSRV.TLB, and ORAIPSRV.REG. These should be located in \WINDOWS\SYSTEM subdirectory. If missing, follow the steps outlined above.

Likewise, the following redistributable files, required for OLE applications, should exist solely in the \WINDOWS\SYSTEM directory. Depending on the technology employed to develop your OO4O application, the following DLLs are also required.

Language	File
Borland C++ 4.0	ORACLB.DLL
Borland C++ 4.5	ORACLB45.DLL
Microsoft C++	ORACLM.DLL
Visual Basic 3.0	ORADC.VBX, VBOA300.DLL, VBRUN300.DLL

Property and Method Name Errors

OO4O is designed to enable simple replacement of the standard Visual Basic data control. As such, especially when Access 2.0 is also installed on the same machine, a number of Oracle Data Control methods and properties have names different from those of the default ones. For the most part, these names are the same but are preceded with "db."

CAUTION
Incorrect selection will lead to anomalous results often appearing only at runtime as connectivity errors.

Additionally, the data type for all of the Oracle objects are of the data type object.

Incorrect Database_Name, Connect Property, or Argument to OpenDatabase Method

The formal syntax for the OpenDatabase method is

```
Set oradbval = orasession.DbOpenDatabase(database_name, connect_string, options)
```

where the arguments are as listed here:

Argument	Description
database_name	SQL*Net identifier used to connect the data control to a database
connect_string	Username/password to be used when connecting to the Oracle database
options	Bit-flag word used to set optional modes; 0 accepts defaults

The following syntax should be employed to properly use the OpenDatabase method:

```
Dim OraSession As Object
Dim OraDatabase As Object
Dim OraDynaset As Object

Set OraSession = CreateObject("OracleInProcServer.XOraSession")
'Create the OraDatabase Object by opening a connection to Oracle.
Set OraDatabase = OraSession.DbOpenDatabase("ExampleDb", "scott/tiger", 0&)
```

NOTE
As recommended, the OpenDatabase method in the previous listing was referred to as DbOpenDatabase to ensure no name conflict occurs.

Slow or Hung Connections

These may be caused by the mode employed in the OpenDatabase method. The Lock Wait mode is of interest for connectivity considerations. The default mode, Wait mode, employs a SELECT...FOR UPDATE to lock the row in the database when dynaset rows are about to be modified (using Edit). This means that if the row about to be changed has been locked by another process, SELECT ... FOR UPDATE will cause a wait until the row is unlocked before proceeding. Lock Wait mode also affects any SQL statements processed using ExecuteSQL.

Alternatively, NoWait mode may be employed. With NoWait mode, an error code is immediately returned if the row about to be updated is locked.

The Visual Basic identifiers for the flags are ORADB_NOWAIT and ORADB_LOCKWAIT.

NOTE
If a connection exists within the same OraSession object, identified by the same connect_string and database_name arguments, it will automatically be shared. Each database object will remain distinct. An OraConnection object is then created automatically, appearing within the OraConnections collection of the session. Be aware that opening a database has the effect of opening a connection, should one not already exist. It does not, however, perform any SQL actions.

Missing Files or Files Not in Path, GPFs, and Other Windows Problems

See the following section on operating system-specific problems for other Windows-specific conditions and their solutions.

Operating System-Specific Problems

Certain classes of problems are related to aspects of the operating system that the client node or the Oracle7 server is running. The following sections highlight a number of vagaries specific to the major operating systems on which Oracle technology is run.

Windows 3.1, 3.11, and Windows for Workgroups 3.11

The most common problem in 16-bit Windows implementations is that of dynamic link library (DLL) usage. Another one is that of blocking operations. General Protection Faults round out the list.

Dynamic Link Libraries (DLLs)

Many applications share DLLs but unwittingly rely on version-specific properties of them. To this end, most well-behaved applications check for conflicting DLLs at the time of installation. If any are found, the setup program should provide the user with a choice of replacing the DLL, using the older one, or placing the one known to work with the application being installed in a directory local to the application so as to not conflict with other applications using the extant version of the DLL.

TIP
Don't forget that applications you develop for distribution to end users may rely on certain redistributable files. It is up to you to ensure they are copied to the target machine along with your application. This is especially important when running applications reliant on SQL*Net or OLE on end-user machines where the required files may never have been installed.

Duplicate or Missing Files   Remove any duplicate Oracle Required Support Files (RSFs). The Oracle RSFs should typically reside in the BIN subdirectory under ORACLE_HOME (e.g., \ORAWIN\BIN). The DLL RSFs are named ORA7*.DLL, CORE*.DLL, and NLS*.DLL.

If RSFs are missing, you should run Oracle Installer (or the setup program for non-Oracle Installer applications such as Oracle Power Objects, Oracle Mobile Agents, and Oracle Objects for OLE) to ensure the files are properly reinstalled. If Oracle Installer indicates the files are already installed, then ensure that the files are in directories included in your PATH environment variable. The PATH variable is typically set in the AUTOEXEC.BAT file or in another DOC batch file CALLed from AUTOEXEC.BAT.

The problem with the Required Support Files is also a possibility with the SQL*Net files. As with the RSFs, ensure SQL*Net files are either in the PATH or the PATH is modified to include their location.

Blocking Operations

Depending on the version and implementation of Oracle software, certain network functions are *blocking operations.* This means that until a query and response cycle has been completed, all input and output on the node is disabled. Although Windows supports multitasking, the keyboard will be locked up until the blocking operation has completed. The solutions are to either patiently wait until the operation is completed or to upgrade to a nonblocking version of the SQL*Net API .

General Protection Faults (GPFs)

Most GPFs occur in Oracle environments when installing new software while other programs are running. Other applications may be sharing objects that are being overwritten. When this occurs, the information in the Windows Registration Database gets out of sync with that of running code, resulting in GPFs.

To prevent this condition, always install new software immediately after starting Windows and before running any other application. Check the LOAD= and RUN= lines in WIN.INI file along with the STARTUP program group in Program Manager to ensure no applications are being started automatically. In the case of the STARTUP group, you can move the icons to another group temporarily, or select File | Properties for the STARTUP group to change its name temporarily.

You can comment out the LOAD= and RUN= lines temporarily by placing a semicolon (;) at the beginning of each of the lines. This functions as a comment. Don't forget to remove them when you have finished installing new software after checking to ensure new LOAD= and RUN= lines were not inserted by the installer.

Windows NT and Win95

The most common problem for users of Windows NT is that of 32-bit versus 16-bit library coexistence. Most applications developed for use with 16-bit Windows are incapable of connecting to remote databases under the 32-bit implementations of Windows NT and Win95. This has been most evident with the ODBC drivers. This is caused by libraries employed to create the drivers being different from those used to create the run-time libraries installed with the 16-bit applications.

You will notice also that the Oracle home directory defaults to a different location that is incompatible with that of the 16-bit software. This is necessary to enable dual-boot configurations to operate properly.

NetWare

Novell's NetWare is the most popular network operating system in use. A network operating system is one where central coordination of resources takes place. (Another popular network operating systems is Banyan VINES.) When using

NetWare, the SPX/IPX protocol is typically employed. When a node running on Novell is started, it establishes a relationship with the NetWare server closest to it. It will rely on this server to provide file sharing, naming services, and service status notification. NetWare employs a technology they call Server Advertising Protocol (SAP) to perform these and other functions.

Most important to consider in NetWare are the two TNS support programs required to support the server-based operations. The primary ones are *ntspxctl* and *ntisbsdm*. The first, ntspxctl, is used to start and stop the SAP broadcast daemon. The second, ntisbsdm, is used by SQL*Net to register and remove names, and to query a NetWare *bindery*, the directory service providing name-into-address translation.

Solaris

A well-known problem with Solaris is related to temporary files created in the directory /var/tmp/o. Removal of this directory and its contents resolves a slew of connection problems. This problem has been resolved in later versions of the SQL*Net software, but from time to time it is known to crop up on re-installations of older versions of the software by unwitting users.

Macintosh

The introduction of the Power Macintosh computers, employing the RISC PowerPC chipset, significantly boosted the capabilities of the Macintosh architecture. Unfortunately, there are problems that beset certain applications expecting the traditional Motorola 68000 family of microprocessors. The PowerPC does support the 68K instruction set in emulation mode. Some applications, however, cannot run on the PowerPC for reasons related to timing differences between the 68K and the much faster PowerPC chip.

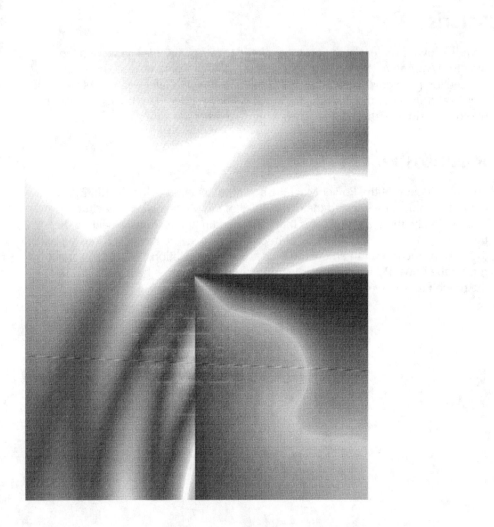

CHAPTER 10

Oracle Enterprise Manager

Big Brother is watching.

—George Orwell

Chapter 9 demonstrated how to track down and resolve problems in your TNS network; it explained that a relatively small number of conditions are responsible for the majority of problems. In the early life of a network, most of these conditions are related to the network configuration and are caused by incorrectly defined parameters. Employing solid configuration management practices helps prevent such problems. In network deployment, as in most things, proper planning is essential. However, abnormal events such as hardware failures cannot always be prevented. As your distributed database system grows, so the frequency of abnormal events is likely to grow as well. Each new software program, node, network segment, and database increases the complexity of your enterprise network. You must keep vigil on your network to ensure all of its functions are normal; otherwise, a single failure may lead to a cascade of failures. As the saying goes, "a chain is only as strong as its weakest link," and all that.

Clearly, no one can afford the number of technicians required to monitor each individual component in an enterprise network around the clock. Fortunately, it is not necessary to do so, as there exists technology to automate both network oversight and configuration management. Supporting industry-standard network management technology, Oracle Enterprise Manager (OEM) provides a platform from which to manage your Oracle network elements, either locally or for the entire enterprise.

Oracle's original network management plan envisioned two distinct add-on products—one for workgroups and software distribution, code-named Battlestar, and another for the enterprise, code-named Mission Control. Mission Control became OEM, and Battlestar became a component of OEM that provides a single solution for both workgroup and enterprise networks. OEM is a standard component of all Oracle Workgroup and Enterprise Servers starting with release 7.3.

Network Management

Network management encompasses far more than failure notification and configurations. Software distribution and license management, statistics acquisition, job scheduling, preventative maintenance, and capacity planning are all aspects of enterprise management. OEM comes bundled with tools for some of these needs and vendor-independent tools for supporting the others. To appreciate the benefits OEM provides, an introduction to network management is an appropriate place to start.

Why Do You Need Network Management Technology?

Network management technology serves to automate operations. By automating operations, the best practices can be consistently followed and the dangers of human intervention, especially operator errors, can be mitigated. The following list describes characteristics of operations suitable for automation.

Time-Consuming Operations

Backups are an excellent example of this type of ideally automated task. Once properly crafted and tested, a backup process should be automated. Otherwise, operations staff periodically will need to remember to check on its status and perform whatever is required for the backup to complete. With automation, many process steps, likely of varying duration, are accomplished in order and without delay.

Critical Operations

Two types of critical operations should be automated. The first is fault handling. Most faults should be processed immediately with automation. If not, multiple unattended fault conditions can quickly escalate into a systemwide failure. The second type of critical operation that should be automated is a scheduled event, such as a replication task or a clean-up task. In increasingly tight 7*24 schedules, a missed task launch may mean the difference between performing an operation slightly behind schedule and not performing a critical scheduled task until the next cycle. Automating such functions renders the need to make this sort of decision rare.

Complex Operations

Certain types of operational tasks, such as determining resource allocations or load balancing, may be computing intensive. While easily described, these tasks lend themselves to multiple points of failure if performed by hand. Automation of such tasks, once properly tested and verified, eliminates the likelihood of failure—especially if the tasks need to be performed near the end of a shift!

Frequently Performed Operations

When you perform an operation frequently, there is a tendency to begin to perform it without thinking. With the monotony of repeated operations comes the danger of not foreseeing the consequence of an action, or even carelessness. Automating these types of functions is one of the reasons people employ computers.

Infrequently Performed Operations

If frequently performed operations are subject to mind-numbing repetition, infrequent ones are often forgotten. A real-world example: checking your smoke alarm. By taking advantage of scheduling facilities in network management technology, infrequent but likely important tasks may be performed without fear of unfamiliarity degrading the operation or forgetfulness overlooking it entirely.

ISO Network Management Framework

As network management is such a broad charter, functional frameworks have been developed to describe the scope and divisions of management components. The most prominent vendor-independent network management framework is that of the International Organization for Standardization (ISO). It describes the following functional characteristics of network management:

- Fault management
- Configuration management
- Performance analysis
- Security management
- Accounting

For each functional characteristic, a network management implementation may provide either *advisory* capabilities or *control* capabilities, or both. Advisory network management capabilities alone guide the development of standards and the retention of status information. Control network management capabilities enable automated responses to changes in network status.

The Railway System as a Metaphor

The following sections will describe what each of these functional characteristics encompasses. We will use a railroad system to illustrate aspects of a managed network. Think of the railroad system as an X.25 packet network. Each train is analogous to a data packet. Each car in the train is analogous to a message. To ensure efficient network utilization, all traffic destined from point A to point B is aggregated on the next train going out, roughly, in the direction of the destination. At each junction, decisions are made as to the most optimal train configurations for getting each car to its destination. Each junction is similar to a router. At each train yard, cars are added and removed, perhaps attached to different trains to complete their journeys. The train yard is analogous to a packet assembler/disassembler (PAD). Segments of the railway system are owned by various entities and are therefore subject to local vagaries. This is analogous to the various types of network media employed and the constraints each place on traffic over them.

Fault Management

Networks have traditionally been centrally monitored. Since the earliest significant managed networks, the railroad systems of the 1800s, personnel have been employed to monitor them. Monitoring is performed for two reasons: to track network traffic and to ensure network integrity. In the case of railroads, network traffic is monitored primarily to avoid collisions. Network integrity is monitored to ensure there are no continuity breaks. Similarly, we monitor computer networks to ensure that traffic does not overwhelm the network components' ability to efficiently move data and that there are no failures preventing a message getting from node a to node b.

Events   As with certain other media, railroad tracks may work bidirectionally. At any one instance, however, each track segment is unidirectional. Switches control the entry and exit of trains from track segments. This switching is an example of an *event*. An event is a key concept in network management and is any occurrence or state change that is identifiable. Some events are scheduled; others occur as required. In a computer network the analogous event is that of a packet being routed. It results in counters being updated and load being smoothed.

Faults   A *fault* is a type of event that should not normally happen. Two trains on the same network segment traveling in opposite directions is a fault. Simple vector arithmetic fails to capture the undesirability of this situation!
   Faults generally arise for one of two reasons:

  1. A component or process has failed, either directly causing a fault or failing to prevent one.

  2. An unanticipated condition has occurred.

   Fault management is intended to alert the network manager of a failure. Certain faults can be *trapped;* that is, the fault event can be identified and a sequence of corrective events activated to mitigate the effects of the fault. For example, a train failing to stop at a signal before a track switch may automatically have its brakes applied, preventing it from colliding with another on the same segment. This is a foreseeable event for which a component has been implemented, preventing the fault from occurring. Likewise, a power failure's effects may be mitigated by employing uninterruptible power supplies (UPS). The UPS generates a fault event when the power fails, and it takes over providing power to the unit. If this event is trapped, the management practices in place may direct the affected units to perform an orderly shutdown until power is restored.

Configuration Management

As mentioned earlier, proper planning mitigates the effects of future problems. Likewise, standards help ensure that proven solutions are implemented and that the wheel is not reinvented with each new component installation. The primary goal of configuration management is to ensure that known successful combinations of hardware, software, and their parameters are maintained and to ensure that only successful combinations are deployed.

Configuration management is generally implemented to fulfill the following subfunctions:

- Dependency management

- Asset management

- License management

Dependency Management   This aspect of configuration management concerns itself with ensuring that all required combinations of components are accounted for. In this manner, successful deployment of systems may be ensured. Otherwise, unreliable or untested combinations of technology may be deployed, leading to systemic problems.

Oracle Network Manager (ONM) is a technology-specific configuration management tool crafted to perform dependency design. ONM ensures that the Oracle TNS configuration meets minimal requirements for connectivity. However, ONM neither knows whether the configuration has been successfully deployed nor monitors the network. Similarly, ONM cannot dynamically reconfigure components. Like most dependency management tools, ONM functions solely as an advisory network management tool.

Asset Management   Asset management is the tracking of hardware and software components and their locations. Where necessary, serialized tracking of each element is performed. This is often required for proper regulatory reporting, for example, when calculating depreciation and applying it to the correct business unit. Successful asset management also enables network managers to calculate the impact and cost of technology changes, such as when upgrading or replacing certain types of devices. Asset management is by definition an advisory function.

License Management   Closely associated with asset management, license management capabilities are employed to track the number of contractually authorized users for each component. Generally, license management is limited to software. Although mostly used in an advisory manner, license management may be used to control access to either a fixed number of users or a set of named users where the software itself cannot provide that function. As a result, license management is minimally provided in the form of an advisory tool but yields its greatest benefit when employed as a control tool.

An example of a license management control implementation is that used to manage stand-alone horizontal applications such as word processors and spreadsheets. If a single copy is shared on a server, the license management component of a network management system will ensure that the number of simultaneous users licensed is not exceeded. Additionally, it may ensure that only certain users are allowed to use the software. Events are used to determine how many people are actively using a managed software program and who they are.

Performance Analysis

There is another reason for monitoring traffic. By tracking the movement of data, or railcars in the train example, analysis leading to more efficient deployment of resources is possible. Management can plan for growth by extrapolating from current traffic patterns. When the telephone network was deployed, its rolling stock, the phone call, was similarly monitored to prevent congestion and manage growth. Reams of data were created, helping the network architects determine how to more efficiently deploy each new segment.

In your own network, you can configure your network components to generate event data for later performance analysis. As such events themselves can create network traffic, careful consideration must be given to ensure that event generation does not itself lead to network congestion.

Security Management

Network security management concerns itself with ensuring that the following aspects of the network are properly overseen:

- Authentication
- Privacy
- Integrity

Security-related events may be generated to create audit trails of activity. At the very least, faults should be processed whenever a security breach is detected.

Authentication   Authentication management serves to ensure the network is only available for use by authorized users.

Privacy   Privacy management serves to ensure that network traffic is not subject to unauthorized viewing or capture.

Integrity   Integrity management serves to ensure that network traffic is not delayed, removed, retransmitted, or subject to unauthorized modification.

Accounting

Accounting management provides a means of capturing utilization statistics on a per-user or per-account basis. The purpose of accumulating this information is to determine the load distribution among users and accounts. In many cases, users and/or accounts will pay a prorated portion of network component expenses based on utilization. Other times, asset management information is used to assess network component cost allocations.

Network Management Implementations

The most successful network management implementations have been the Simple Network Management Protocol (SNMP) and the Common Management Information Protocol (CMIP). Why two? SNMP predates CMIP but is limited in its abilities. SNMP was originally devised as a truly simple means of managing network hardware components. CMIP is part of the Open System Interconnect (OSI) model, the same one that provides a seven-layer protocol stack. Partly because OSI was promoted as part of the U.S. federal systems standard, the Government OSI Profile (GOSIP), and partly because it supports greater functionality than SNMP, CMIP has endured.

The ISO functional model describes the types of tasks network management technologies perform. Management implementations such as SNMP and CMIP describe the technology required to collect and process the data required for those tasks.

SNMP

The simple network management protocol (SNMP), briefly described in earlier chapters, provides the technology most often implemented to manage network devices. SNMP's growth has been primarily driven by that of TCP/IP, as SNMP is implemented as a User Datagram Protocol (UDP) service under TCP/IP.

SNMP was originally intended to manage devices. The flexibility of its design, however, allows it to be used to manage applications as well. To understand SNMP, a few definitions are in order.

Managed Device   A managed device is a node or other network component that is running one or more programs called SNMP agents. Managed applications are those with data and/or parameters accessible by SNMP agents. Each managed device is referred to by its IP address. Managed applications are referred to by their Object ID on the managed device.

NOTE
The term *managed device* will be used for the remainder of this chapter. However, keep in mind that managed applications are essentially equivalent.

Object ID   This is the unique identifier for a managed device/application data element or parameters. Each OID has a datatype and access rights associated with it.

Abstract Notation Syntax 1 (ANS.1)   This is the format in which OIDs and SNMP actions are transmitted.

Management Information Base   Each OID is a leaf on the management information base (MIB) tree. The tree contains public OID branches and technology-specific, or private, OID branches. The MIB structure as proposed in RFC1157 was supplemented with the RDBMS MIB branches proposed in RFC 1697.

SNMP Agent   The SNMP agent is the software residing on a managed device that provides parameter data to the management station when requested and sets local parameters when instructed to do so by the management station. Each SNMP agent processes only the OID values it has access to.

Master Agent   Some managed devices run multiple agents. The master agent is used as a single connection point for all agents on a managed device.

Management Station   The management station is a node used to monitor and control managed devices and applications. It also enables the network management staff to refer to MIB objects by name and not by OID. SNMP management stations monitor and control managed devices using a small set of commands. These commands are GET and GET NEXT, SET, and TRAP.
      SNMP does not specify what data is maintained. SNMP specifies how data requests are made and the format of responses. As a result, the management station generally runs software that maintains information about each managed device and application and the data and parameters accessible through SNMP.

NOTE
Oracle SNMP agent support is implemented using Oracle Network Manager. Refer to Chapter 4 for an example of SNMP configuration.

SNMP V2

SNMP's success has highlighted its failings. There are three primary shortcomings to SNMP, as follows:

1. It is primarily a polling protocol. Agents wait to be polled to notify the management station of the managed device's status. Traps, of course, are immediately transmitted, but despite their name, the event does not necessarily wait for resolution. Think of traps as *alerts,* not suspensions.

2. An intentionally lightweight protocol, SNMP requires many interactions to check and/or update many MIB variables.

3. SNMP is not secure. There is no means of authenticating SNMP commands. Therefore, SET operations on many managed devices remain unavailable to prevent unauthorized modification of parameters.

Two SNMP-like technologies have been proposed to replace SNMP. They both provide a means of securing SNMP traffic and an aggregate GET verb, also called GET BULK. Without the former, any managed device was open to unauthorized access and perhaps modification. The latter lessens SNMP traffic load on a network by permitting an entire set of MIB variables to be retrieved with a single command.

Unfortunately, the two camps, known as SNMPv2* and SNMPv2U, continue to squabble over which solution is better. SNMPv2* sports encryption innately. Proponents of SNMPv2U say their approach is peppier, but it requires that the user's implementation provide the encryption technology. Ironically, the fragmentation in the camps is between the two chief proponents of SNMP, Jeff Case of SNMP Research and Marshall Rose of Dover Beach Consulting. Regardless of which proposal succeeds, the promise of SNMP as a viable network management implementation will continue to be fulfilled.

Common Management Protocol

Common Management Protocol (CMP) is a recent remote procedure call (RPC) specification from Ki Networks with support from IBM and Sun Microsystems. Unlike the SNMP mechanism, where a verb is provided and values are returned or set, CMP calls for processing to be distributed across each subnet. This is intended to reduce SNMP traffic and enable local nodes to perform management station operations. CMP is a standard proposed to the X/Open standards consortia.

Remote Monitoring (RMON)

RMON was introduced as a means of improving efficiencies in network management. Whereas SNMP is based on polling of managed devices using UDP, RMON functions at the data link layer of a network. RMON implementations generally are supported alongside SNMP and complement it. The next revision of RMON, RMON2, will define how to monitor network and application-layer traffic.

Management Stations

Once a technology has been selected for network management, the functions of the management stations themselves must be understood. Once again, a framework devised by ISO describes the aspects of a technology. In this, ISO provides a framework for management operations rather than functions. These operations describe what is done to the data collected and processed by management stations in a network management system.

ISO Network Management Operations

The following operations describe the occupational processes performed on data collected from and on managed devices themselves.

Problem Management   Also known as help desk management, problem management is concerned with logging events requiring human response, assigning responsible parties, and tracking the resolution of the event. Information captured should be categorized to aid in future events on the affected and similar managed devices.

Instrumentation Management   Instrumentation management concerns itself with the analog and digital representation of captured data. It enables the network manager to view graphs, drill down on data points, and otherwise view data in more informative ways than just numbers.

Event Management   Event management concerns itself with tracking the universe of events known and the actions that should either be automatically performed or result in action recommendations.

Inventory Management   Inventory management concerns itself with physical location and description information for all hardware components. It is generally associated with the Problem Management operation to ensure tracking of events to equipment.

Asset Management   Asset management transcends inventory management in that software items and their licensing are also accommodated. It also concerns itself with access considerations, which inventory management does not.

Automated Discovery Tools for Topology Mapping   Automated discovery covers operations related to diagramming the network topology. This operation may feed data to the inventory operation to keep the information in sync.

> **NOTE**
> Oracle Names release 2 Dynamic Discovery Option is an example of an automated network management discovery tool.

Software Management   Software management concerns itself with the proper distribution and installation of software and its associated parameter files.

Workload Management   It is important in any distributed processing network to account for fluctuations in network component load. Workload management concerns itself with anticipating and reacting to changes in workload so that no one component bears an inappropriate amount of the load at any point in time.

Data Management   Data management concerns itself with the compilation, aggregation, and storage characteristics of network management data. There are likely millions of data points collected in the modern enterprise network. How they are maintained to ensure their greatest utility is the concern of this operation.

Reporting   The means, frequency, and detail in which network management data is reported is handled by the Reporting operation.

Change Management   This operation concerns itself with the orderly transition of hardware, software, and operational changes. Examples include the reconciliation of data captured under previous practices with that captured under new parameters. Others concern themselves with the orderly migration of data and users to new hardware components.

Capacity Planning   Taking the data captured and the plans entered for change management operations, capacity planning operations attempt to divine the appropriate accommodation requirements for changes in operational levels. Operational levels include user counts, application load, data volume, and time considerations.

License Management   License management affects the operational process based on data captured in the asset operation. This is where users may find themselves locked out of operations due to too many simultaneous users.

TIP
Keep an eye on this aspect of network management. As network computing gains prominence, an anticipated successful model will rely on just-in-time access to software. No more buying licenses to accommodate expected volume. Each use is charged separately. You only pay for what you use.

Device Management   The original reason for network management, the controlling of network devices, is implemented by the device management operation.

Management Station Topology
Although you may have settled on a network management implementation, questions remain. How will the managers be laid out—centralized, decentralized, or distributed? These questions should be considered, as the cost and effort required to later change to another model may be prohibitive.

Centralized Management Stations   Centralized management, where a single, centrally located management station console oversees the entire network, sounds like a good idea. Each managed device is either polled or automatically sends event data to the management station. Unfortunately, as the network grows, the amount of processing required, both automated and human, may begin to exceed the capabilities of the management station and the operator.

Decentralized Management Stations   Multiple management stations throughout the enterprise control, collect, and analyze data from their respective managed devices. This distributes the load to each management station and not to a single monolithic one. Additionally, the single point of failure a central management station creates is eliminated. The problem with decentralized management, however, is simple and troublesome: how do you look at the big picture when information is not aggregated network-wide but is processed locally?

Distributed Management Stations   Distributed management seems to provide the best means of managing distributed operations. Processing is decentralized but central analysis is still possible through aggregated management stations. However, although the impact of measurement and event overhead are mitigated, the difficulty of properly managing throughput is exacerbated. This is certainly the case in frame-relay environments, where end-to-end analysis is problematic as the routes are not easily analyzed. RMON2 is inteded to help here.

Network Manager Checklist
So, now that all of the network management characteristics have been outlined, what do you do as a network manager? You plan. Plan for what you can expect,

what to do when the unexpected happens, and how to keep track of and learn from this wealth of data. The following steps are necessary to ensure events are handled consistently:

1. Define the events.
2. Define the severity levels:
   a. Advisory
   b. Minor
   c. Serious
   d. Critical
3. Define the levels (instrumentation thresholds. for each level.
4. Define the responses for each level.
   a. Ignore
   b. Log
   c. Alert manager
   d. Run recovery process
   e. Alert manager and run recovery process
   f. Escalate
5. Define the logging frequency.
6. Define the reporting frequency.
7. Define the event frequency for regular events.
   a. Job scheduling
   b. Load balancing
   c. Backups
   d. Other preventative maintenance events

Oracle Enterprise Manager

Drawing on the work of the Oracle's Systems Management Tools Initiative (SMTI), Oracle Enterprise Manager (OEM) provides single-console management of Oracle resources using industry-standard technologies. OEM works cooperatively with major network management platforms, including IBM NetView and HP OpenView, to ensure seamless integration with existing management stations. Additionally, an open interface is provided so that third-party tools can be developed to interoperate with OEM.

NOTE
The Systems Management Tools Initiative (SMTI) is a vendor consortium chartered to ensure cross-technology network management compatibility of Oracle and Oracle-related products. Oracle has long recognized the importance of integrating distributed database technology operations management with network management in general. So, in addition to driving the development of the RDBMS SNMP MIB, RFC 1697, Oracle formed SMTI.

As described by Oracle, OEM supports the following functions:

- Asset management
- Database monitoring
- Job scheduling
- Listener monitoring
- Software distribution

However, this set of bullet points is insufficient to fully appreciate OEM's capabilities. OEM extends many of the capabilities already provided by SQL*DBA, Server Manager, and the new 32-bit Navigator by providing customizable, schedulable capabilities to each of the existing function sets. OEM can manage the Oracle7 Server, Oracle Mobile Agents, and Oracle MediaServer, in addition to all SQL*Net and TNS applications.

OEM provides a platform supporting two key tools to the network manager:

1. Intelligent agents do your bidding, both at the Oracle level using SQL and PL/SQL, and at the operating system level using any host tools available. The agents can be developed and saved to both monitor and set your configuration. Examples using the Tool Control Language (TCL) and perl are included with the base OEM product.

2. A robust framework for monitoring instrumentation and schedules and for crafting agents and profiles. The framework enables you to deploy agents and assemble result sets in meaningful ways, both graphically and contextually.

OEM extends your network and database manager's reach both geographically and across 24 hours, making the ease of local database and network operations possible for remote components. The image in Figure 10-1 shows the Oracle Enterprise Manager console.

OEM Components

The following tools are part of the OEM standard distribution:

- Backup and Recovery Manager
- Import/Export Manager
- Instance Manager
- Schema Manager
- Security Manager
- Software Manager
- SQL Worksheet
- SQL*Loader
- Storage Manager

The following tools are part of the OEM Power Pack, an optional set of tools that greatly enhances Oracle technology management.

- Oracle Diagnostics
- Oracle Events
- Oracle Expert
- Oracle Performance Monitor
- Oracle Tablespace Manager
- Oracle Top Sessions Monitor
- Oracle Trace

TIP

Use Oracle Expert extensively. Without proper baseline determination, the metrics returned by the network management tools are not useful. You can only turn data into information if you

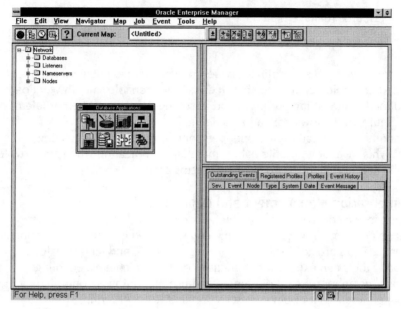

FIGURE 10-1.   *Oracle Enterprise Manager console*

have a context on which to base it. Fortunately, as part of Oracle
Expert, a complete methodology is provided in the online
documentation, aiding you in collecting your data.

OEM Network Management Operations

Using the operational framework previously described, the following is an
overview of key features OEM provides.

Problem, Workload, and Device Management

OEM enables you to design and execute SQL and host scripts on all the items
in a group when problems are detected. Problems may be defined in the
following realms:

■   Fault management

■   Performance management

- Resource management

- Space management

Additionally, with job scheduling services, preventative maintenance jobs can be scheduled chronologically. Together, these services enable smooth workload distribution by preventing problems and lessening downtime when problems do occur. Figure 10-2 shows how a job is defined.

In addition, notification of proper personnel is made through paging and e-mail systems when available. Profile data is maintained indicating when and how to reach the appropriate manager when problems arise.

Instrumentation Management and Reporting

OEM provides a console with alterable windows. Windows may be docked, floating, hidden, maximized, or minimized as required by conditions or operator preference. Tools are accessible from menus, toolbars, and launch palettes. Third-party tools can expose their functions on the same items, enabling a consistent metaphor for ease of training and use. Reporting is controlled by the jobs and user preferences for both item selection and result ordering.

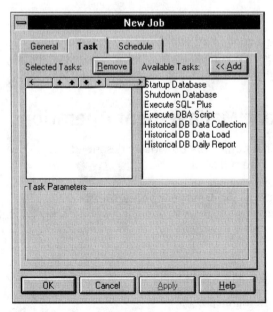

FIGURE 10-2. *New Job Creation dialog box*

Event Management and Automated Discovery Tools for Topology Mapping

Using OEM's map feature, problems at nodes or groups of nodes for which events are being monitored are highlighted. Each object displays a signal flag per event or event set. The flag graphically depicts the status of the object. Status is indicated as follows:

- A green flag means there are no problems detected.

- A yellow flag means there is a condition detected that should be checked.

- A red flag means there is a severe problem detected requiring immediate attention.

- A circle with a slash through it indicates the item is down or unavailable.

Additionally, drilling down by clicking on the affected node will provide details on the source of the alert. Figure 10-3 shows how an event is defined. This is also where you optionally specify the job to be run to fix or mitigate the problem when the event occurs.

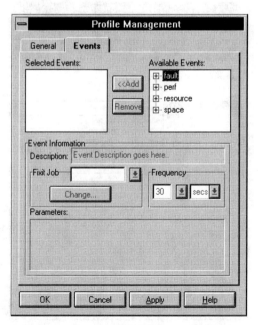

FIGURE 10-3.   *Event Definition dialog box*

Automatic node and service discovery can be accomplished using a combination of the OEM communications daemon, Oracle's plug-and-play name server (i.e., Oracle Names release 2 Dynamic Discovery Option in SQL*Net 2.3), and topology files.

Data Management

The following tools are provided to aid in data-controlled data management:

- Backup and Recovery Manager
- Import/Export Manager
- SQL Worksheet
- SQL*Loader

Capacity Planning and Change Management

Oracle Expert provides effective means of planning for changes in throughput and storage needs. Capacity planning scenarios may be developed and saved for further analysis. Figure 10-4 shows how Oracle Expert is used to set up a tuning session.

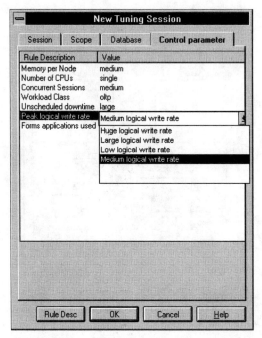

FIGURE 10-4.   *Specifying control parameters for an Oracle Expert tuning session*

Oracle Expert responds with recommendations for improving performance within the parameters indicated, as shown in Figure 10-5.

Software and License Management

Software distribution, license management, and event processing for software on individual nodes and groups of nodes is provided through Oracle Software Manager, an OEM add-on.

Inventory and Asset Management

Open APIs for integration with OEM enable third-party developers to integrate inventory and asset management tools using OEM's API, snap-in console with OLE integration, and SNMP.

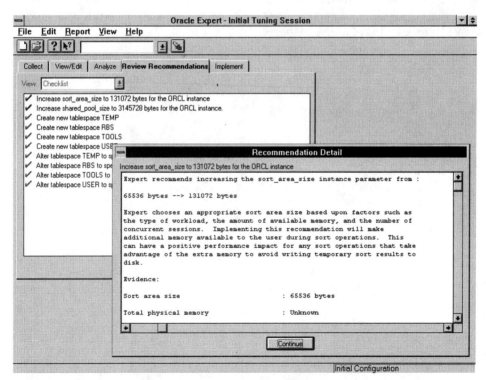

FIGURE 10-5. *Oracle Expert recommendations and detail*

Conclusion

Enterprise management includes software distribution, job scheduling, preventative maintenance, backup performance, and component oversight. Reliable performance of these tasks is necessary to ensure your Oracle technology implementation both remains robust and performs efficiently.

Just as you can't have network technicians at every node, you likely can't have a DBA for each database. It is cost prohibitive. Ideally, you should have just-in-time expertise—a DBA who is only there when you need her. How do you do this? How do you leverage your investment in your DBA staff without resorting to hiring more DBAs?

The key to enterprise management is to plan for these faults, or failure events, and determine the appropriate response. The known faults and their resolutions are then made part of the enterprise management technology's tasks. When such faults occur, automated responses may be triggered to resolve the problem. Agents enable such automated responses to occur reliably.

You must employ proactive technology if you want to keep your job. What you need is an omniscient, omnipresent network component manager. Fortunately, one is available: Oracle Enterprise Manager. And, best of all, it's free!

CHAPTER 11

Oracle Mobile Agents

What used to be wireless is now wired. What used to be wired is now wireless.

–Nicholas Negroponte

Once upon a time, the only path to your enterprise data resources was through your LAN wiring. Today, business demands require certain users to have access to enterprise data regardless of their location. Dial-up access to the corporate LAN adequately extends the network to some users, provided they have a phone line to plug into. However, for a segment of your user population, an even less restrictive technology must be employed. Mobile computing technology makes this possible.

Global deployment of wireless networks has created a viable physical infrastructure for mobile users. But wireless networks are not like their wireline counterparts. Wireless networks have vague boundaries prone to occlusion by tunnels and hills. Wireless networks are also much slower than wireline networks. As a result, the client/server model does not perform well on wireless networks. How do you effectively communicate across low-speed networks? How do you accommodate network service fluctuations?

Oracle Mobile Agents (OMA) solves these problems, providing a means of developing and deploying applications optimized for mobile users. The typical mobile user works in a variety of environments. OMA components enable mobile applications to reliably and efficiently communicate across wireless networks, circuit-switched telephone lines, and local area networks. From a moving vehicle to a hotel room, OMA applications transparently connect to corporate data resources. This is a key feature of OMA technology—regardless of the medium employed, OMA applications can present the same appearance to the user. There is no need to train the user on different approaches based on connectivity measures. OMA takes care of resolving underlying differences in the network media employed.

OMA applications may be developed using a wide variety of client application technologies including Oracle Power Objects and Developer/2000, Microsoft Excel, Visual Basic and C++, and Powersoft's Powerbuilder. And OMA-enabled applications can interact with practically any information source, not just Oracle7 databases.

NOTE

It is important to realize that wireless networks are not inherently unreliable. It is just that their medium is prone to the same problems experienced by other radio transmissions: line-of-sight requirements affected by geography and architecture, and climate-related interference.

What Is a Mobile Application?

Nicholas Negroponte, founder of the MIT Media Lab, pointed out how the shift from broadcast television to cable television has been echoed by a shift from the wire media of telegraphs and telephones to the wireless medium of modern telephony and data communications. This has come to be known as the "Negroponte Flip." This shift has enabled a similar change in our increasingly mobile workplace, from strictly static LAN solutions to mobile ones.

Mobile applications are those where the user interacts with enterprise data sources but is not tethered to the corporate LAN. The mobile application user may need to operate from a variety of environments such as the shop floor, a delivery vehicle, or a client's office. Mobile applications are not "mobile" because the user is necessarily in motion. Mobile applications are so named because the user cannot be constrained to a stationary location.

This means mobile applications must be able to handle the problems mentioned earlier. Well-crafted mobile applications work across telephone lines, LANs, and wireless networks. Likewise, the effective mobile application accommodates wireless network outages, permitting operation to continue while a connection to remote data is unavailable. Most importantly, a mobile application must be able to perform well across a low-speed network. Such requirements form a very tall order.

Types of Mobile Applications

Typical mobile applications include sales force automation, service dispatch, and fleet management. The types of programs such applications require include electronic mail, scheduling, and broadcast messaging. With Oracle Mobile Agents, development of less prosaic applications such as on-site event registration, mobile point of sale systems, and financial market monitoring is made easier.

Certain classes of applications are clearly not appropriate for use in mobile environments. These include most horizontal applications such as word processors, spreadsheets, and highly graphical programs. The high variability of the data conveyed in such programs makes them inappropriate for use across low-bandwidth networks.

Field Force Automation
Mobile applications generally enable one or more of the following needs of a nomadic worker:

- To provide data immediately to the enterprise
- To complete a business process remotely

■ To access corporate data remotely

A nomadic worker is one working away from a central location. Generally, the term *field force* is used to collectively describe such users. Here are how two typical field force workers' days are laid out.

Fleet Applications

Mobile data systems were first generally deployed to support fleet workers such as service technicians and delivery drivers. Mobile data communication was typically limited to transmitting work order messages to the field, such as "go to this location and fix copier X" or "pick up two boxes from customer Q." As more sophisticated devices and networks were deployed, field workers could perform minor updates and transmit data back to the base station.

Today, the typical fleet worker's day goes something like this:

1. Travel to dispatch location to replenish stock or pick up load.

2. Travel to first stop.

3. Continually inform dispatch of your location and status.

4. Travel to next stop.

5. If required, alter your plans to accommodate new schedule from dispatch.

6. Notify dispatch of incoming repairs or items to be delivered elsewhere.

Steps 3 through 6 are then repeated throughout the day with perhaps occasional returns to a central location. Without mobile technology, tracking down employees and alerting them of routing changes is problematic. Without mobile technology, the streamlining of processes such as reloading and replenishing supplies is hindered as you have to wait for the vehicle to return to determine what is needed to turn that vehicle around. With mobile technology, your resources can be dynamically allocated because it is possible to have a global view of your operations status.

Such mobile technology is effectively employed by package delivery services. Couriers alert their central office of inbound parcels and their final destinations. With this information, simultaneously collected from multiple couriers in the field, the delivery service's operations team can determine how to most efficiently allocate the resources required to deliver each package—on time, worldwide. This fulfills one of the key reasons for deploying mobile applications: to enable nomadic workers to provide data immediately to the enterprise.

Field Sales Applications

Every organization sells something. Whether offering a product or a service, a sales force is required. Sometimes the sales force is not a distinct group but is comprised of employees with other roles. Regardless, most organizations have mobile workers out selling their companies' offerings. Here is how a typical field sales employee's day may go.

1. Start your business day by dialing into the office to update your e-mail and appointment schedule.

2. Travel to your customer.

3. Meet with your customer.

   a. Resolve outstanding issues.

   b. Promote new offerings.

   c. Close deals.

4. Travel to your office for sales meeting.

5. Connect to corporate LAN to update mail and appointment schedule.

Here, steps 2 and 3 are repeated throughout the day. Without mobile technology, real-time access to corporate data is not possible. Likewise, without OMA, the ability to use the telephone line, the wireless network, and the corporate LAN without having to alter your way of doing business is not likely. You have to be able to solve problems and close the deal quickly because, to the field sales force, time is definitely money. Mobile technology gives the ability to have the information you need while your customer is ready, willing, and able. This fulfills the other key reasons for deploying mobile applications: to enable a nomadic worker to remotely complete a business process and access corporate data.

Other Types of Mobile Applications   Not all mobile applications are for "mobile" users. An example of one such "stationary" mobile application is the on-site event registration system. Oracle uses such a system internally for some of its training seminars. The users managing the event do so from a fixed location throughout its duration. There is not, however, a fixed network infrastructure in place. By employing OMA technology, trade show management may be performed completely wireless.

TIP
Most trade shows require their own laborers to perform all equipment installation, regardless of how trivial the work is, at exorbitant prices. By using OMA technology, you can deploy an event system without having to lay cable or bring in numerous telephone lines. Laptops with wireless modems can do most of the work. This speeds up setup and loadout time and can lower the cost of deploying a local, networked solution.

Why Not a Client/Server Solution?

As you learned in Chapter 8, client/server systems tend to be of the data management, decision support, or resource sharing kind. The needs they fulfill and their requirements are quite different from those of mobile applications. Most importantly, several of a client/server architecture's primary underpinnings exclude its direct application in a mobile solution.

Limitations of a Client/Server Architecture

The ubiquity of client/server architectures does not mean that it is the design of choice for all applications. The following points illustrate how the hallmarks of client/server architectures are actually limitations to mobile computing.

Reliance on High-Speed Networks
The need for a high-speed pipeline in client/server architectures effectively ties users down to their networks if not to their desktops. Wireless technology cannot offer anywhere near the same throughput as wireline technology. Wireless data devices communicate at about 9600 bits per second. This is less than one thousandth the speed of 10BaseT Ethernet. The diagram in Figure 11-1 illustrates the disparity in bandwidth.

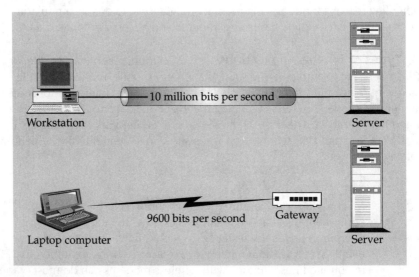

FIGURE 11-1. *Network throughput disparity*

Reliance on Connection-Oriented Protocols

Client/server applications are typically connection oriented. This means a couple of things. First, when a client establishes a connection with the server, a session is active until an explicit sign-off is performed. Until the session is concluded, the server will periodically check for the presence of the client. Another aspect of connection-oriented protocols is that, unlike the mobile applications that typically are message oriented, client/server applications exchange many messages as part of a single connection.

These properties of connection-oriented protocols cause three problems. First, the already slow wireless link is burdened by the overhead each additional message adds in the form of acknowledgments. The second problem arises when the data link is temporarily unavailable, not uncommon in wireless networks. In a client/server application, the typical response is to terminate the session and roll back any transactions in process. Again, as a single connection is composed of multiple messages, each of which may be a transaction, multiple operations may be undone as a result of a temporary signal loss.

One-Way Session Establishment

In client/server environments, it is the client that initiates contact with the server. Generally, there is no means of a server application initiating contact with a client application. This is acceptable in most environments but not in mobile applications, where broadcast messages must typically be supported.

The OMA Advantage

Mobile applications must contend with network media differences, fluctuating service areas, and, most importantly, significantly slower throughput. Fortunately, the race does not always go to the most fleet of foot. Applications developed with OMA work smarter, not harder.

OMA was originally introduced as Oracle in Motion, and it was later renamed to Radio Agents before its current name was finally settled on. These changes underscore the flexibility of the product. Envisioned to provide the globally expanding market of wireless network users with an efficient and reliable messaging infrastructure, OMA's innate ability to function across wireline networks has broadened the product's appeal. Even stationary users requiring an efficient messaging system find OMA's client/agent/server technology appropriate to employ.

Mobile Application Design

When users are mobilized, their data processing needs typically change. They do so for a good reason: business needs have changed. The mobile user is more likely to be conducting core business functions such as selling or delivering than performing decision support operations. As a result, rather than performing ad hoc queries and receiving hundreds of rows of data, the typical mobile application is requesting and updating smaller, predetermined sets of information.

Message-Based Mobile Applications

In a decision support application, the user may very likely alter the columns and the sort order of rows returned by a single query. This means that a SQL query is built, sent to the database server, processed, and the rows returned to the client application. The client application must be able to accommodate an unknown number of columns and rows.

Mobile applications are message based. They typically permit a limited range of operations to take place. Of course, limited may mean hundreds, but, nonetheless, still limited. Rather than transmitting a whole slew of information about the desired columns and sort order, a well-designed mobile application need merely specify which of a number of predefined operations is to be performed and any key values required to perform that operation. Each operation is indicated by a message type. Knowing beforehand what operations will occur allows the designers of mobile applications to limit the amount of information that must be exchanged and optimize for those operations.

For example, the typical field sales force worker needs to perform only the following data operations:

- Maintain contact information—customers, appointments, and so on.

- Enter and update orders.

- Check on order status.

- Synchronize local databases.

Limit Interaction Between Client and Server

As in most client/server architectures, the bulk of the data selection and ordering takes place on the server. However, this scheme only works for the simplest of operations. There are requirements that may not be easily supported by a call-and-response framework. For example, suppose you have a mobile order entry application. The user attempts to fulfill the order from the closest of 50 or so warehouses. The application is smart enough to know that when a message is received indicating the warehouse is back-ordered, it should try the next one, and so on until the order can be filled.

This is a reasonable approach for a client/server system. However, each interaction across the wireless network may take five seconds. On average, it may take over two minutes to fill the order if most of the warehouses are typically back-ordered. The solution is to not come back to the mobile client until an order can be filled. How is this done?

Exploit Server Technology

One solution is to use stored procedures. This presumes, however, that Oracle Mobile Agents is used with an Oracle7 database server. This is not necessarily the case. One of the key success factors of OMA is its independence from any data source.

Exploit the Link

A better solution is to employ an agent, or a proxy, to handle the interaction with the database server. The proxy will not trouble the client application until it is necessary for a decision to be made at the client end. Agents exploit the high-speed link found on the corporate LAN where the agent and the data server both reside.

The Structure of OMA Systems

OMA provides a messaging infrastructure for mobile applications. It does so by breaking up an OMA application into a framework consisting of the following components.

Component	Description
Client	The client application is solely concerned with presentation and local processing of data.
Messages	Instead of queries and result sets, OMA applications exchange messages. Message header data enables the client and agent to handle each message properly.
Message Manager	This is the OMA-supplied program responsible for managing the dispatch and receipt of messages. It manages the connection to the mobile link. Each client runs one in the background.
Mobile link	The mobile link may be the wide area network, a dial-up connection, or even the corporate LAN.

Message gateway	This is the OMA-supplied program running on the corporate LAN to manage connections between the mobile link and each agent.
LAN	The corporate LAN is the high-speed connection shared by the message gateway, agent, and server applications.
Agent	This is the client's proxy application that performs all highly interactive operations with the server and exchanges messages with the client.
Server	This is the server application through which corporate data is accessed. This is not necessarily an Oracle7 server.

OMA and Client/Agent/Server

OMA capitalizes on each component's efficiency and employs something called client/agent/server technology. It is this inclusion of agent technology into the traditional client/server architecture that enables OMA to provide effective communication across a medium far less available than your office LAN.

OMA applications are designed to distribute work across the client, agent, and server components. They are intended to extend your corporate resources to those who are outside the boundaries of your corporate LAN. They do so by constraining highly interactive processing within the server side of the architecture. A component called the agent acts as the client application's proxy. It is as if you took the traditional client/server client and broke it into two pieces, a GUI component and a processing component. The OMA client provides mostly GUI operations, although it is not constrained to, and likely does provide local processing as well. The agent performs all of the interactions with the server required to ensure that operations are properly performed and that data is exchanged between the client and the server (see Figure 11-2).

As mentioned in Chapter 1, client/server applications generally exchange queries and result sets. In OMA applications, performance limitations are overcome by instead exchanging messages. Messages are relatively short data packets. Each message contains a header identifying the type of data it contains. This header information is used to both exchange data and to manage the flow of packets. You see, in client/agent/server applications, the data flow is not necessarily synchronous. Responses may not immediately follow requests. In fact, there is no guarantee that a request has been dispatched. This may be the case when either the wireless network is unavailable or the user chooses to work offline.

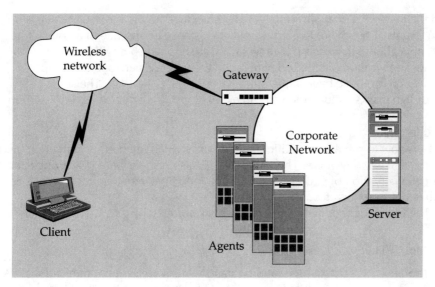

FIGURE 11-2. *Low throughput client/agent and high throughput agent/server connections*

Client Application

The client application is one that can exchange messages with the OMA Message Manager. Any of the following can be used as client applications. (This is not an exhaustive list.)

Oracle Forms	Oracle Power Objects
Visual Basic 3.0	Microsoft Access 2.0
Microsoft Excel 5.0	SQL Windows
Powerbuilder 3.0	Visual C++

Messages

Messages contain preformatted information and are exchanged between a client and its agents. A header indicates to the recipient what the message contains through a field called the message type. The agent and client applications independently know how to pack and unpack the contents of each message type.

OMA Message Manager

On the client side there is also software referred to as the Message Manager. Its purpose is to manage the dispatch and reception of packets between the application and the network. An application hands off messages to the Message Manager and then forgets about them. Regardless of the existence or absence of a connection, the application behaves as if the message was sent, which it will be once a connection is again established either with the wireless network, a dial-up connection, or, once back at the office, connected to the LAN. The simplicity of this design masks a much more complex relationship, of course.

Mobile Link

OMA is able to run across multiple mobile links, enabling users to remain in touch from practically anywhere. The mobile link is also responsible for securing data through encryption of packets across its network. Be aware that not all traffic across mobile links is encrypted.

The following mobile links are currently supported by OMA.

Mobile Link	Description
Mobitex	An international standard for wireless communications, RAM Mobile Data runs the Mobitex network in the United States.
CDPD	Cellular Digital Packet Data (CDPD) is a wireless network built on top of existing cellular telephone network bandwidth. It is not the same as using a modem across a cellular phone line.
RD-LAP	Ardis is IBM and Motorola's combined effort at a wireless network. RD-LAP is Ardis's network protocol.
CSC	Circuit-switched cellular is the use of a modem on a cellular line.
PSTN	Public-switched telephone network is the conventional wireline telephone network. Also called Plain Old Telephone Sytem (POTS).
LAN	Local Area Networks running TCP/IP are supported by OMA.

OMA Message Gateway

In practice, there are many clients communicating with many gateways over the wireless network. These gateways in turn communicate with corporate LANs via X.25 packet-switching networks. Then, upon reaching the corporate network, each packet is routed to the appropriate agent for processing. Responses and unsolicited messages are likewise handled. This store-and-forward behavior provides both survivability and scalability.

The message gateway also has an additional feature: authentication. Users are authenticated in two forms. First, the device identifier for the mobile modem authenticates the device to the mobile link. Second, the id and password supplied by the Message Manager identify the user to the message gateway.

Agents

A client's proxy, which handles requests on the client's behalf, is called an agent. It takes advantage of its proximity to the corporate data source to provide improved performance. The agent performs all conditional operations required to convert a message requesting information into a set of messages providing that data. Should any questions arise during the processing of the request, the agent "knows" how to respond so that no additional processing is required by the client to complete the request.

Data Server

OMA is not limited to use with the Oracle7 Server. Any application that can communicate with your agent application can be designated a server application. Only the agent is required to follow OMA standards. Beyond the agent, anything is possible.

Limitations of Mobile Computing

Clearly the greatest limitations of mobile computing are coverage area and bandwidth. Mobile networks are still not universally available. In the United States, RAM Mobile Data's Mobitex network and the IBM/Motorola Ardis network provide the greatest coverage. CDPD, however, is provided by local cellular carriers. Unlike the national networks, CDPD coverage is not contiguous across the U.S. On the other hand, CDPD coverage, where available, is more complete with fewer weak spots than RAM's network. This is because CDPD benefits from piggybacking on extant cellular infrastructure.

Limitations in both networks are ameliorated by OMA's support for alternative dial-up access as well as support for more than one wireless network. Remember, regardless of which is used, the application can look the same to the user. You merely instruct the Message Manager to use another network.

CAUTION

On the client side, OMA does not support active connections on multiple networks simultaneously. The Message Manager listens and dispatches on a single network at a time. On the enterprise LAN, however, multiple gateways may be enabled for simultaneous access to corporate data stores.

Oracle Power Objects and OMA

When OMA version 1.1 was released, Oracle Power Objects (OPO) had not yet gone into production. However, even then it was known that OPO would be the platform of choice for many OMA applications. There are several reasons for this, among them:

- OPO is very data aware and provides visual development capabilities for data objects. Unlike with Visual Basic, data management software may be developed in OPO with very little coding required. OPO is an object-oriented tool and, as such, makes use of inheritance to automatically bind data sources to controls.

- OPO comes with its own local data store, Blaze, a SQL database manager that requires only 300K of memory to run. Blaze is upwardly compatible with Oracle7. An integral data store makes OPO far more attractive a development tool as it simplifies local data management. Soon, OPO will work with Oracle Lite, the object-oriented database currently under development. Oracle Lite will offer a vast improvement to Blaze performance, making OPO an even better platform for OMA application deployment.

- OPO comes with clsOMA, an OPO user-defined class providing OMA-specific methods and properties to greatly simplify OMA development.

- OPO comes with a sample application, MOBSALES, which is described in the Oracle Power Objects Sample Applications Guide. This guide is also provided in Adobe Acrobat PDF as a file from the Oracle Power Objects program group in Windows.

Using the Class

There are five steps in successfully using the Oracle Mobile Agents class in Oracle Power Objects. These operations are similar regardless of the client platform technology employed.

Step 1: Initialization
This establishes contact with the Message Manager and initiates a session with the appropriate agent.

```
udpServiceName : Service_name
udpAgentName   : Agent_name
udmOMAInit()
```

Step 2: Set Notification Window

Next, set the notification window to receive the results of the OMAMsgRcvd( ) method call.

```
udmSetNotify( Form1 )
```

Step 3: Create and Send a Message

This is the outbound portion of your application, where you iteratively pack the contents of your message, including the header information, and send it. Remember, the message is only guaranteed to have made it to the Message Manager. Dispatch to the agent is handled by the Message Manager.

```
Set udpAddress, udpUserName
[optional: Set udpStable, udpAtMostOnce, udpCompress]
Call udmNewMsg
For each value in message, call udmPack( object/value )
Call udmSendMsg
```

Step 4: Read and Clear a Message

The analogue of step 3, here you retrieve any messages waiting from the Message Manager. You unpack the contents according to the header. Finally, indicate the successful reception of the message by clearing it from the Message Manager.

```
Call udmReadMsg (sets udpFromAddress, udpFromUserName to be used to reply )
For each value in message, call udmUnpack( object/value )
Call udmDoneReading
```

Step 5: Deinstall OMA

When finished using the application, deinstall the OMA components, effectively signing off from the Message Manager and the agent.

```
udmOMADeInit()
```

Conclusion

Oracle Mobile Agents is the preferred solution if you require the following:

- *Wireless Data Communication* Communication between a mobile client and a corporate agent using wireless, radio, or dial-up communication.

■ *Network Media Flexibility* Communication across the highest throughput connection available—a directly connected LAN, a dial-up LAN, or a wireless network.

■ *Disconnected Processing* The ability to run an application that can queue up transactions for dispatch while disconnected.

■ *Asynchronous Messaging* The ability to receive and process unsolicited messages as well as transmit messages not requiring an acknowledgment.

■ *Store-and-Forward Processing* The ability to handle messages that queued up while disconnected.

■ *Agent Processing* The ability to have agents perform functions for the client on a higher-speed link to the data store than that of the client application.

■ *Prototyping and Visual Development Capabilities for Rapid Application Development* Oracle Mobile Agents applications may be developed using a variety of popular technologies, including Visual Basic, Oracle's Developer/2000, and PowerBuilder.

CHAPTER 12

Oracle and the Internet

Information wants to be free.

—Marshall McLuhan

The Internet is successful precisely because it serves information freely and through a number of technologies. In order to successfully leverage the Internet, a means of connecting Oracle to the Internet effectively, supporting diverse data access methods while retaining security and reliability, is required. The success of Oracle's World Wide Web (WWW) Interface Kit, described at the end of this chapter, heralded the second stage of Oracle/Internet integration.

The first stage saw use of the Internet as an inexpensive and convenient, though insecure, means of communicating with Oracle servers using *Telnet* or perhaps SQL*Net. However, both required coordination between the nodes' users. Contrary to the Internet's model for success, Oracle-based information was not freely available.

The third stage sees Oracle and Internet technologies effectively combined to capture, serve, and manage data stored in relational databases. The WWW Interface Kit led directly to the development of Oracle's commercial implementation of Web/RDBMS integration technology, called Oracle WebServer. And with Oracle Web Applications, based on WebServer technology, secure user access to Oracle financial data, such as Order Entry information, is ensured.

NOTE

The key component of the WWW Interface Kit was the WOW Gateway, described in detail later in this chapter. One year after the release of the gateway, despite the fact that the source code was provided and Oracle released the technology to the public domain, not one of the other major relational database vendors had as effective and simple a technology. Most continue to rely on external, custom applications to achieve their integration with the Internet. Oracle's solution is server-based, and applications are written using PL/SQL, Oracle's procedural SQL development language.

It is crucial to understand how to use Oracle to serve data across the Internet. There are a number of ways to accomplish this. The World Wide Web gets the most attention, but the Web itself is mostly a combination of standard Internet technologies melded to perform magic.

The following sections provide an overview of the technologies that preceded the World Wide Web. Each solved a particular problem that was hindering the free exchange of data. Most are still in use. As you read each section, keep in mind that the current solutions build on the older ones and in some cases may merely put a new face on them. But, first, a little history.

A Brief History of the Internet

The Internet grew up with Usenet, Ethernet, and TCP/IP. In the last 15 or so years, it has thrived alongside Unix, the two of them together fostering many of today's open networked computing systems. Some of these technologies were developed cooperatively. Others simply burst on the scene as if from nowhere. The ones that survived did so in large part because they were agreed upon, standardized. It is these standards that define the Internet and its capabilities. But even before the Internet, there was ARPANET.

ARPANET

In 1969, the Department of Defense's Advanced Research Projects Agency (DARPA or ARPA) undertook an experiment in nationwide packet-switched networking. Intended to demonstrate the feasibility of a survivable network, ARPANET was initially implemented across four western United States research centers. Much as Eisenhower's Interstate Highway System was developed to ensure a reliable, redundant, high-speed national roadway network, ARPANET's goal was to determine which networking technologies would ideally provide a similar means of ensuring reliable, redundant, high-speed national data communication.

NOTE

The term *redundant* as used here means a network with multiple paths between nodes. This is necessary to ensure efficiency and survivability, or robustness. Efficiency is achieved by providing parallel paths, thus limiting congestion on the way to heavily trafficked destinations. These multiple paths also ensured a means of reaching nodes regardless of network segment losses. This was during the Cold War. In the case of both the Interstate Highway System and ARPANET, the Department of Defense was thinking of survivability in case of nuclear attack.

By the early 1970s, ARPANET was successfully living up to the concept. Using then high-speed, 56Kbps, dedicated leased-line circuits between nodes and packet-switching software to route messages, the network enabled its members, mostly academics performing government-sponsored research, to reliably communicate among themselves. Communication methods included mail messages, remote logon, and file transfers. Once the concepts were implemented reliably, the development of more sophisticated, standardized technology such as wide area network file sharing was undertaken.

TIP

An excellent history of the Internet, with pointers to others, is Robert Hobbes Zakon's Internet Timeline. You can find the file on the Internet at **http://gopher.well.sf.ca.us:70/0/matrix/internet/hobbes.internet.timeline**.

TCP/IP

Through the 1970s, ARPA heavily funded the development of packet-switching technology. It sponsored other projects including *ALOHA*, a wireless packet technology whose principles were later applied to the wired technology called *Ethernet*. Just five years after ARPANET was launched, a new standard network protocol was in development. This technology later became the Transmission Control Protocol /Internet Protocol (TCP/IP), from which the name *Internet* was derived.

Unix and Usenet

Concurrently, the emergence of Unix as the operating system of choice among university students, in large part because it was free for the asking, led to the development of other popular networking technology such as Usenet, a broadcast discussion system built on top of Unix's UUCP (Unix to Unix CoPy) facility. The growth of Usenet, spurring the use of Unix, signaled the start of a growth spurt in internetworking.

The Great Confluence

In 1983, several very important events took place. AT&T was forced to divest. As a result, it was no longer bound by a consent decree that enjoined it from selling computers and software. Unix was now a commercial product, one with thousands of devotees just hitting the workforce.

Also in 1983, the switchover of all of ARPANET to TCP/IP took place. In order to make this a more palatable event, ARPA had funded the development of TCP/IP technology for Unix, thus easing the transition. This meant too that computers not on ARPANET could take advantage of TCP/IP and its applications for their own networking needs. Internetworking was now considered universally viable and desirable.

Finally, 1983 also saw the Department of Defense split ARPANET into a civilian section and a military section. The latter was called MILNET, while the former remained ARPANET. The separation of the two, with a firewall/gateway between, marked the beginning of the end for ARPANET.

NSFnet

The number of ARPANET nodes—with ARPANET still a single network and limited to a small number of members—was dwarfed by other networks using TCP/IP. To facilitate access among non-ARPANET researchers, an internet called CSNET was funded by the National Science Foundation (NSF), and a gateway to ARPANET was provided to facilitate e-mail between the respective sites.

In 1986, the NSF established a high-speed network backbone, NSFnet, to support traffic among five supercomputing centers nationwide. This led to a spike in the number of academic networks connecting to NSFnet. ARPANET was effectively overshadowed by the Internet.

Commercial Internetworking

One year later, Usenix, the preeminent Unix users group, funded the creation of UUNET, the first commercial gateway to Usenet and UUCP. The same year, NSFnet entered into commercial agreements with IBM and others to support and extend the network. In the next five years, the Internet saw steady growth from commercial mail traffic and the development of commercial technologies such as the Wide Area Information Service (WAIS). By 1990, there was no turning back. By 1995, the Internet had gone commercial and the Web had gone Hollywood.

NOTE
The Internet Society is a non-profit organization chartered with fostering the development of the Internet. Visit them at **http://www.isoc.org**.

Internet Protocols

Now that you know, roughly, how the Internet came to be, an explanation of its components is appropriate. As described earlier, the identity of the Internet comes from its primary network protocol, TCP/IP. In Chapter 1, the TCP/IP concepts of IP addresses, well-known ports, and services were examined. In the following sections, the primary protocols used to serve data on the Internet are explained.

Standards

The Internet has been able to evolve rapidly because it is standards-based. Each growth spurt captures the imagination and brainpower of many in a very short period of time. It is therefore all the more important that the advances be coordinated to ensure synergy and not anarchy. Internet standards come about in the form of Requests For Comments (RFCs). They are so named because it is understood that they are rarely static.

Most of the Internet's advances are now in the public domain. Even WAIS, which began as a commercial venture, has entered the world of the public domain and standards, through freeWAIS. And despite the commercialization of the Internet, it is the noncommercial organizations that continue to help manage the exponential growth of the Internet and its underlying standards. The following standards are at the heart of the WWW's success.

NOTE:
Want to know more about standards organizations? Check them out on the Internet at **http://www.w3.org and http://www.ietf. cnri.reston.va.us**. Or *archie ANSI, archie WWW,* and *archie IETF.* For the head standards organization, visit ISO, the International Organization on Standardization (not the International Standards Organization, as you will learn when you go there!), at **http://www.iso.org/**.

Telnet

Telnet is the primary remote login protocol for TCP/IP. It provides a means of connecting to a remote computer using TCP segments. The connection appears as if it were from a local terminal. The port for this service is typically 23. Telnet may be used to access Oracle's character-based applications across the Internet. The following listing shows a Telnet session in which SQL*Plus is used. It is like being on a local terminal.

```
UNIX(r) System V Release 4.0 (saraswati.com)

login: oracle
Password:

Last login: Thu Jan 18 02:12:26 from bti-6
Sun Microsystems Inc.   SunOS 5.4      Generic July 1994
You have mail.
$ . oraenv
ORACLE_SID = [OIS] ?
$ sqlplus scott/tiger

SQL*Plus: Release 3.2.2.0.0 - Production on Thu Jan 18 02:58:10 1996

Copyright (c) Oracle Corporation 1979, 1994.  All rights reserved.
```

```
Connected to:
Oracle7 Server Release 7.2.2.3.0 - Production Release
With the distributed, replication and parallel query options
PL/SQL Release 2.2.2.3.0 - Production

SQL> select * from dept;

    DEPTNO DNAME          LOC
---------- -------------- -------------
        10 ACCOUNTING     NEW YORK
        20 RESEARCH       DALLAS
        30 SALES          CHICAGO
        40 OPERATIONS     BOSTON

SQL> quit
Disconnected from Oracle7 Server Release 7.2.2.3.0 - Production Release
With the distributed, replication and parallel query options
PL/SQL Release 2.2.2.3.0 - Production
$ exit
```

Telnet operates on virtual devices it calls Network Virtual Terminals (NVT). The capabilities of NVTs are negotiated when the session is established. When you start Telnet, a message is sent to port 23 of the remote computer. There, a background process called a *daemon* listens for connection requests. On some Unix systems, a general-purpose daemon called *inetd* listens on all ports; on others, a specific Telnet daemon is used.

The daemon and the Telnet client then enter a session negotiation phase. Session properties include the geometry of the display and the behavior of the backspace key, destructive or not. Each end of a Telnet session maintains a map of the current terminal state. It is presumed but not guaranteed that the maps are in sync. Once the session capabilities are agreed upon by both sides, the connection is handed over to the login process to complete.

The negotiation phase takes place using a simple set of instructions passed between the client and the daemon. These instructions are in the form of a three-digit number and text. This method of session control is used in other TCP/IP applications as well.

NOTE
Telnet is a very convenient application. When connecting to any other port, if the port does not respond with Telnet messages, it functions as a simple terminal and can be used to *spoof,* or imitate, another application. Telnet is often used in this manner to debug connections to other TCP/IP applications. In Chapter 13, you will see how to use this capability of Telnet to test the Oracle WebServer.

FTP

The File Transfer Protocol (FTP) is a more sophisticated application and an integral part of the TCP/IP suite. The primary application program incorporating the protocol is the eponymous ftp. The program ftp enables file transfers across machines through TCP segments on port 21. FTP uses the Telnet protocol to establish the initial connection and validate the user. Unlike Telnet, in which the user does not directly issue commands to the application, the user does issue commands to ftp. These commands may specify data conversions, such as between ASCII and EBCDIC, and identify and initiate the transfer of individual files and groups of files. World Wide Web client programs, called *browsers*, often also function as ftp clients. An example of ftp being used to retrieve the SQL*Net listener log file from a remote system is shown in the following listing:

```
$ ftp saraswati.com
Connected to saraswati.com.
220 saraswati.com FTP server (UNIX(r) System V Release 4.0) ready.
Name (saraswati.com:oracle): oracle
331 Password required for oracle.
Password:
230 User oracle logged in.
ftp> cd network/admin
250 CWD command successful.
ftp> ls
200 PORT command successful.
150 ASCII data connection for /bin/ls (204.137.229.36,32776) (0 bytes).
listener.log
listener.ora
sqlnet.log
sqlnet.ora
tnsdmn.ora
tnsnames.ora
tnsnav.ora
226 ASCII Transfer complete.
90 bytes received in 0.018 seconds (4.9 Kbytes/s)
ftp> get listener.ora
200 PORT command successful.
150 ASCII data connection for listener.ora (204.137.229.36,32777) (590 bytes).
226 ASCII Transfer complete.
local: listener.ora remote: listener.ora
618 bytes received in 0.003 seconds (2e+02 Kbytes/s)
ftp> quit
221 Goodbye.
$
```

NOTE

In the preceding listing, you see ftp's session control messages. Like Telnet's, each begins with a three-digit number.

Oracle and FTP

FTP is often used to move files between nodes on TCP/IP LANs. Perhaps the
greatest use of ftp along with Oracle is performing backups directly across a LAN. It
is generally a simple process to develop batch programs that systematically perform
hot backups to remote file systems. As this is generally faster than backing up
directly to tape, it lessens the amount of time the database is not completely up.

FTP Archives and Anonymous FTP

An *ftp archive* is a file system or file/directory hierarchy set up primarily for
anonymous access using the File Transfer Protocol. FTP archives generally serve as
public repositories of data and software. FTP archives may be set up to require user
authentication, but most allow *anonymous*, or unauthenticated, access to all files
below the archive's root directory. The cataloging of FTP archives is discussed in
the next section on Archie.

   High-traffic FTP archives are often *mirrored* on multiple, geographically
separated computers. Mirroring means duplicating or reflecting the contents of a
container. Physically, containers include storage and memory devices. Logically,
containers include file systems and machine state. Mirroring helps secure
information from loss by duplicating it in a space separate from its twin, where
simultaneous damage to both data stores is extremely unlikely. Mirroring also aids
by distributing the load when continual multiple access to the resource is required.

> **NOTE**
> Oracle maintains a public ftp archive at **ftp://ftp.oracle.com**. From
> this site, you may download trial software and information on
> Oracle's products and services.

Archie

Archie is an Internet service that provides information about ftp archives.
Although ftp itself is a very old IP service, the utility of and idea for a database of
information archives across the Internet is fairly recent. Archie provided the first
wide area information indexing and retrieval mechanism across the Internet in
1991. Archie servers may exchange information with each other to facilitate
cross-Internet consistency of Archie servers. As with ftp servers, Archie servers may
also be mirrored.

   Archie can only tell you about archives that have been registered. Most such
archives are registered with the main Archie database at *bunyip*, Internet home of
the originators of Archie. Administrators register their archives by sending e-mail to
archie-admin@bunyip.com requesting addition to the Archie database.

   Once registered, the Archie server will periodically refresh its database with the
listing of the contents of the archive, *not* the contents of the archive itself. This

listing is created using a command such as Unix's "ls -lR", and is referred to eponymously as the "ls -lR" file. The phrase "ls" is Unix's file and directory information listing command. The "l" argument specifies a long-format listing, which provides ownership, access, creation date, and/or date of last access. The "R" argument specifies a recursive search of the directories encountered, ensuring that all branches below and including the originating directory are listed.

Archie was designed to search for file and directory names and not file contents. It has been extended to allow for searches based on information provided by the archive administrator. The quality of this information is problematic, as it is beyond the control of the Archie server administrator. Therefore, the name of the file is usually the best means of determining what is on a site.

Using Archie
The following listing shows the Archie command line options.

```
$ archie
Usage: archie [-[cers][l][t][m#][h host][L][N#]] string
        -c : case-sensitive substring search
        -e : exact string match (default)
        -r : regular expression search
        -s : case-insensitive substring search
        -l : list one match per line
        -t : sort inverted by date
        -m# : specifies maximum number of hits to return (default 95)
        -h host : specifies server host
        -L : list known servers and current default
        -N# : specifies query niceness level (0-35765)
```

To find publicly accessible information on Oracle, for example, using Archie, perform a case-insensitive search for the string "oracle" as shown here:

```
$ archie oracle

Host ftp.deakin.edu.au

    Location: /pub/snm/mibs
        DIRECTORY dr-xr-xr-x        1024  Nov 12 10:57   oracle

Host ftp.mty.itesm.mx

    Location: /pub/banner/infraestruct/u00
        DIRECTORY drwxr-xr-x         512  Jun 22 07:40   oracle
    Location: /pub/banner/infraestruct/usr/local
```

```
        DIRECTORY drwxr-xr-x           512  Jun 22 07:52    oracle
```

Host vivaldi.belnet.be

```
    Location: /pub/usenet-faqs/usenet-by-hierarchy/rec/humor
        DIRECTORY drwxr-xr-x           512  Sep 18 15:06    oracle
```

This is a subset of the data returned. However, it is apparent that not all of the archives identified are related to Oracle Corporation and its products. The last entry returned refers to the Usenet Oracle, a source of humor on the Internet.

In addition to checking for each entry's relevance to the information sought, care must be taken to ensure that text substrings and case are sufficient to limit the number of hits returned, but not so limiting that useful records are eliminated from the search. For example, note differences in the number of records returned by the Archie command as different arguments are provided. The Unix utility program *wc* is used here to count the number of rows returned for each invocation of the command. In this first example, the proper-case string "Oracle" is sought and six rows are returned.

```
$ archie -l Oracle | wc -l
        6
```

Here the lowercase string "oracle" is the search key, and twenty-one rows are returned.

```
$ archie -l oracle | wc -l
       21
```

Finally, specifying the case-insensitive "oracle", eighty-four rows are returned.

```
$ archie -sl oracle | wc -l
       84
```

TIP
For more information on Archie, you can use the Archie command itself to search. The command is *archie archie*. Or, crawl the Web to **http://bunyip.com**.

Wide Area Information Search (WAIS)

As the 1990s began the inexorable push to end another millennium, personnel from the leading computer companies Thinking Machines and Apple Computer, and the global information service providers Dow Jones and KPMG Peat Marwick, combined to produce the Wide Area Information Search (WAIS) technology. This was no longer an academic exercise. Commerce needed better means of managing the vast amount of information being compiled across the world. Apple Computer was the best at the Graphical User Interface (GUI) metaphor, Thinking Machines' Unix-based Connection Machine was unequaled in raw computational power, and Dow Jones and KPMG Peat Marwick needed to ensure their information and talent were as up-to-date as possible.

Using the Connection Machine, a massively parallel supercomputer, the four companies strived to implement the ideas that had been fermenting in the ANSI draft standard Z39.50. A work in process, Z39.50 covers the protocol for bibliographic searches and retrievals. WAIS performs both the indexing and searching of documents. For the first time, Internet users were treated to the ability to adaptively search and acquire information rather than just grab files. A graphical WAIS client is shown in Figure 12-1.

WAIS is particularly remarkable for two Internet innovations. First, it not only processes information requests entered by the user, but also can take the documents the user determines are relevant and use the text within those qualified documents to acquire even more applicable data. Also, WAIS provides the ability to search for text containing any of the strings the user enters, not just the complete set of words entered. This is often not desirable as it lacks complex conjugational

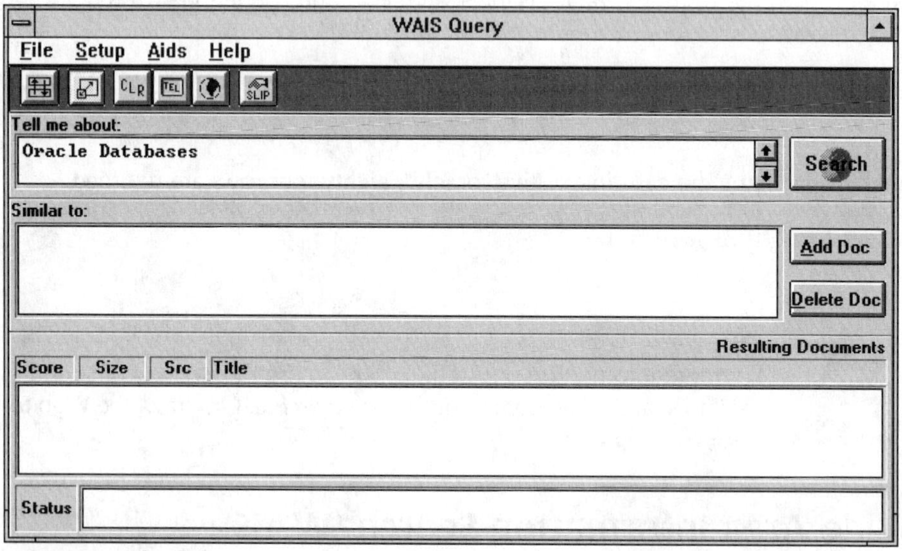

FIGURE 12-1. *A traditional WAIS search*

capabilities, but it set the stage for the coming agents, including web crawlers and spiders, that would improve on the idea.

WAIS lives on today in three forms: a shareware version, WAIS 2.0; a freeware browser technology called freeWAIS; and the commercial server/browser technology produced by the eponymous WAIS, Inc., called WAISserver.

NOTE
WAIS, Inc., was bought by AOL Productions, Inc., in late 1995. The WAIS, Inc., web site may go away as a result. Until it does, for more information visit **http://www.wais.com**. You can obtain freeWAIS, maintained by the Clearinghouse for Networked Information Discovery and Retrieval (CNIDR), via ftp from **ftp.cnidr.org**. And, as with all standard Internet technologies, freeWAIS is also mirrored throughout the world, so you can perform the command *archie wais* to learn more. Then, once you have it, *wais wais*.

Regardless of the implementation you use, however, a problem with WAIS libraries remains. WAIS libraries are significant undertakings. They are "real" libraries. This means critical thought must be applied to the collection and registration of relevant material. To that end, WAIS collections are often quite focused. Unfortunately, many areas of knowledge are not yet available under freeWAIS for all to freely traverse.

TIP
Many of the concepts WAIS's creators explored are an integral part of Oracle's TextServer3 and ConText technologies. ConText, Oracle's natural language processing technology, identifies key concepts and themes, and can extract the core concepts from a text block. It can use this information to determine the key points and generate condensed versions of processed files. And, unlike WAIS, it is readily interfaced with the Oracle7 database technology. For more information on TextServer3 and ConText, surf over to **http://www.oracle.com/info/products/newMedia/textserver.html**.

Gopher

For a short time it appeared as if Gopher would become the "killer" or driving application for which the Internet had patiently waited. Developed at the University of Minnesota, and released in 1991, Gopher was ostensibly named for either the school's mascot or as a pun on "go for." Gopher is a client/server technology that relies on a hierarchical client interface to Gopher servers' information bases. The universe of all Gophers servers is called *gopherspace.*

Gopherspace comprises the file systems through ftp-like services, Internet services such as Telnet, and even WAIS where allowed by the Gopher server manger. Gopher provides a common metaphor for running Internet applications and performing information searches on all of the major protocols.

In Figure 14-2, the left side of the window contains the hierarchical view of gopherspace, while the right contains the expanded view of the item highlighted on the left, which in this case is Veronica. Gopher's rapid growth led to the creation of other tools to help manage the search for data in gopherspace. Veronica and Jughead are two of these tools. Veronica is to Gopher what Archie is to ftp. Veronica is a searchable archive of all the resource descriptions found in gopherspace. An Internet service, Veronica is itself part of gopherspace, as the figure also shows.

Continuing the allusion to the *Archie* comic strip, Jughead is a compact, Veronica-like indexing and search tool limited to its own server resources. As Gopher grew in popularity, it expanded beyond its original Unix-based audience out to the Windows and Apple worlds, where GUI versions blossomed. Although Gopher innately is based on a text metaphor, it demonstrated the appeal of using a graphical client for finding and retrieving information. The next step was the handling of nontextual information as efficiently and seamlessly.

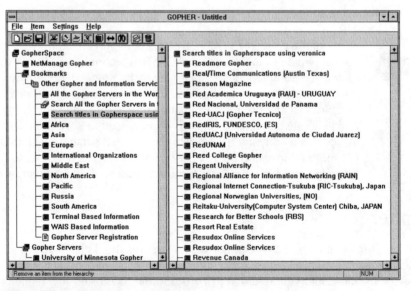

FIGURE 12-2. *A graphical Gopher client*

TIP
For more information on Gopher, burrow your way to the main Gopher server at **gopher.micro.umn.edu**, or *archie gopher* for other resources.

As useful as ftp, Gopher, and their associated technologies were, however, these methods were merely file serving. Clearly, better means were needed to more efficiently serve and secure access to multiple types of information, including programs, raw text files, formatted text files, images, audio, video, and compound documents.

DEFINITION
Compound documents: These are data sets that may include multiple element types. Elements of a compound document include text, images, audio, video, links to other compound documents, links to other places within the compound document, and embedded software. OLE (Object Linking and Embedding) and OpenDoc are two important compound document technologies.

Multipurpose Internet Mail Extensions

Traditionally, mail communication was limited to 7-bit, or printable, portions of the 8-bit character sets. Two forces conspired to improve on this. One was the need to support multibyte character sets, required for National Language Support where the character set exceeds 256 elements. The other was the increasing need to support transmission of binary file attachments such as executable programs, images, and audio files. Such files were moved around by first converting them in such a way that only the printable character set was used. This method, called *uuencoding*, causes files to increase by roughly 33 percent. As the Internet grew, this was clearly unacceptable. The solution was to implement a protocol called the Multipurpose Internet Mail Extensions (MIME). MIME provides for a header describing the type of file, such as stream data, audio, movie, and so on, and the particular method of encoding, such as MPEG, GIF, or AU. Then the file is transmitted with a unique character string bracketing it. When the receiving program sees this character string, printable and guaranteed not to exist in the file itself, it knows that transmission is complete.

The World Wide Web

In 1989, a researcher assigned to improve communications among his peers began work on a technology for serving files containing both formatted and unformatted text, hypertext links, and binary data including audio, and still and motion images. The embodiment of this technology is called the *World Wide Web (WWW),* or simply *the Web.* Its development would lead to the Internet's killer app, the web browser Mosaic.

DEFINITION
Hypertext: Conceived at SRI International and popularized by Ted Nelson while at Xerox Corporation's Palo Alto Research Center, PARC, hypertext is a navigation and viewing metaphor where textual data contains highlighted words or groups of words. When these words are selected or clicked on with a pointing device such as a mouse, more information about the highlighted text, or link, is immediately provided. This concept was soon embodied in a variety of forms, the most ubiquitous being Windows Help files. Not entirely coincidentally, the mouse, too, was conceived at SRI International by Douglas Englebart and Bill English.

Tim Berners-Lee, then a researcher at CERN, the European Laboratory for Particle Physics, needed to provide immediate and universal access to all participating members in accordance with his institution's charter. He devised the combination of an Internet service, the HyperText Transport Protocol (HTTP), and a document tag/value formatting scheme, the HyperText Markup Language (HTML), to effect his solution. A server-based application called an HTTP server and a client-based application called a web browser are used to implement the WWW.

Web Browsers
The WWW's client software, browsers enable users to navigate via a GUI metaphor. Using a pointing device, usually a mouse, to jump between hypertext links, users browse, rather than search, for information. Unlike Gopher, where navigation is performed only among the descriptions of the resources, web browsers can navigate using pictures, icons, or other graphical elements. And, unlike WAIS, where you request a result set and then retrieve it, web browsers immediately retrieve an item when it is selected. Oracle's own web client, PowerBrowser, offers these features and more. Figure 12-3 shows PowerBrowser on Oracle's own home page.

If you don't have or cannot use a graphical interface, text-only web browsers are available, Lynx being the best known. Admittedly, the Web is pushing the envelope on graphical creativity and metaphor extension. Virtual Reality Markup Language (VRML) is an example of this. As useful as text-based metaphors have been, they have been superseded by GUIs, which retrieve and present not only text but also images and other binary data such as video and audio streams. Text browsers will likely not disappear, however. Much as Telnet remains an integral part of the Internet, so will HTTP's textual components.

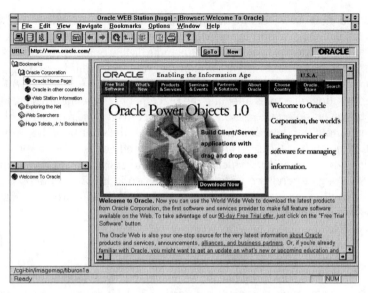

FIGURE 12-3. *PowerBrowser displaying Oracle Corporation's home page*

HTTP

The current standard for web servers, the HyperText Transport Protocol version 1.0 (HTTP/1.0), is managed by the Internet Engineering Task Force's (IETF) HTTP working group. It is a simple client-server protocol that provides for the orderly exchange of documents between server and client and the definition of document identifiers. Generally, web servers are called *http daemons*, or *httpd* for short. Daemons is the historical Unix term for persistent background processes.

HTTP is traditionally configured as an application or service running on port 80.

Web servers primarily concern themselves with two things: file serving and security. The file-serving part is rather straightforward; the security is more complicated as you look at means of limiting access to certain files and even then only to certain groups of users.

HTML

Web pages consist of a title and body text. They may also contain hypertext links, inline images, and fill-in forms. HyperText Markup Language (HTML) is the language or syntax used to develop web pages. It is a standard maintained by several groups. It is (mostly) a Standard Generalized Markup Language (SGML) application defined via a Document Type Definition (DTD). SGML is itself an ISO Standard, 8879:1986. Support for HTML is provided for in two other standards, "text/html" Internet Media Type (RFC 1590) and MIME Content Type (RFC 1521).

SGML provides for a consistent markup description standard much as Backus-Naur format is used to define programming language syntax. HTML provides formatting directives affecting the placement of text and images. HTML does not, however, determine absolute appearance. The size, typeface, color palette, and output window dimension are all under the control of the client.

HTML is *mostly* an SGML DTD because it currently does allow some display characteristics to be provided, which is anathema to SGML tenets. An example is the "<BLINK>" tag currently considered for inclusion in HTML v3 but used perhaps too frequently. Blinking is a display characteristic. SGML standards suggest the use of a "blink" attribute within another tag, such as an <ALERT> or perhaps a <WARNING> tag.

TIP
Oracle Book provides the tools needed to develop SGML applications. Oracle Book Version 2 Designer comes with many DTDs, of which HTML is one. Additionally, Rich Text Format (RTF), which is used to create Windows Help files, is also supported. This allows both multiplatform and multimetaphor development of hypertext applications.

Uniform Resource Locators

Another very useful standard is that of the Uniform Resource Locator, or URL. This is the means of requesting particular documents and establishing particular connections. URLs specify the service, domain name, and document identifier. Examples include

- **http://www.oracle.com/overview.html**
- **ftp://ftp.oracle.com**
- **news:comp.databases.oracle**

The general form of a URL is *service:hierarchical location/filename* where *service* is the TCP service name, *hierarchical location* specifies the domain name of the server to which to connect, and a *filename* is included if appropriate. The first example above requests HTTP service from Oracle's WWW site and, in particular, the **overview.html** web page. The next establishes an ftp connection to Oracle's ftp archive, and the last requests access to the **comp.databases.oracle** newsgroup in Usenet.

In the example shown in Figure 12-4, the elements are as follows:

- The underlined characters are *hypertext links.* You navigate to other Web resources by clicking on these links with your mouse.

- The picture at the top is a *bitmap* or *image,* usually to show a logo or other graphic element. Some images are *clickable image-maps.* These return to the server the x-y coordinates of the location clicked on the image, allowing a single image to display multiple hypertext links graphically. These are covered in greater detail in Chapter 13.

- At the bottom are four bitmaps that resemble buttons. They are visual equivalents to the character hypertext links. They are not image maps. Regardless of where you click on one of the buttons, the action taken will be the same each time.

Dynamic Web Pages

A problem with web pages is that they are mostly static. This leads to a lack of stimulation and certainly diminishes the likelihood of repeat visits to a web site where the content rarely changes. Much information acquires its utility from its

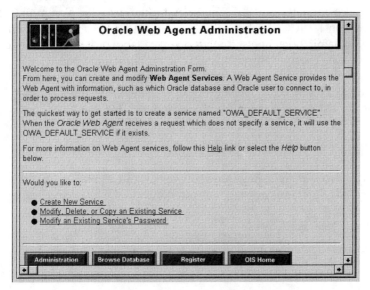

FIGURE 12-4. *An example of a web page with hypertext links*

timeliness. Such information is not generally provided from static web pages. Examples of timely information include updated stock quotations, inventory levels, and delivery status. This is also the type of data you are likely to store in a database. You must be able to serve dynamic data, not just static data.

Server-Side Includes

Server-side includes partially solved the problem of timeliness by providing a means of inserting request time information into the web page. Server-side includes use the following syntax:

```
<!--#command tag="value"-->
```

In this example, the tag value is a program to be executed or a file to be inserted at that location. However, server-side includes are discouraged as they open up the server to security violations. Improper site management could allow someone to perform exploitative commands using the feature. As a result, better means were devised.

CGI

Clearly, server-side includes are limited and their security implications generally rule them out. Fortunately, there is another Web standard, the Common Gateway Interface version 1.1 (CGI/1.1 or just CGI), which facilitates the generation of completely dynamic documents. It relies on executable programs that reside on the server to generate dynamically populated and properly formatted HTML.

CGI works by executing programs rather than transferring existing text pages. The URL for a CGI script may not appear any different than one for general processing. In fact, the URL may even look incorrect. For example, here is a typical CGI URL:

```
http://www.saraswati.com/cgi-bin/showtime
```

This refers to the executable program *showtime*, located in the cgi-bin directory. The shell script commands in *showtime* are shown in the following listing:

```
echo "Content-type: text/html"
echo "<TITLE>This is the output of the showtime program</TITLE>"
echo "<BODY>"
echo "<B>The time is now"
date
echo "</B>"
echo "<\BODY>"
```

This will run the program *showtime* and send its output, which is properly formatted as an HTTP/1.0 data stream, to the user's browser. Of course, the server must be set up to allow CGI scripts, the CGI script must be in the proper location as specified in the server's configuration file, and the script and its directory path must be accessible by the user.

Passing parameters to CGI programs relies on an unusual behavior of the CGI standard. Should the CGI program specified in the URL refer to a directory that is actually a file, the server will attempt to run the program specified as a directory with the file or subdirectory components being arguments to the program. For example, a link to the URL **http://www.saraswati.com/cgi-bin/timeconv/EDT** results in the command "timeconv EDT" being run on the **www.saraswati.com** computer with its results sent back to the requester in the form of a properly formatted web page. The timeconv script is shown in the following listing.

```
echo "Content-type: text/html"
echo "<TITLE>This is the output of the timeconv program</TITLE>"
echo "<BODY>"
TZ=${1:-"EDT"} # set the TZ environment variable to EDT if no arg was passed
echo "<B>$TZ time is now</B>"
echo "</EM>"
date
echo "</EM>"
echo "</BODY>"
```

CGI and Security Considerations

Several problems arise when using CGI. First is the trouble of launching and managing other programs on the system. CGI programs are traditionally shell scripts or C. This introduces the potential for an ill-behaved program to run amok on the server. This is complicated by the need to develop nontrivial CGI programs with variable parameters.

Parameters are managed in one of two ways. These are called the GET and the POST methods. The GET method relies on CGI programs expecting parameters following the URL. The POST method is preferable and relies on standard input passing of tag value pairs.

GET Method   The National Center for Supercomputing Applications (NCSA) and other organizations involved in HTML CGI standards development say the GET method programs should be considered deprecated. GET programs have always been troubled by two problems: length limits on environment variables and the awkwardness of very long URLs. GET values are appended to the URL. For example, if you are running a program *add-newpart*, which takes a part number and a description from HTML, you may end up with the following command:

```
add-newpart?hammer+6
```

Suppose you have a CGI program accepting many fields, some of which may be text fields of a few hundred characters, not unusual in customer service applications. You then end up with a URL such as this, or worse, one that fails as the maximum length is exceeded on the browser or on the server.

```
add-comment?I+have+a+problem+with+my+brand+new+framajazz.+It+seems+
that+each+time+I+start+it+smoke+pours+out+of+the+front.+I+thought+t
hat+it+was+supposed+to+come+out+of+the+back+and+flames+were+suppose
d+to+shoot+out+of+the+front.+It+is+not+what+I+expected.+Can+you+fix
+this?
```

Regardless of the method, there remains the need to escape out characters which, upon passage through the command line processor, could be misinterpreted or, worse, used to subvert normal processing. A simple example is the need to pass quotes as part of processing. In practice, most CGI software will pass such special characters escaped to prevent initial interpretation. The problem arises as the data makes its way through various subprograms. Those final programs must undo all of the escape characters to use the correct data.

POST Method   The POST method avoids some of these problems by passing information through the standard input stream. Most well-behaved CGI programs work in this fashion, including all but one in the WWW Interface Kit. POST method programs expect to receive variable-value strings in their input stream. The CGI program then extracts the value portion of the strings and stores it for later use. Additionally, embedded spaces, which are replaced with plus (+) signs for backward compatibility with GET programs, along with escaped special characters, must be handled.

Despite the improvement POST method CGI programs provide, there remains the traditional difficulty of interfacing external programs with core business functions. To this end, the best solutions rely on interacting with data in the database through stored procedures and triggers where business rules are best maintained centrally. Several of the WWW Interface Kit solutions, including the best one, WOW, provide such means of managing data.

The Oracle World Wide Web Interface Kit

Oracle constantly strives to solve the problem of combining core business functions with emerging data access technologies. To this end, the Oracle World Wide Web Interface Kit was composed. Bringing you the best of third-party CGI processing solutions, the WWW Interface Kit was placed on the Internet at Oracle's home site in early 1995.

Overview of the Kit

The Web Interface Kit provides gateways, a text search system, and links to other companies' products that are useful to the WWW software developer. The primary components are discussed here.

Gateways

- **WOW**   PL/SQL-based gateway by Magnus Loennroth of Oracle Corporation, originally of Oracle/Sweden but now developing Oracle Web solutions with Oracle/US. This is the best of the gateways and is covered fully later in the section titled "WOW."

- **WORA**   An excellent ad hoc table database browser by Constantin Ocrainets of Russia. WORA uses a Pro*C executable as its CGI interface. It then connects to the Oracle database and uses the data dictionary tables to manage its lists of tables and columns. It provides three screens where users may view the list of tables, columns and query conditions, and the result set of the query. A downside of WORA is that it is implemented using CGI's GET method, one of two means of exchanging information. As such, there are system limits that constrain the number of parameters and their lengths, as well as those of the query condition. For most simple browsing requirements, however, it is a fine example of Web-database integration.

- **DECOUX**   A postprocessing gateway by Guy Decoux of France, DECOUX relies on several configuration files that specify which predefined query and action to perform. It is accessed via a Pro*C executable. An Oraperl solution is also available. DECOUX relies on another CGI parameter called ISINDEX to perform its functions. ISINDEX is simply a GET tag that causes the browser to display a standard input box with a message prompting for keywords. Unfortunately, it is subject to the same problems as any other GET method CGI program.

- **ORAYWWW**   An Oraperl-based gateway and form builder by Arthur Yasinski of Canada, ORAYWWW facilitates the creation of HTML forms dynamically. The forms may allow queries only or may be written to update and delete data as well. Its strength is in its ability to selectively specify both allowed user functions and the columns displayed.

Search Engine

- **TSS Demo**   Free-text indexing and search system with a PL/SQL front-end by Peter Larsson of Sweden. TSS is a complicated system to use but simple to get up and running. It uses several Oracle Call Interface (OCI) daemons to perform its functions of searching and indexing. The actual API for the software is in PL/SQL. The interaction required between Oracle and the operating system is performed using the DBMS_PIPE package. This provides the means of reading documents through a user-developed function.

PL/SQL Compiler

■ **pls.sun4 (or PL/Web)** A stand-alone PL/SQL compiler for the SunOS 4 operating system, pls.sun4 contains built-in extensions to PL/SQL to provide HTML processing. It gives developers a means to produce PL/SQL applications without an Oracle7 database. It also provides the ability to interactively develop PL/SQL HTML applications. To do so requires use of HTML pages provided with the compiler. The code may then be saved as source files on the server. Unfortunately, this compiler is only available for SunOS 4.1.3.

Acquiring the Kit

Oracle continues to forge ahead in innovative computing directions. The WWW Interface Kit was the first of now many products available either first or exclusively through the WWW. Of course, many people limit their use of Internet technology to internal networks. These internal networks, which may be completely inaccessible from the Internet or perhaps behind a firewall that traditionally limits their utility but increases security, have driven the creation of more robust, corporate-quality development tools and techniques.

Now that Oracle has a commercial implementation of the technology, WebSystem, the WWW Interface Kit is no longer available from the main web site, **www.oracle.com**. There are other sources for the Kit, either in its entirety or in individual components. You can search for them by name on the WWW using any of the popular searching engines.

TIP
If you are having trouble locating the WWW Interface Kit, you may email the author for a list of current locations at **hugo@mcs.com**.

Installing the Kit

The WWW Interface Kit's components are provided in compressed tar formats. *Tar* is a common method of combining multiple files into a single file called an *archive.* The word "tar" comes from its original purpose of creating *tape archives.* Each tar file is further compressed using the Unix compress utility. Both tar and compress are available for other platforms as well. You do not need to be running Unix to use the technology, although it will take a bit more work to implement the concepts.

After downloading, copy each file to an empty directory where you wish the code to reside. Uncompress each using the following command, and then follow the instructions provided in the .doc and .html files that accompany each product.

```
$ zcat <filename> | tar xvf -
```

Depending on the gateway, both compilation and importation of information into database tables using SQL*Plus or some other utility may be necessary. This is because some of the technologies depend on stored procedures, written in PL/SQL, to be entered into Oracle tablespaces.

WOW

In early 1994, Oracle became the first major RDBMS vendor to release a gateway for the WWW. Called WOW for Web-Oracle-Web, it was released into the public domain and remains the best means of getting Oracle databases on the Internet for little or no cost. For commercial operations that require more robust and supported operation (WOW is an unsupported product), users need to use the Oracle WebServer, which is covered fully in Chapter 13.

Most gateways have traditionally been coded in C, perl, or shell scripts. WOW is remarkable in that it provides the ability to develop all Web applications in PL/SQL. This means that the same language developers already use to write other Oracle applications may be harnessed to the power of the Internet and the World Wide Web. And this is all done using traditional CGI call mechanisms so that the programs are called as if they were files in the CGI directory.

WOW consists of several components:

- **wow**   This is a shell script, provided in C-shell format but easily converted to Bourne or Korn shell to provide the same functions, namely, setting environment variables related to the database connection.

- **wowstub**   This is an OCI program that converts POST data into calls to stored procedures with arguments passed correctly as entered, that is, with + replaced by space, and so on.

- **HTP**   This is the hypertext package containing all procedures used by the WOW gateway.

■ **HTF** This is the hypertext package containing all functions used by the WOW gateway. The functions return values, whereas the procedures do not. The functions are required to check error conditions and alter behavior as needed.

A Demonstration of WOW Using SQL*Plus

To grasp what WOW does, look at a simple example using SQL*Plus. PL/SQL until recently did not provide a means of exchanging data except through tables. In Oracle7, there are a number of packages that extend the facilities available to the language. One of these new packages is DBMS_OUTPUT. Within this package are several functions including put_line(), which sends its arguments to a buffered stream. The following examples illustrate its use.

```
DBMS_OUTPUT.PUT_LINE('Your total order comes to ' || TO_CHAR(total_order));
```

DBMS_OUTPUT specifies the package name, and PUT_LINE specifies the particular function within that package. A single character-string value or expression is required. In this case, an expression is used concatenating a character string and a total value that is first converted from numeric to character-string type.

In addition to DBMS_OUTPUT, a program that knows to extract such buffered information is required. The likely choice is SQL*Plus. Whenever a PL/SQL stored procedure is called or an anonymous PL/SQL block (an inline program) is executed, and provided that the SET SERVEROUTPUT ON command had been previously issued, upon completion of the block or procedure the output will be sent to the standard output of the application.

In fact, to appreciate how WOW works, an example in SQL*Plus is called for. For purposes of this example, assume the htp and htf packages have been installed under a user id called wowuser. A call to the bold procedure results in the following output with the appropriate HTML bracketing tags for boldface output.

```
$ sqlplus wowuser
enter password: *****
Connected.
SQL> SET SERVEROUTPUT ON
SQL> EXECUTE htp.bold('This is a test');
<B>This is a test</B>
PL/SQL procedure successfully completed.
SQL>
```

wowstub: the Agent Component

Of course, you do not want to have to invoke SQL*Plus each time you want to produce HTML, so instead, wowstub fills the need as the primary CGI interface program. The wowstub program itself does not perform the application functions but acts as a pipeline between the HTML server and the Oracle database. Be aware that the program need not be called wowstub. However, if the name is changed, references to that program name must also be changed. They will be found in HTML files and in the wow shell script.

When invoked, wowstub evaluates several environment variables and determines whether the GET or POST method will be used. Additionally, it checks to see if the program was invoked in debug mode. Finally, it reads the parameters from standard input for POST or from the INFO environment variable for GET and ISINDEX requests and connects to the database using the name and password specified in the environment variables. It is very important that the gateway be installed such that the contents of the agent are not visible to unauthorized users. Otherwise, as the name and password are in plain sight, wowstub and the data with which it interacts will be compromised. Count on it!

The CGI programs specified will actually be packaged procedures in the database. So when the following URL is performed,

```
http://www.saraswati.com/cgi-bin/wowstub/newuser
```

the wowstub program will connect to the database and call the function passed on the command line, newuser. This is in keeping with the aforementioned CGI behavior regarding programs in nonexistent directories. The directory name is assumed to be the program name, and all remaining directory levels are passed as command line arguments to that program.

The wow Shell Script

In order for the wowstub program to be properly executed, a wrapper program is required that takes care of setting up environment variables and any other desired functions to be performed each time the gateway is called. This is the purpose of the wow shell script. As in the case of the wowstub program, this name may be changed to one more appropriate to the application it performs. You may also create a different one for each user/password/service to which you need to connect. For the following examples, however, we will use the name wow.

Extending WOW Using PL/SQL

PL/SQL is Oracle Corporation's procedural SQL-based programming language. Based on ADA, PL/SQL offers object-oriented features to fully harness SQL's potential. Combining polymorphism and encapsulation with SQL data manipulation language (DML) statements, users may craft the most sophisticated business rules and execute them efficiently within the Oracle7 engine. Additionally, PL/SQL is used to develop the procedural code within Oracle's development applications such as Forms, Graphics, and Reports. As such, Oracle developers need not learn a new language to process HTML.

In the WOW gateway, PL/SQL packages such as htp.bold and htp.italic are written in two pieces, the called procedure and a matching function. This is due to the inability to call a function without capturing the result. It is consistent with strongly checked languages such as ADA and with current solid code practices. Frequently, in less rigorous languages, errors arise from unchecked result codes and return values. You will also notice that all of the functions conclude with a call to the print, or *p*, procedure. This places the output in the put buffer from which the application, wowstub in this case, will extract the results.

```
function bold   (ctext  in varchar2) return varchar2 is
begin return('<b>' || ctext || '</b>' ); end;
procedure bold   (ctext  in varchar2) is
begin p(htf.bold(ctext)); end;
```

Now, when desired features are not available in WOW, a user must add that feature by adding it to either the application or, better yet, the HTP and HTF packages. An example with a common limitation will further illuminate this.

When developing HTML forms using WOW, you may specify input fields in the following forms:

```
procedure formField(cname in varchar2, nsize in integer);
procedure formField(cname in varchar2);
procedure formField(cname in varchar2, cvalue in varchar2);
```

All of the forms require the name of the field as the first argument. This is how values are tagged before being passed through to the CGI program. Then, depending on whether the next argument is missing, an integer, or a varchar2 field, PL/SQL expects to set the field to a default width, to the specified width, or to the default width with an initial default value. What is missing is the ability to create a field with a specified width *and* an initial default value. To do this, we extend WOW by adding the following procedure prototype, function prototype, procedure, and function. All are required.

```
function formField(cname in varchar2, nsize in integer, cvalue in varchar2) return varchar2;
function formField(cname in varchar2, nsize in integer, cvalue in varchar2) return varchar2 is
begin
   return('<input type="text" name="' || cname || '" size="' ||
          to_char(nsize) || '" value="' ||
          cvalue || '">');
end;
procedure formField(cname in varchar2, nsize in integer, cvalue in varchar2);
procedure formField(cname in varchar2, nsize in integer, cvalue in varchar2) is
begin p(htf.formField(cname,nsize,cvalue)); end;
```

WOW's Limitations

As groundbreaking as WOW is, however, it is not sufficient for commercial utilization without considerable extensions to the feature set. And, since WOW product support is not available from Oracle, feature extension is left up to the individual developer as the HTML standard evolves. Additionally, WOW requires manual setup for each web server's implementation. Ideally, there should be a one-stop solution: web server, gateway, agent. Oracle has such a product in WebSystem.

The Future of Oracle and the Web

The topics covered in this chapter are only the beginning. From these origins, Oracle has grown products far more sturdy and sophisticated than those that preceded them. With these products, Oracle WebServer and Oracle PowerBrowser, the World Wide Web, widely distributed information processing, and the Internet as a whole will see the rise of true online commerce. The key was providing a way for businesses to securely manage their affairs while effectively throwing a perpetual open house on the Internet. In Chapters 13 and 14, you will see how to use these tools most effectively, reliably, and securely.

CHAPTER 13

Oracle WebServer

Forget the ladder. Learn the web.

–*Robert Reich*

The rapid growth of the World Wide Web (WWW), driven by the favorable customer acceptance its ease of use engenders, has many enterprises considering the use of internal web applications. Many enterprise networks are already running TCP/IP, a key requirement of web technology. On these internal TCP/IP networks, called *intranets* to differentiate them from the global *Internet*, increasing numbers of web applications are being developed and deployed to provide nimble solutions to many problems.

This was not the case, however, before February 1995. Up until then, web applications integrated with distributed database management systems were homegrown and unwieldy. And web applications without databases behind them tend to be little more than electronic billboards, often more effectively deployed using other technologies.

Then, Oracle introduced the WOW gateway. This groundbreaking software, developed by Magnus Lonnroth of Oracle Sweden, provided a simple and effective means of generating dynamic web pages from Oracle stored procedures. This meant that an organization's investment in Oracle technology and enterprise class implementation, including server-enforced business logic using PL/SQL and optimized distributed databases, could easily be leveraged to quickly develop web applications.

Oracle now provides two offerings for Oracle/web integration. The first is WebServer 1.0, a standard component of the Oracle Universal Server. Included with WebServer 1.0 are applications for managing both the Oracle7 server and WebServer components. Increasingly, more distributed management applications will be deployed on the web. Oracle intends the Web to be an important part of its distributed management framework.

WebServer 2.0, providing enhanced capabilities for higher performance, extends the product line and supports a wider variety of technologies for reliably and securely serving your information on the web. WebServer 2.0 does not make WebServer 1.0 obsolete. Oracle intends to remain the clear leader in the integration of enterprise database systems with the Web. Each version will be developed and extended to fulfill distinct needs.

To appreciate what WebServer brings to the enterprise, this chapter begins with coverage of WebServer 1.0, including how to convert applications developed for the WOW Gateway for use with WebServer. A detailed survey of the additional features of WebServer 2.0 and the various means of partitioning applications with it concludes the chapter. Using the information in this chapter, you will improve your management of the web applications and your distribution of the workload on your network.

Oracle WebServer 1.0

As described in Chapter 12, Oracle has always had a home on the Internet. Integration of Oracle technology with the World Wide Web began with homegrown solutions, usually crafted in C, perl, and with shell scripts. Oracle gathered the best approaches, including their own internally developed technology, the WOW gateway, and made them all available on Oracle's home page on the Web, **http://www.oracle.com/**. Following its highly successful release, the commercial market clamored for a completely bundled and supported Oracle/web integration product. To fill that need, Oracle took what it had learned from the WOW Gateway, bundled in an HTTP server and Oracle7 database, and released Oracle WebServer 1.0 into production in late 1995.

WebServer 1.0 is comprised of four primary components:

- Oracle Web Listener
- Oracle Web Agent
- Oracle WebServer Developer's Toolkit
- Oracle7 Server

The following sections describe the role each component plays in WebServer. The diagram in Figure 13-1 shows how they are logically arranged.

TIP
For sites currently running an Oracle7 server at a release level earlier than 7.3.2, the Oracle Web Option is available. Oracle Web Option provides the Oracle Web Listener and Web Agent only. All other functionality remains the same.

Oracle Web Listener

Oracle's Web Listener is a high-performance server suitable for use both on the Internet and within corporate intranets. Like the SQL*Net Listener, the Oracle Web Listener program is a server application. It does not initiate contact but solely responds to requests from client applications called *web browsers*. These requests are provided in the format specified by the Hypertext Transport Protocol (HTTP).

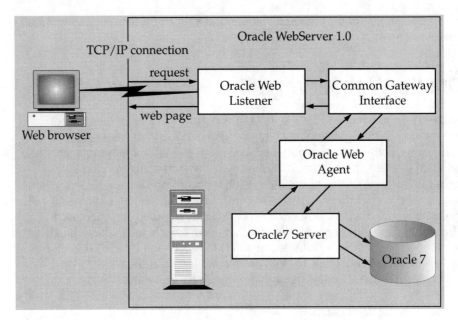

FIGURE 13-1. *Oracle WebServer components*

The Web Listener is also known as the HTTP listener. The response to HTTP requests is a text stream referred to as a *web page.* The web page is in Hypertext Text Markup Language (HTML) format.

TIP
If you are already running another vendor's HTTP server, you may elect not to employ the Oracle Web Listener. All other Oracle WebServer functionality remains the same.

Oracle's Web Listener serves web pages both traditionally, from static files, and dynamically, from Common Gateway Interface (CGI) applications. A special CGI program, designed for effective and reliable access to Oracle7 servers, is provided with WebServer. This program is part of the Oracle Web Agent and is described later in this chapter. The following section will describe how static file access is managed by the Oracle Web Listener.

Managing File Access
The Web Listener manages file access in various ways. The most basic is through the user id assigned to the Web Listener. When it is configured, you specify the user id employed to run the Web Listener program. The permissions set for a web

page must allow access by the Web Listener or an error results. Likewise, the directories in the file's path must allow access by the Listener as well. When you install WebServer, you configure this and other values using the web page shown in Figure 13-2.

CAUTION
In its installation instructions, Oracle specifically discourages configuring the Web Listener to belong to the dba group or to have Oracle software owner privileges. Such permissions compromise database security by allowing anyone gaining access to the Listener to craft applications to circumvent security. Heed this warning!

The Web Listener also facilitates location transparency. When a URL is requested, the Web Listener determines the actual location of the file. To help limit access to certain paths, file locations may be aliased. For example, most URLs are in the form

```
http://www.hostname.com/dirname/dirname/.../filename
```

The first directory in the filename portion of the URL, /dirname, is not likely to be located in the root directory of the web server computer. The Web Listener has

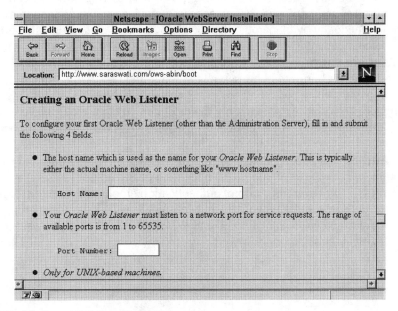

FIGURE 13-2. *WebServer configuration*

a configuration file that specifies where the root directory for requested files is. With WebServer 1.0, this directory defaults to $ORACLE_HOME/ows/doc.

As with HTML documents, the location of CGI programs is specified in the Web Listener configuration files. As with HTML files, there may be multiple aliases provided. Generally, there is at least one alias, cgi-bin, provided. This alias defaults to $ORACLE_HOME/ows/cgi-bin.

When a URL is specified as http://www.saraswati.com/cgi-bin/fred, the Web Listener will spawn the program *fred.* The results of fred are returned to the web client. If fred does not return a properly formatted web page, an error will result. Otherwise, the page is returned and the connection to the client terminated.

If a URL is specified as http://www.saraswati.com/cgi-bin/fred/argone/argtwo, the Web Listener, upon detecting that fred is an executable program and not a directory, will spawn the fred program with each subsequent filename component provided as an argument on the command line. In this case, the spawned command line would be

```
fred argone argtwo
```

Limiting Access

In addition to aliasing the locations of files, access to files may be further limited by only certain users, authenticated by name and password, or by the IP addresses or domain name of the requester. The following sections describe how authentication and IP addresses are employed to limit access. In each case, the protection may be specified individually by filename or by specifying a set of files using wildcards.

Basic Authentication   *Basic authentication* requires that a user provide a name and password prior to being served the requested URL. Unfortunately, the name and password are passed across the IP network in the clear, that is, unencrypted. This is acceptable in only the most benign of cases. However, it may be necessary where other means, such as digest authentication, are not supported.

Digest Authentication   Similar to basic authentication in use but not in action, *digest authentication* also prompts for a name and password prior to serving a requested URL. However, this form of authentication employs encryption. This means that the name and password exchange is not in clear text. There is little danger of the exchange being captured and exploited later. Not all browsers support digest authentication, however.

IP Address and Domain Name Restriction   Files may be further protected by only allowing access from certain IP addresses or domain names.

> *TIP*
> On the subject of files and access to files, you may wish to configure the Web Listener to have access to the SQL*Net listener log and trace files for ease in debugging connections. You can do so in two ways: add the directories to the list of available paths to the Web Listener, or alter the Listener's configuration files using Oracle Network Manager to place log and trace files in a directory accessible to the Web Listener.

Oracle Web Agent

The Oracle Web Agent enables access to Oracle7 databases using applications written in PL/SQL and saved as stored procedures on the server. It is a program named *owa,* run through the Common Gateway Interface (CGI), that provides a connection from a Web Listener to an Oracle7 server. This program is similar in design and purpose to the wowstub program included in the WOW Gateway of the Oracle World Wide Web Interface Kit. The Oracle Web Agent connects to an Oracle7 server, runs the specified stored procedure, returns the output of the stored procedure as an HTML-formatted web page, and terminates the connection to the Oracle7 server. WebServer applications are usually developed using the Oracle WebServer Developer's Kit, described later in this chapter.

The key to the Oracle Web Agent is PL/SQL. More precisely, the ability of PL/SQL to generate output using the DBMS_OUTPUT package enables applications to be written that interact with the Oracle7 server and result in text output. The Oracle Web Agent provides the conduit across which input from a web browser is passed to a stored procedure and processed. The result, a character stream containing HTML tags, is returned to the browser. All of the extensive capabilities of PL/SQL, unmatched by any other RDBMS technology, are then available to craft dynamic web applications.

As with other Oracle applications, you must provide a service name, username, and password to connect to an Oracle7 server. With WebServer, you can further specify the environment under which an application is run. The parameters that describe the environment are called a *Web Agent Service.* Web Agent Services enable a single Web Listener to serve as an access point to multiple Oracle7 servers (see Figure 13-3).

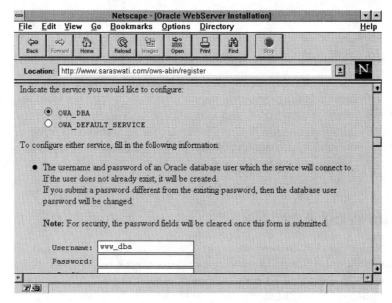

FIGURE 13-3. *Oracle Web Agent installation*

Each Web Agent Service defines the following parameters:

- Web Agent Service name
- Oracle7 username and password
- ORACLE_HOME
- ORACLE_SID for a local database, or SQL*Net V2 service name or V1 connect string for a remote database
- Filename of the HTML page returned when an error occurs
- IP ports that are supported by this service
- Log directory into which message will be written for this service
- NLS language for national language support

A local database, as used here, is defined as one residing on the same server as the Web Listener. A remote database is one requiring SQL*Net to access. Web Agent Service parameters are stored in a configuration file called OWA.CFG managed through WebServer itself.

CAUTION
It is imperative that the contents of the OWA.CFG file be kept secure. This file contains several parameters that may be exploited, including the username and password combinations and the valid IP ports. Also, the IP port specifications should not be considered security parameters. They are solely a means of limiting service requirements.

Here is an example of a URL for a WebServer application.

```
http://www.saraswati.com/ows-bin/oranet/owa/sample.startproc
```

When Oracle's Web Listener receives a request for a web page, it determines whether the page requested is stored in a file or is generated through the CGI. In this example, ows-bin alerts the Web Listener to the fact that a CGI program is being called. The directory ows-bin is one of several identified as containing CGI executables. The next element, oranet, specifies the name of the Web Agent Service to be employed (oranet is one directory below ows-bin). The element owa refers to the Oracle Web Agent executable program. Finally, sample.startproc is the name of the stored procedure, startproc, in the package sample, to be run. If you wished to run this program from the operating system, you would merely enter

```
owa sample.startproc
```

Of course, web applications generally require input. This is usually provided through HTML forms. The field/value pairs of the fields on the form are passed through standard input to the Oracle Web Agent. The owa executable then passes them to the stored procedure by name.

Because owa conforms to CGI specifications, it inherits all of the exported environment variables known to the Web Listener. These environment variables include the name of the host on which the client application is running, the username of the account under which owa is running, and other values used to craft targeted responses such as the type of web client the user is running. The values of many of these environment variables are made available to the developer to provide context-specific responses. Access to the environment variables is through the routine owa_util.get_cgi_env( ), part of the WebServer Developer's Toolkit.

WebServer Developer's Toolkit

To significantly ease the development of web applications using PL/SQL, Oracle provides a software development kit (SDK) called the *WebServer Developer's Toolkit*. It is comprised of a set of PL/SQL stored routines, provided in the form of packages named HTP, HTF, and OWA_UTILS, that are compiled and saved by an Oracle7 server. These utilities enable easy coding of standard HTML tags, plus many proposed tags and enhancements, including tables and forms. Although free to do so, the Oracle web applications developer does not have to directly code HTML syntax into the application. These procedures do much of the work of coding HTML for you.

NOTE
The division of the packages into three sets is historical and related to PL/SQL requirements. The HTP and HTF packages originated with the WOW Gateway. Although they are very similar, in some cases identical, the WebServer packages contain greatly improved code with increased flexibility and without the limitations that existed when WOW was released.

The first package, HTF, consists of PL/SQL functions. It is very modular in its design, the intention being that each function returns an HTML-formatted string enabling functions to be recursive. Additionally, the packages significantly exploit *polymorphism,* PL/SQL's ability to overload an identifier, so that a single function name may in fact be multiple functions. At runtime, the number and type of arguments passed to the function determine which version of the function is actually used. This feature extends to functions and procedures. When executing PL/SQL code, the Oracle7 engine determines if an *lvalue,* or *return value,* is expected. If so, the function by that name is run; otherwise, the procedure by that name is called.

Here is an example of how this works. Suppose there is a function to create a boldface item, bold(), and another function to produce a hard line break on the web output page. To output an item in boldface and terminate it with the HTML <P> tag, you simply call the function print(bold('string')).

The following listing shows the function bold(). Note how it expects to be called with one or two values of type varchar2. If the second value is not passed, a NULL is substituted in its place. This function merely takes the first value passed, returns the text "<B" followed by any attributes specified in the second value, followed by ">". This completes the start of the tag. Next, the first passed value is appended. Finally, a terminal "</B>" tag is appended.

```
function bold   (ctext  in varchar2,
                 cattributes in varchar2 DEFAULT NULL) return varchar2 is
begin return('<B'||
             IFNOTNULL(cattributes,' '||cattributes)||
             '>'||ctext||'</B>'); end;
```

The procedure bold() merely calls the procedure p(), passing as its value the output from the function bold() using the passed text as its value to process. The htf.bold() function returns a boldface string that is passed to the p() procedure, a variant of the print() procedure.

```
procedure bold    (ctext  in varchar2,
                   cattributes in varchar2 DEFAULT NULL) is
begin p(htf.bold(ctext,cattributes)); end;
```

The second package, HTP, consists of the same operations, but in the form of procedures that call the HTF functions. HTP is required to get around the requirement that all functions must return a value. Procedures do not return values, making the process of crafting PL/SQL web applications much easier.

The third package, OWA_UTIL, consists mainly of non-HTML operations. These include functions to return CGI environment variables, get_cgi_env( ), and a procedure to return the source of a PL/SQL routine as an HTML-formatted page, showsource( ). Some operations in OWA_UTIL do provide HTML output, such as the single table print function tableprint( ).

OWA PL/SQL Package

There is an additional package, OWA, that is comprised of PL/SQL routines solely for the use by the owa executable. The Oracle web application developer will never call any routine in the OWA package directly.

CAUTION
The contents of the OWA package may be changed without notice. By using only the HTP, HTF, and OWA_UTIL routines, the developer will be protected from differences in the underlying OWA package contents.

Oracle7 Server

Oracle WebServer provides a one-stop solution to serving enterprise data through web technology. Unlike other solutions, which require the acquisition of each web technology component from a different vendor, WebServer enables you to install a single CD containing all of the required components, including an Oracle7 server. The Oracle7 server delivers the most important components of WebServer, the database and PL/SQL engine.

The combination of PL/SQL and enterprise data enable effective use of an existing investment in resources—the corporate data repository, business rules, and a distributed database management infrastructure. A single WebServer can support multiple Oracle7 servers. This feature should be exploited for performance and security.

CAUTION
The Oracle7 server provided with WebServer trial versions does not include the distributed option. It cannot participate in distributed updates. This is appropriate as most sites will segregate their web server database from the rest of their enterprise data server for security reasons.

Optimizing WebServer 1.0 Applications

The following recommendations will improve overall network performance when using WebServer.

- Monitor hits and cache files appropriately.

- Although dynamic pages are generally better from a life-cycle point of view, use static pages where appropriate.

- Consider running multiple Web Listeners.

- Consider distributing applications across multiple servers. Partitioning is achieved in one of two ways: distributing a single application across multiple servers, or multiple applications across multiple servers, each application on a single server. The latter is certainly easier from a management point of view.

- Take advantage of replication services where possible. Refer to Chapter 8 for details on replicated databases and using a single TNS listener for multiple copies of a replicated database, called listener load balancing.

NOTE
The Oracle WebServer distribution does not include a web browser, the application required to view WWW sites. A browser is necessary to install and maintain WebServer. You may use any browser capable of supporting HTML tables and forms. Oracle's own web browser, PowerBrowser, may be downloaded for free from Oracle's web site, **http://www.oracle.com/**.

Converting WOW Applications to WebServer 1.0

In order to extend the facilities in WebServer and to resolve some earlier architectural vagaries, the Oracle Web Agent packages contain many extended and renamed package components. In order to use existing WOW applications with the Oracle WebServer, the following differences must be accommodated.

- The WOW "C" program, wowstub, is now called owa.

- Existing WOW code may be accommodated using OWA_DEFAULT_SERVICE. This is the default service owa will use if the URL refers to an unknown service.

- The default signature procedure, wow.sig, is now called owa_util.signature.

■ The WOW procedure, wow.showsource, is now called owa_util.showsource.

■ The procedures and functions listed in Table 13-1 have been renamed. To accommodate these differences, change the names of the affected subprograms in your application, as shown in the table.

The use of the following procedures and functions may also require coding changes.

The procedure *formText* is now called *formTextArea*. This is to accommodate the presence of a new single-line text field by use of the procedure formText. Text areas are scrollable sections of *n*-rows by *n*-columns. In addition to the name, the new formTextarea will also accommodate initialization of the text area. To do this, issue a text outputting call between the formTextareaOpen and the TextareaClose statements.

```
...
htp.formTextareaOpen('comments',10,60);
htp.print('This text will appear in the comments field as the default text.');
htp.formTextareaClose;
...
```

As mentioned previously, the formField procedure required extension to set both its width and initial value. This still applies. However, another modification is required. In cases where only the initial value is provided, the following form should be used:

```
formText(cname, NULL, NULL, cvalue);
```

WOW Name	OWA Name
url	anchor
gif	img
formUndo	formReset
item	listItem
ddef	dlistDef
dterm	dlistTerm

TABLE 13-1. *Subprograms to Rename*

Fixing a previous limitation, the formDo button has been renamed and extended. It is now called *formSubmit* in keeping with the HTML name for the object it represents, a submission button. What was previously missing was a means of setting both the name associated with the name/value pair passed to WOW and the label displayed on the button. If desired, existing calls to formDo may just be recoded as follows:

```
formSubmit(NULL, label);
```

To fully utilize the feature and enable multiple buttons to be dealt with in a single form, the following form should be used instead:

```
formSubmit(cname, cvalue, cattributes);
```

Oracle WebServer 2.0

Oracle WebServer 1.0 is a standard component of the Oracle7 server beginning with release 7.3. It provides the standard means of integrating Oracle7 databases with web applications. However, despite its many strengths, there are features it lacks that would enable it to provide even better performance, especially when serving across the Internet.

WebServer 2.0 is an optional product providing extensive improvements to the WebServer technology base. In addition to supporting all of the functionality of Web Server 1.0, Web Server 2.0 provides the following additional features:

- Secure Sockets Layer (SSL)
- Proxy support
- Web Request Broker
- LiveHTML
- Java
- New PL/SQL library packages with routines for text manipulation, pattern matching, image map, and HTML cookie

The following sections describe the features and how to manage them for a better Oracle network. The richness of WebServer 2.0 is illustrated in the main page shown in Figure 13-4.

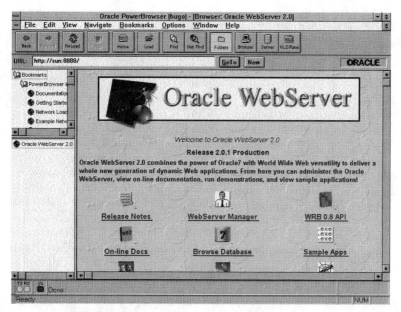

FIGURE 13-4. *WebServer 2.0 main page*

Secure Sockets Layer (SSL)

In addition to the file security mechanisms provided with WebServer 1.0, WebServer 2.0 now supports the Secure Sockets Layer (SSL) protocol. SSL provides connection encryption so that point-to-point communication is secured. Unlike authentication that limits access by page or group of pages, when used in conjunction with SSL, all communication and access is secure.

Use of SSL is specified through the URL identifier HTTPS instead of HTTP. A digital certificate is required to employ SSL. Certification of authorized users is enabled through RSA public-key algorithms. Verisign is the agent for the technology. WebServer 2.0 administrators must contact Verisign to obtain certification for using SSL. There is additional information on obtaining this certification from the Web Listener Administration page as shown in Figure 13-5.

> **NOTE**
> The trial version of WebServer 2.0 employs 40-bit keys. This is due to federal regulations regarding the exportation of encryption technology. A domestic 128-bit key version is available.

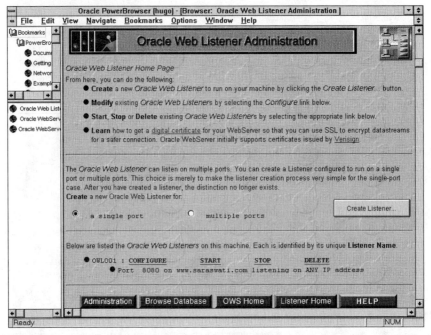

FIGURE 13-5. *Obtaining a Verisign digital certificate through Web Listener Administration*

Proxy Support

An additional means of securing access to resources, *proxy support* makes it possible to use different IP services rather than the well-known ports. This enables the use of firewall applications that secure access to certain ports and applications. Oracle's WebServer 2.0 Listener implements the WWW Consortium (W3C) proxy behavior as specified by the authors Luotonen and Altis.

NOTE
Additional information on proxy services is found at the following web site: **http:://www.w3.org/hypertext/WWW/Proxies/**.

Web Request Broker

New in WebServer 2.0 is the Web Request Broker (WRB) technology. An extension of the HTTP listener configuration, WRB is a more sophisticated means of determining the appropriate application to service a request. Unlike WebServer 1.0, dynamic generation of HTML through applications is not limited to single-threaded CGI calls. WebServer 2.0 enables multi threaded connections to persistent applications, lowering the time required to establish and service a request. A process called the *WRB dispatcher* handles requests. Connections are then handed off to WRB executable engines, WRBXs; these are the persistent applications.

Configuration of the Web Request Broker and other WebServer 2.0 features is through the enhanced management web page shown in Figure 13-6.

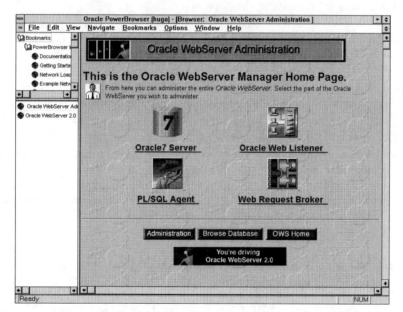

FIGURE 13-6. *WebServer 2.0 Manager Home Page*

WRB Cartridges

The WRB applications programming interface (API) is designed for open development of WRB-compliant applications, called *cartridges.* This allows both users and third parties to develop WRB plug-ins. Currently, three cartridge types are supported:

- PL/SQL
- Java
- LiveHTML

PL/SQL   The PL/SQL cartridge effectively replaces the Oracle Web Agent for most applications. The others are described below. As with the Web Agent and Web Agent Services, there is an equivalent cartridge and WRB API combination. It is called a *WRB service.* As with Web Agent Services, the WRB services also require parameters specifying their scope. In the case of the Oracle7 WRBX, these are called *Database Connection Descriptors* (DCDs).

LiveHTML   Many times it is desirable to provide a somewhat dynamic web page, that is, a web page with a few fields dynamically generated. This is the role *server-side includes* fill. Unfortunately, in the past, server-side includes have posed security risks. With the LiveHTML cartridge, you have improved server-side include processing, speeding up, simplifying, and securing simple dynamic page creation.

Java   WebServer 2.0 introduces server-side Java processing. This 32-bit implementation of Sun's Java language is expected to be widely deployed. Java offers many of the features of object-oriented languages in a safer, network-optimized framework. It is much easier to take up and use than other traditional OOP languages such as C++. Additionally, the Java WRB cartridge enables access to PL/SQL from Java programs on the server.

Extended PL/SQL Function Library

Oracle has extended the function libraries, adding routines for text manipulation, pattern matching, and image map operations. The new packages are

- OWA_PATTERN
- OWA_TEXT

- OWA_IMAGE
- OWA_COOKIE

Pattern Matching Utilities (OWA_PATTERN)
OWA_PATTERN is a PL/SQL package containing procedures and functions for performing string matching and substitution. A key feature is the ability to employ regular expressions, wildcards, with them. As with all PL/SQL packages, non-WebServer applications can also take advantage of the package contents.

Text Manipulation Utilities (OWA_TEXT)
OWA_TEXT is a package comprised of procedures, functions, and datatypes used by OWA_PATTERN for manipulating large data strings. They are externalized so you can use them directly if you wish. As with OWA_PATTERN, non-WebServer applications are likely to benefit from their use as well.

Image Map Utilities (OWA_IMAGE)
OWA_IMAGE provides a set of datatypes and functions for manipulating HTML image maps. *Image maps* are images that, when clicked on by the user, result in the coordinates of the cursor being sent to the Web Listener. The position of the pointer determines the resulting URL processed. Image maps may be processed locally or at the server. OWA_IMAGE provides the features needed to process image maps at the server.

Cookie Utilities (OWA_COOKIE)
One of the greatest hurdles in developing web applications is that of the persistent logical connection. As each connection to web interface effectively terminates a connection to the server, users have had to craft their own means of maintaining persistence from page to page. Now, a method called *HTML cookies* is available. HTML cookies are client-side variables used to capture and maintain state information. The OWA_COOKIE package provides a set of datatypes, procedures, and functions for manipulating HTML cookies. They eliminate the need to continually exchange state information with the server. New PL/SQL functions have been added to support cookies.

Conclusion

The choice between employing WebServer 1.0 or WebServer 2.0 is likely to come down to this: WebServer 1.0 is effectively free, WebServer 2.0 is not. However, considering the relatively low cost of the WebServer 2.0 product and the wealth of features it provides, the cost is quickly recovered.

Regardless of the choice you make, both provide excellent features and a useful set of technologies for your Oracle network.

TIP
There are two user-maintained sources of information on WebServer. I highly recommend Thomas Dunbar's site, **http://gserver.vt.edu/**. While there, sign up for the samples mailing list. Another source on WebServer is the Oraweb-L mailing list. Pointers to these and other sites are found on my Oracle Page at **http://www.mcs.net/ ~hugo/oracle.html**.

CHAPTER 14

Oracle PowerBrowser

Where do you want to go today?

—*Microsoft*

The technology found in Oracle's WebServer provides an elegant means of integrating the Web with the Enterprise database. It seamlessly integrates with your existing investment in business rules, role-based security, and other standing PL/SQL resources. However, as was discussed in Chapter 1, there is a spectrum of client/server application partitioning. While Oracle WebServer provides extensive facilities for server-side processing, some applications lend themselves better to processing on the client side. To meet this need and to ensure complete coverage of application development requirements, Oracle developed PowerBrowser.

Leveraging the object-oriented database access technology from Power Objects, Oracle's PowerBrowser and PowerBrowser OCX enable developers to deploy applications that effectively provide client-side processing. PowerBrowser technology provides broad client-side processing abilities through Network Loadable Objects (NLOs) including Oracle Basic scripts, Java applets, and plug-ins. Supporting the latest HTML features, PowerBrowser provides something else—built-in distributed processing capabilities through client-side database integration and a lightweight HTTP server. PowerBrowser is shown displaying Oracle's home page in Figure 14-1.

NOTE
Chapter 12 covers the basics of the World Wide Web including HTML, HTTP, and web browsers. It is recommended that you familiarize yourself with the information provided in that chapter before diving into PowerBrowser.

Browser Technology

The web browser is being touted as the universal client. This is because a web browser can serve many different functions: directory service, file transfer (albeit download only), GUI client, multimedia viewer, and character display. This flexibility is a result of the Internet standards in place. The following section describes how to get up and running with PowerBrowser. You will see what each standard brings to the client and why it enables the browser to function as the interface of choice.

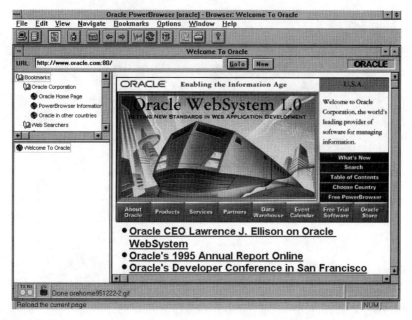

FIGURE 14-1. *PowerBrowser on Oracle's home page*

Oracle PowerBrowser Quick Start

To limit its size and to simplify end-user installation, PowerBrowser does not use the sophisticated Oracle Installer technology provided with its server products. Instead, PowerBrowser comes as an *executable archive.* An executable archive is a single file consisting of a program preamble that extracts files compressed within its data area. When run, PowerBrowser prompts for the destination directory and proceeds to install itself where specified.

The first time PowerBrowser is run after installation completes, it provides several dialog boxes to facilitate its setup. The first dialog box presented, PowerBrowser Setup, is shown in Figure 14-2. Unless you are an Oracle employee, select from either Generic Setup or one of the Internet Service Providers listed.

The next dialog box, New User, prompts you for your username. PowerBrowser provides for multiple users and stores information such as the full name and e-mail address for each user separately. Enter the information in the dialog box, shown in Figure 14-3.

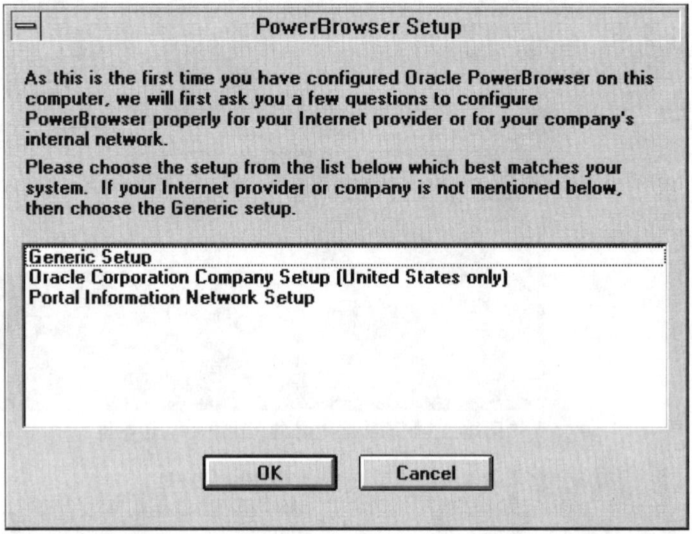

PowerBrowser Setup

As this is the first time you have configured Oracle PowerBrowser on this computer, we will first ask you a few questions to configure PowerBrowser properly for your Internet provider or for your company's internal network.

Please choose the setup from the list below which best matches your system. If your Internet provider or company is not mentioned below, then choose the Generic setup.

Generic Setup
Oracle Corporation Company Setup (United States only)
Portal Information Network Setup

[OK]   [Cancel]

FIGURE 14-2. *PowerBrowser Setup dialog box*

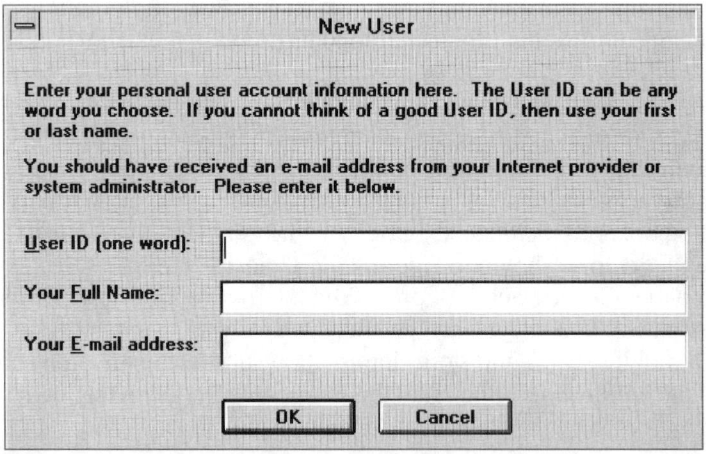

New User

Enter your personal user account information here. The User ID can be any word you choose. If you cannot think of a good User ID, then use your first or last name.

You should have received an e-mail address from your Internet provider or system administrator. Please enter it below.

User ID (one word): [   ]

Your Full Name: [   ]

Your E-mail address: [   ]

[OK]   [Cancel]

FIGURE 14-3. *New User dialog box*

Finally, the setup process provides an opportunity to further configure
PowerObjects. It is recommended that you click on Yes, as shown here:

Setting Preferences

You are then presented with the Preferences dialog box, consisting of several
tabbed sections. It is here that you customize most of PowerObjects' attributes. The
tabs allow you to set up the proper values for your proxies and to enter the names
of your mail and news servers, as shown in Figure 14-4.

TIP
Before you actually try to set up your preferences, it is recommended
that you read the rest of this section. Some of the items may require
you to contact your system administrator for the proper value.
Compile all of the values you need ahead of time, and then enter the
information once.

FIGURE 14-4.   *Preferences dialog box*

Proxies

As described in Chapter 13, *proxies* are programs that protect your internal network from unauthorized access from the Internet. They are part of *firewall strategies* that enable relatively unencumbered access to the Internet while providing a reasonable level of security to resources within the firewall. The proxy numbers specify the TCP/IP port number to be used for each service in place of the standard port number for that service. Proxy numbers may be provided for the following services:

HTTP
FTP
Gopher
WAIS
News

Additionally, you may disable proxies on certain addresses by entering them into the text box labeled "No Proxy On." If proxies are to be temporarily disabled, check the box labeled "Disable All Proxies Temporarily." This is usually only checked by mobile users who are connecting to the Internet through a dial-up modem when they are disconnected from their home LAN.

Servers

In order to send and receive mail, you must provide the name of your mail server. The server should be running the Simple Mail Transport Protocol (SMTP). Likewise, to read and post news items, you must provide the server name for your Net News Transport Protocol (NNTP) server. NNTP is sometimes still called Usenet.

User

The User tab contains two sections, User Details and Preferences. The first three fields in the User Details section are those that were entered when PowerBrowser Setup first ran. An additional field, Reply-To, is provided. This is used in mail messages and news posting to specify a different e-mail address to which replies should be sent. This is generally for users who have a preferred e-mail address different from that from which PowerBrowser is typically run. The User tab is shown in Figure 14-5.

The Preferences section contains the Home Page URL, or default URL. This is the URL loaded when the Home button on the toolbar is clicked. You can specify to automatically load the Home Page by checking the Auto Load Homepage check box.

The next three check boxes determine how images are handled. The first, Display Images While Loading, specifies whether images should be incrementally displayed as their bits are received. If not checked, a placeholder icon will appear in place of the image until it is completely received. Once received, the

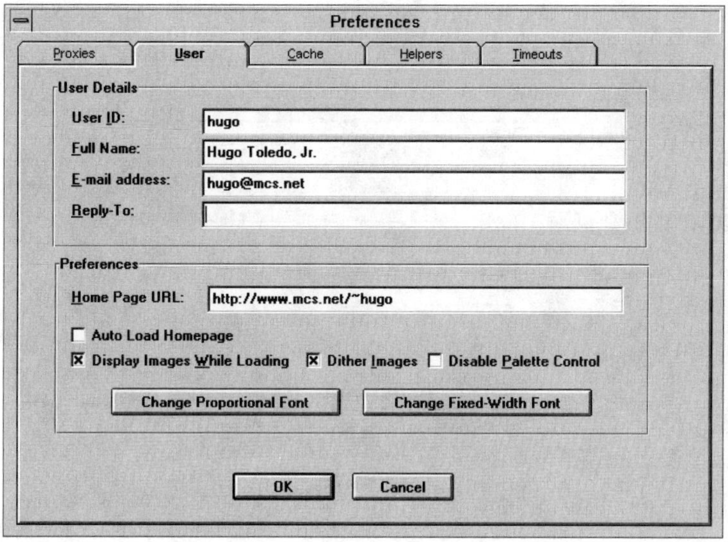

FIGURE 14-5.   *User tab in Preferences dialog box*

placeholder is replaced with the image. The next check box, Dither Images, specifies how images with greater color depth than that provided by the computer should be *dithered.* Dithering is where adjacent bits are altered to achieve the effect of greater color depth. However, dithering is more CPU intensive than the nearest color selection, which is what happens if the box is left unchecked. Finally, checking Disable Palette Control prevents the modification of the color palette.

The last two items in the Preferences section of the User tab are the font buttons. If clicked, both bring up the standard Windows Font dialog box. The first, Change Proportional Font, changes the font used for proportional text, which is all text except for that marked as preformatted, bracketed with the HTML tags <PRE> and </PRE>. Preformatted sections are shown in Fixed Font, which may be changed by clicking on the other button, Change Fixed-Width Font.

Cache

The next tab contains two sections, Base Directory and Cache. The former contains a single field, Base Directory, which controls from where files with relative pathnames are sought. An example of the Cache tab is shown in Figure 14-6.

The Cache section of the tab contains information related to the disk cache. In order to improve performance, PowerBrowser *caches,* or retains, a certain volume of HTML and images for a period of time. In this way, icons that are repeated across a web site are loaded only once from the remote server and will be reloaded

Preferences

| Proxies | User | Cache | Helpers | Timeouts |

Directories

Base Directory: `C:\ORAPB`

Cache

Cache Directory: `C:\ORAPB\CACHE`

Cache Size: `1024` kilobytes

Don't Reload Before: `24` hours

☐ Disable Cache Temporarily

Clear Cache Now

OK   Cancel

FIGURE 14-6. *Cache tab in Preferences dialog box*

from the cache. Also, as you tend to visit certain sites frequently, it makes sense to retain elements that may not change often.

The first field, Cache Directory, contains the name of the directory in which the cached files are stored. The next, Cache Size, expressed in kilobytes, sets the maximum amount of storage all of the cached files may take up. If space is not a problem and you have a large number of frequently visited sites, increase this parameter. Otherwise, keep it low but expect to trade off space for time as you wait for each page and image to load from the remote server. The third field specifies the expected latency of most material. Even if a manual reload is specified, unless this period of time has passed, the cache is used. The check box, Disable Cache Temporarily, is useful to reload only certain sites or pages from sites. Finally, there is a button labeled Clear Cache Now, which empties the cache, freeing up space on the disk. Here is the resulting dialog box that prevents accidental clearing of the cache.

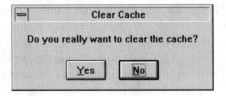

Clear Cache

Do you really want to clear the cache?

Yes   No

Helpers

As described in Chapter 12, there is an Internet standard called Multipurpose Internet Mail Extensions, or MIME. MIME types indicate what sort of data is embedded in a file. When a file is processed by PowerBrowser for presentation to the user, it first determines what type of file it is. Sometimes the file is preceded by a MIME type identifier, such as image/gif. Other times, PowerBrowser determines the MIME type from the file extension.

Some MIME types are properly presented to the user by PowerBrowser. Other MIME types require *helper* applications to properly process their contents. If necessary, PowerBrowser launches the appropriate helper application as identified by information maintained through the Helpers tab, shown in Figure 14-7.

NOTE

The term "process" rather than "display" is used above because not all MIME types are visual. Examples include audio data, which are played, and applets, small software programs, which are executed.

The MIME types listed in Table 14-1 are processed internally by PowerBrowser. You generally add or update helper programs to accommodate new MIME types. To update a helper program, select the affected MIME type in the listbox at

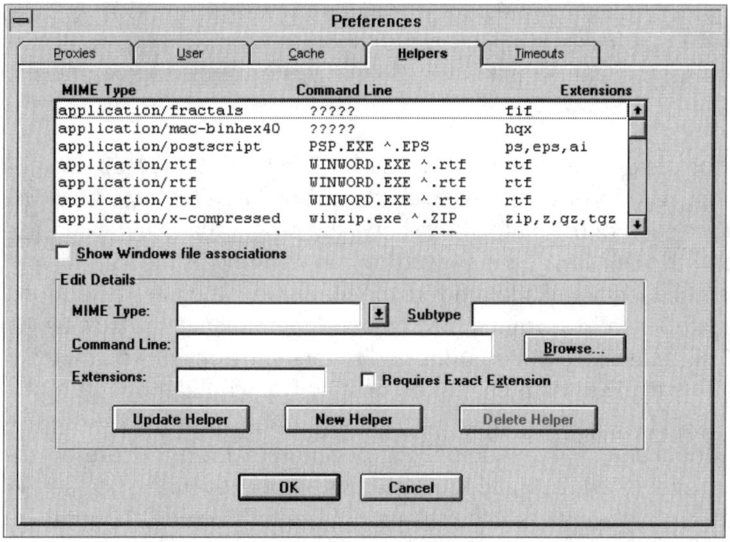

FIGURE 14-7. *Helpers tab in Preferences dialog box*

MIME Type	Extension
audio/basic	.au, .snd
audio/x-aiff	.aiff, .aifc, .aif
audio/x-voc	.voc
audio/x-wav	.wav
image/gif	.gif
image/jpeg	.jpg, .jpeg
image/pcx	.pcx
image/tiff	.tif, .tiff
image/x-windows-bitmap	.bmp, .dib
image/x-windows-rle-bitmap	.rle
image/x-xbitmap	.xbm
text/html	.htm, .html, .mdl
text/plain	.txt
audio/avi	
video/msvideo	.avi
video/x-msvideo	

TABLE 14-1. *MIME Types and Their Extensions*

the top of the dialog box. In the previous image, the MIME type application/rtf, used for Rich Text Format data, was selected. When a MIME type is selected, the Edit Details section of the dialog box shows the program and file extensions associated with that MIME type. PowerBrowser determines the MIME type from either an embedded MIME identifier in the file or from the file's extension. To accommodate operating systems with limited-length filenames, such as Windows, where the file extension is often truncated to three characters, you may deselect the Requires Exact Extension check box or specify each likely subset such as .htm or .html.

In the Command Line text box, the application that is run to present the MIME type is specified. In this case, application/rtf is associated with Microsoft Word for Windows. The ^. at the end of the command line tells PowerBrowser to launch Word with the filename appended. To change the associated application, enter the name of the new application or click on the Browse button to select the application using the standard Windows File Open dialog box. You may also add additional extensions, separated by commas, in the Extensions text box. When you have finished making changes, click on the Update Helper button to save the changes.

Occasionally you may need to delete a helper program association if the type is no longer valid or the associated application is problematic. To delete the association, select the MIME type from the listbox, and then click on the Delete Helper button.

NOTE
Clicking on the Delete Helper button does *not* delete the helper program. Only the association is deleted. Consult the helper program's documentation for uninstallation details.

Using PowerBrowser

PowerBrowser is Netscape-compatible and behaves like most browsers. One enhanced feature requiring a brief explanation is the use of multiple window panes. As shown in Figure 14-8, when you launch PowerBrowser, it displays multiple panes. The upper-left pane contains your *bookmarks*. Bookmarks are Uniform Resource Locators saved to enable quick access to web resources. Double-clicking on a bookmark causes PowerBrowser to load that URL's contents. Below the bookmarks is your *URL history list,* which contains the URL of each web resource you have visited. Finally, the right side of PowerBrowser's window contains the main browser pane in which web pages are displayed.

PowerBrowser may also be run as a single pane. To do so, click on the pane icon, which looks like this:

The resulting single-pane view of PowerBrowser is shown in Figure 14-9.

Personal Server

In addition to its browsing abilities, PowerBrowser enables anyone to publish on the World Wide Web. Within Oracle PowerBrowser is a lightweight HTTP server called the Personal Server. To start the Personal Server, click on the icon, shown here:

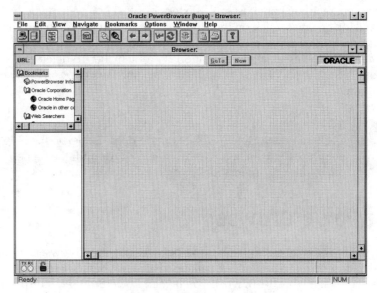

FIGURE 14-8. *PowerBrowser's multiple panes*

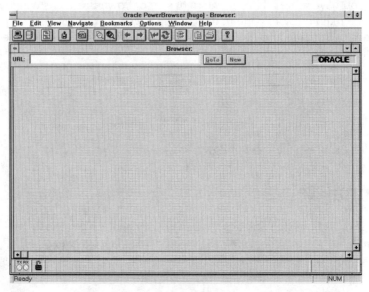

FIGURE 14-9. *PowerBrowser in single-pane view*

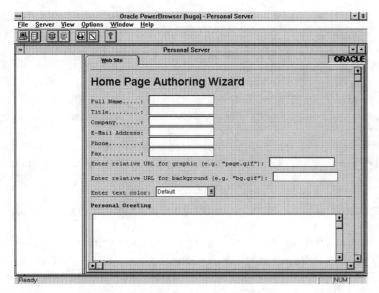

FIGURE 14-10. *Setup screen for Personal Server*

You will be presented with the Personal Server setup screen, shown in Figure 14-10.

PowerBrowser Programming

The means by which the Personal Server is configured is a PowerBrowser script. Here is the listing for the default Personal Server home page. You see that some of the action tags call a script file, WIZARD.SCR.

```
<html>
<head><TITLE>Personal Home Page</TITLE></head>
<body>
<FORM METHOD="CSP">
<HR>
<H1>Home Page Authoring Wizard</H1><P>
<KBD>
Full Name.....: <INPUT NAME="name"      SIZE=20><BR>
Title.........: <INPUT NAME="jobtitle"  SIZE=20><BR>
Company.......: <INPUT NAME="company"   SIZE=20><BR>
E-Mail Address: <INPUT NAME="email"     SIZE=20><BR>
Phone.........: <INPUT NAME="phone"     SIZE=20><BR>
```

```
Fax..........: <INPUT NAME="fax"          SIZE=20>
<BR CLEAR=LEFT><P>
Enter relative URL for graphic (e.g. "page.gif"): <INPUT
NAME="graphic" SIZE=20><P>
Enter relative URL for background (e.g. "bg.gif"): <INPUT
NAME="background" SIZE=20><P>
Enter text color: <SELECT NAME="textcol">
    <OPTION
SELECTED>Default<OPTION>Black<OPTION>Red<OPTION>Green<OPTION>Yellow
<OPTION>Blue<OPTION>Magenta<OPTION>Cyan<OPTION>White</SELECT>
<HR>
<B>Personal Greeting</B><P>
<TEXTAREA NAME=greeting TYPE=TEXTAREA ROWS=5 COLS=80></TEXTAREA>
<P>
<INPUT TYPE="SUBMIT" METHOD="CSP:SCRIPT" ACTION="wizard.scr"
VALUE="Save Home Page Using Wizard">
<INPUT TYPE="SUBMIT" METHOD="CSP:SCRIPT" ACTION="twizard.scr"
VALUE="Save Home Page Using Template">

<HR>
</KBD>
</FORM>
</body>
</html>
```

WIZARD.SCR is a database markup language (DBML) application. Here is what it looks like:

```
Begin Client

    If name.value = "" then
       Browser.bas_messagebox("Please enter your name")
         Exit Sub
    End If

    If greeting.value = "" then
       Browser.bas_messagebox("Please enter a personal greeting message")
         Exit Sub
    End If

    Dim TextColor As String
    Dim HTMLColors As String
```

```
   TextColor = ""
  HTMLColors = "<OPTION
SELECTED>Default<OPTION>Black<OPTION>Red<OPTION>Green<OPTION>Yellow
<OPTION>Blue<OPTION>Magenta<OPTION>Cyan<OPTION>White"

    If UCASE$(textcol.value) = "BLACK" then
         TextColor = "#000000"
         HTMLColors = "<OPTION
SELECTED>Black<OPTION>Default<OPTION>Red<OPTION>Green<OPTION>Yellow
<OPTION>Blue<OPTION>Magenta<OPTION>Cyan<OPTION>White"
    End If
    If UCASE$(textcol.value) = "RED" then
         TextColor = "#FF0000"
         HTMLColors = "<OPTION
SELECTED>Red<OPTION>Default<OPTION>Black<OPTION>Green<OPTION>Yellow
<OPTION>Blue<OPTION>Magenta<OPTION>Cyan<OPTION>White"
    End If
    If UCASE$(textcol.value) = "GREEN" then
         TextColor = "#00FF00"
         HTMLColors = "<OPTION
SELECTED>Green<OPTION>Default<OPTION>Black<OPTION>Red<OPTION>Yellow
<OPTION>Blue<OPTION>Magenta<OPTION>Cyan<OPTION>White"
    End If
    If UCASE$(textcol.value) = "YELLOW" then
         TextColor = "#FFFF00"
         HTMLColors = "<OPTION
SELECTED>Yellow<OPTION>Default<OPTION>Black<OPTION>Red<OPTION>Green
<OPTION>Blue<OPTION>Magenta<OPTION>Cyan<OPTION>White"
    End If
    If UCASE$(textcol.value) = "BLUE" then
         TextColor = "#0000FF"
         HTMLColors = "<OPTION
SELECTED>Blue<OPTION>Default<OPTION>Black<OPTION>Red<OPTION>Green
<OPTION>Yellow<OPTION>Magenta<OPTION>Cyan<OPTION>White"
    End If
    If UCASE$(textcol.value) = "MAGENTA" then
         TextColor = "#FF00FF"
         HTMLColors = "<OPTION
SELECTED>Magenta<OPTION>Default<OPTION>Black<OPTION>Red<OPTION>Green
<OPTION>Yellow<OPTION>Blue<OPTION>Cyan<OPTION>White"
    End If
    If UCASE$(textcol.value) = "CYAN" then
```

```
        TextColor = "#00FFFF"
        HTMLColors = "<OPTION
SELECTED>Cyan<OPTION>Default<OPTION>Black<OPTION>Red<OPTION>Green
<OPTION>Yellow<OPTION>Blue<OPTION>Magenta<OPTION>White"
    End If
    If UCASE$(textcol.value) = "WHITE" then
        TextColor = "#FFFFFF"
        HTMLColors = "<OPTION
SELECTED>White<OPTION>Default<OPTION>Black<OPTION>Red<OPTION>Green
<OPTION>Yellow<OPTION>Blue<OPTION>Magenta<OPTION>Cyan"
    End If

    HTML.bas_StartDoc()
    HTML.bas_StartHeader()
    HTML.bas_Title("Personal Home Page of " + name.value)
    HTML.bas_EndHeader()
    HTML.bas_StartBody(TextColor,"",background.value)
    HTML.bas_RawHTML("<HR>")
    HTML.bas_Heading("H1", name.value + " at home")

    If graphic.value = "" then
        HTML.bas_RawHTML("<HR><PRE>")
    Else
        HTML.bas_RawHTML("<HR><PRE><IMG SRC=" + graphic.value +
" ALIGN=LEFT>")
    End If

    HTML.bas_RawHTML(" Name..........: " + name.value)
    HTML.bas_CRLF()

    if jobtitle.value <> "" then
        HTML.bas_RawHTML(" Title.........: " + jobtitle.value)
        HTML.bas_CRLF()
    End if

    if company.value <> "" then
        HTML.bas_RawHTML(" Company.......: " + company.value)
        HTML.bas_CRLF()
    End if

    if email.value <> "" then
        HTML.bas_RawHTML(" E-Mail Address: <A HREF=mailto:" +
email.value + ">" + email.value + "</A>")
```

```
        HTML.bas_CRLF()
    End if


    if phone.value <> "" then
        HTML.bas_RawHTML(" Phone.........: " + phone.value)
        HTML.bas_CRLF()
    End if


    if fax.value <> "" then
        HTML.bas_RawHTML(" Fax...........: " + fax.value)
        HTML.bas_CRLF()
    End if


    HTML.bas_RawHTML("</PRE>")


    HTML.bas_Newline("LEFT")
    HTML.bas_RawHTML("<HR>")
    HTML.bas_Heading("H2", name.value + " says:")
    HTML.bas_RawHTML(greeting.value)
    HTML.bas_Paragraph("ALL")
    HTML.bas_RawHTML("<HR>")
    HTML.bas_EndBody()
    HTML.bas_EndDoc()


    Dim TempHTMLFile As String


    TempHTMLFile = environment.bas_GetProfileValue("USERDIR") & "\index.htm"
    HTML.bas_SaveHTML(TempHTMLFile)


    BROWSER.bas_Load(TempHTMLFile)


End Client
```

Notice that the language is very much like Visual Basic. This is because it is based on Oracle Power Objects Basic. Compared to Java, which PowerBrowser can also run, PowerBrowser scripts are much simpler to develop.

> **NOTE**
> Microsoft licensed Oracle's implementation of PowerObjects Basic for client-side processing for use in its own products. In a cross-licensing agreement, Oracle contracted to support Microsoft's Visual Script.

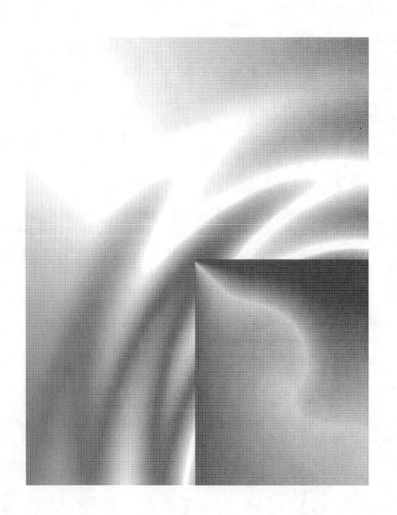

CHAPTER 15

Keeping Up with Oracle Technology

There are two types of knowledge. One is knowing a thing. The other is knowing where to find it.

—Samuel Johnson

Contrary to conventional wisdom, it is *what* you know that counts. Experience will certainly hone your analytic skills; the scars of previous hazards unavoided remind you to exhibit greater caution. But, unlike climbing a mountain where the tools improve but the terrain remains much the same, in networking, the ground is always moving. Underneath shifting sands of ever-changing Oracle technology lie quickly evolving network topologies.

So, as Sir Edmund needed Tenzing to help him scale Everest, you too need competent Oracle guides. Fortunately, there are myriad sources of accurate information for your voyage from installation, through change management, to desupport. Just make sure you and your guide are speaking the same language.

A Wide Variety of Sources

It is important to be both aware of and adept at using each of the many information sources available—before you need to use them. Experience teaches you which questions to ask; here you will learn where to seek answers and how. In Figure 15-1 you see the resource landscape laid out, ranging from nonelectronic sources to those available via electronic media, and from Oracle and other commercial sources to user community-based information sources.

The quality of information served from each of the following sources varies along with the type of information available. You may be surprised at the number of people who take the time to answer your questions. Some are paid to help and some are not. While you should look at information from unmoderated sources with a critical eye, fortunately, most are reliable. In the case of non-Oracle resources you may even find that those replying to your query are actually Oracle employees responding on their own behalf.

TIP
Should you solicit information, regardless of the source, make certain you provide as much information as possible with your request.

Etiquette

If someone provides assistance, be appreciative and thank them. If the information they provided was incorrect, return the favor by pointing out their mistake

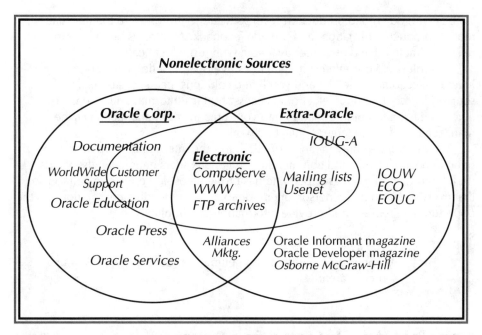

FIGURE 15-1. *The Oracle information sources universe*

privately. If the discussion took place in a public forum, clarify the error publicly so that others do not make a second mistake. The golden rule applies here as well. It is certainly good etiquette and your cooperation will be well rewarded. Besides, it does not help to alienate your information sources, either!

Types of Information Sources

There are two broad categories of information sources: electronic and nonelectronic. There are also Oracle Corporation sources and those outside of the corporation; you can call these "extra-Oracle." All four types intersect as the appropriate medium is employed to best convey information.

Electronic Information Sources

Oracle Corporation's homestead on the Internet, its World Wide Web (WWW) home page, further demonstrates the power of the Internet as an effective vehicle for providing timely information. There you can try out a demonstration of Oracle's

Web Server, download production-level software for 90-day free trial evaluation, request product information, and provide feedback. And this is but one of many reliable Oracle-related resources available with just a local call.

Regardless of your interest in Oracle—developer, reseller, end user, or investor—get out on the Net and you'll find solutions, peers, customers, and sources. Without a doubt, electronic access shortens information lag, enables efficient integration of information into your organization, and facilitates the management of much larger contact networks.

And the Net certainly means more than just the Internet. Dial-up access to bulletin boards locally and commercial service providers nationally also yields useful information. Increased demand has brought cost-lowering competition so that everyone from a one-person operation to a market-leading corporation has the opportunity to retrieve and provide information electronically.

CAUTION
Anyone can put forth a compelling Net identity. So, pick your sources carefully.

Nonelectronic Information Sources

There is a world beyond your monitor. Most of it goes on without you, of course. But, thankfully, in addition to the wonders of an electronic solution, there are still opportunities to meet and speak with people, as well as read books, and otherwise deal with the world as you once did! Nonelectronic information sources include product documentation; third-party information media including Oracle technology magazines and books; Oracle Services consultants; and, of course, Oracle's own support personnel, who—while not quite there with you—are very humanly available at the other end of a phone call.

Oracle Corporation

Need help? Get it right from the fountainhead, Oracle Corporation. Oracle provides the most complete information on their products and their integration. This information comes through several different vehicles:

- Product documentation
- Oracle Press
- Oracle Education

- Oracle Services
- Alliances Marketing
- WorldWide Customer Support

Product Documentation

Oracle's product documentation is not only complete but increasingly accessible as it is delivered in more ways than before. Each type is appropriate at different times and for different purposes. In the following sections you will learn what each of the media contains and how to use it effectively.

TIP
At the Massachusetts Institute of Technology (MIT) there resides an FTP archive of commonly requested information. It is found at **ftp://rtfm.mit.edu/**. You can see by its Uniform Resource Locator (URL), its name, that the archive resides on a computer named *rtfm*. It is so named because, traditionally, when someone asked you for information readily found in the documentation, thus taking up your time needlessly, the only appropriate reply was "RTFM!" Translated, this acronym means "read the manual first." Or something like that. So, please, before asking someone, make sure you RTFM.

Printed Media
Oracle products always come with documentation covering product installation, getting started with and using the product, and supporting reference documentation. The documents contain a table of contents and an index. They often also contain a glossary covering potentially unfamiliar terms found in the documentation. Such documentation, however, is no longer generally distributed in book form.

In February 1994, Oracle began the initial distribution of online product documentation based on Oracle Book along with their CD-ROM–based software distribution media. Eventually, all product and documentation will be shipped on CD-ROM for systems that support CD-ROM and support a Graphical User Interface (GUI). For such systems, both non-CD software media and printed documentation remain an available option for a nominal fee.

Yet, despite the move to CDs as both a product and documentation distribution medium, some printed documentation is always provided. Even where product manuals are not shipped, Oracle always provides documentation covering support options and Release Notes. Release Notes are dated and contain information not available at the time the final documentation for the product was completed. The first page of the Personal Oracle7 Enterprise Edition Release Notes is shown in Figure 15-2.

Personal Oracle7 Enterprise Edition
Version 7.1.4.1.0-Production
Release Notes May 1995
A25116-1

These release notes include updated information and known restrictions to Personal Oracle7 Enterprise Edition operation.

To install your Personal Oracle7 Enterprise Edition, refer to the complete installation instructions in the *Personal Oracle7 Enterprise Edition Installation and User's Guide for Windows.*

Installation Notes
Read this section before you install Personal Oracle7 Enterprise Edition for Windows.

Hardware Requirements
This release of Personal Oracle7 Enterprise Edition is supported running on a 486 or Pentium computer.

Win32s
This release supports Win32s Version 1.20, which is provided on the Personal Oracle7 Enterprise Edition CD. This version of Win32s must be installed on your PC before installing Personal Oracle7 Enterprise Edition.

Memory Requirements
This release requires a minimum of 16 MB of RAM and it requires Windows running in Enhanced mode (virtual memory turned on).

Microsoft Sound System 2.0
Microsoft Sound System 2.0 is incompatible with Personal Oracle7 Enterprise Edition. If Microsoft Sound System 2.0 is loaded on your machine, during the installation of Personal Oracle7 Enterprise Edition you are asked whether or not you want to install an updated driver from Microsoft that is compatible with Personal Oracle7 Enterprise Edition. If you say Yes, the updated driver is installed for you.

Building Control Files
When you are installing Personal Oracle7 Enterprise Edition, you may not have enough memory (RAM) to finish building the control files. If this happens, you are warned by the Installer to look at the build.log file in the ORACLE_HOME\RDBMS71\TRACE directory. If the error message indicates that there isn't enough memory, use the following steps to work around this problem:

1. Either from DOS or from the Windows File Manager, delete ctl1.ora (if present) from your %ORACLE_HOME%\DBS and %ORACLE_HOME%\RDBMS71\ARCHIVE directories.

FIGURE 15-2. *Typical Oracle Release Notes format*

README files

Found on the installation media, and often copied during installation into the ORACLE_HOME hierarchy itself, README files generally cover platform-specific issues more timely than that of the printed media. These are usually related to installation issues and are prominently located in the installation media hierarchy to ensure their being spotted and read during the installation process.

Hypertext Help

As was shown in Chapter 12, "Oracle and the World Wide Web," hypertext is playing an increasingly important role as Oracle expands its product line to include the small work group and departmental arena. There, GUI clients are the norm. From Motif to Windows to Macintosh, users are accustomed to this metaphor for finding answers to application problems.

Other factors make hypertext documentation irreplaceable. Workgroup/2000 products are available for a free 90-day trial period just by downloading them from Oracle's WWW site. If this is not possible or desirable, you may also order CDs containing Workgroup/2000 software. In either case, having to provide bound documentation would render these emerging distribution channels far less useful to both Oracle and its customers.

Moreover, effective documentation is crucial during the products' installation and trial-period evaluation. Oracle recognizes this and provides complete documentation in the form of hypertext help files, which are distributed with the software. Additional installation assistance is provided through the Internet. To help facilitate Internet access, Oracle even provides a web browser with all of the software needed to get up and running on the Internet in 15 minutes. The browser, pointed at Oracle's online installation web page, is shown in Figure 15-3.

Depending on the platform, hypertext files are provided in various formats. On the Macintosh, the files may be in Oracle Book, Microsoft Help, or Foundation Solutions EHelp format. Under Windows, the files may be in Oracle Book, Adobe Acrobat, or Microsoft Windows Help format. Regardless of the authoring tool, the hypertext metaphor is well understood by most GUI users. There still remain two common misconceptions to address:

■ **Misconception One: Unlike paper documentation, you don't have any place to add your own notes when using hypertext.**

Wrong. Certainly, one of the hallmarks of effective documentation is how dog-eared, sticky-noted, and scribble-filled a manual becomes. You know on seeing a well-worn tome that the documentation fulfilled its purpose and was considered an effective component of many a solution. And, although the book metaphor may not seem to be carried through, most hypertext help systems support user annotations.

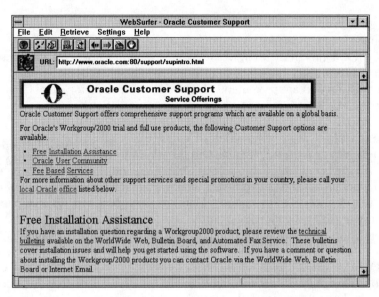

FIGURE 15-3. *Web browser from Oracle Workgroup/2000 90-day trial CD*

In Windows Help, selecting Edit|Annotate from the menu displays the annotation in a dialog box that permits the entry of persistent notes. Once an annotation is entered, a paperclip icon appears at the top of the page, or *topic*. To read, modify, or delete the annotation, click on the paperclip icon. An example of the Annotate dialog box is shown in Figure 15-4.

NOTE
As with printed documentation, should the help file be updated or replaced, the annotations may no longer track properly or may not be accessible at all. Permanent copies of notations must be filed away externally to ensure important annotation data is not irretrievably lost.

TIP
When replacing documentation, either rename or move the old help file containing annotations to another location. Then just cut and paste the old annotations from the old to the new file.

An example of how hypertext is superior to the initial installation and setup of a new product is found in the SQL*Net V2 for Windows 3.1 online documentation. The new user may not be able to establish a

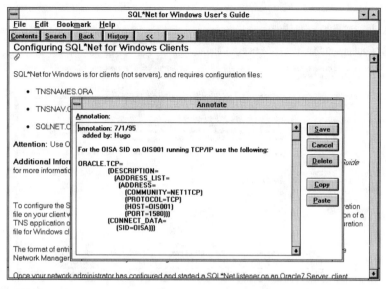

FIGURE 15-4. *Annotating Windows Help files for future reference*

connection with another computer but will be able to view the documentation explaining the required steps and providing an example, in this case through a Windows Help file. Windows Help allows the user to select any or all of the help on a topic, and copy it to the Clipboard. The example in Figure 15-5 shows how a user would copy the boilerplate for a SQL*Net configuration by lifting it directly out of the documentation.

On the Macintosh, Microsoft Help is also available and functions similarly. Where EHelp is used, a similar process is used as demonstrated in Figure 15-6.

Another form of customizing or enhancing your Windows Help files is shown in the following illustration.

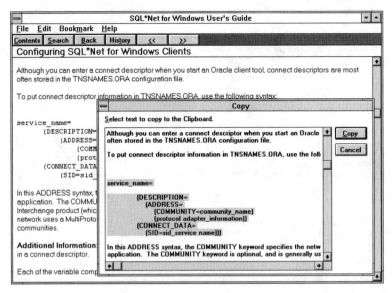

FIGURE 15-5. *Windows Help example showing use of copy to Clipboard process*

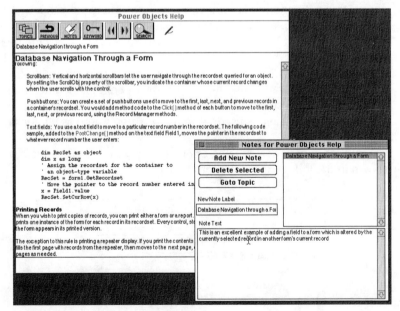

FIGURE 15-6. *Macintosh EHelp annotation example*

You can create bookmarks, which will quickly bring you to a topic by clicking on one of the bookmarks in the list presented when you select Bookmark from the menu.

■ **Misconception Two: You can't take the documentation with you to read while away from the computer or while it is tied up doing something else.**

Of course, if you do not like hypertext, and feel the need to further deforest the planet, all is not lost. Seriously, all of the hypertext formats Oracle uses provide means for printing out the documentation. In Windows Help, each topic may be viewed online or printed. To print a topic, select File|Print Topic from the menu. Oracle Book provides even greater flexibility, allowing you to print as little as a highlighted selection or as much as the whole document in one step. Figure 15-7 shows Oracle Book's print dialog box with all the available options for print scope selection.

Oracle Book

As internetworking drives the RDBMS world harder, Oracle needs to effectively keep product documentation current on disparate platforms. To this end it has required additional tools to manage that growth. Oracle Book is one such tool. It is used to manage electronic documentation destined for multiple platforms and formats. It has both authoring and viewing components and is designed to

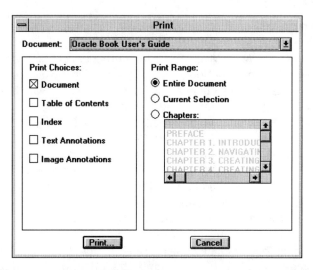

FIGURE 15-7. *Oracle Book Print dialog*

accommodate additional formats and platforms as they develop. Oracle Book also accommodates group development and functions as a document librarian as well. Finally, it also performs format conversions.

Oracle Book V2 is the current incarnation of this product and offers many benefits over version 1. Chief among these is the tighter integration with other Oracle products and the expansion of the API to effect its integration with ConText and other Standard Generalized Markup Language (SGML) tools. Oracle Book is used to manage the development of Oracle documentation, which must be distributed in multiple languages, many of which require multibyte character sets. A somewhat recursive look at Oracle Book in action is presented here:

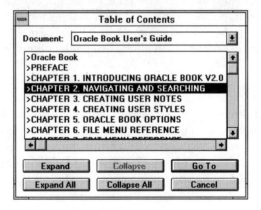

Oracle Press

Oracle Press publishes *Oracle Magazine,* a quarterly publication distributed free to qualified readers, which provides ongoing insight into Oracle technology. Every issue contains articles covering client application profiles, software tuning tips, and technical articles on Oracle platforms and operating environments.

In September 1995, *Oracle Magazine* also included the Oracle Workgroup/2000 90-Day Trial CD, version 4.0, to all of its readers. The CD contains Oracle Power Objects for Windows and Macintosh, Oracle Objects for OLE, Personal Oracle7 for Windows, and the Oracle7 Workgroup Servers for NetWare, NT, and OS/2. So, in addition to articles on these breakthrough products, readers can try out the software for themselves.

With the proven success of Oracle Media Object's interactive multimedia technologies, Oracle Press brings *Oracle Magazine Interactive* to your desktop. A CD-ROM containing the complete contents of all *Oracle Magazine* issues for 1993 and 1994, it comes with a host of other demonstrations and information retrieval tools. All of it is created and run using Oracle Media Objects.

To apply for a free subscription to *Oracle Magazine,* call and request an application form. They are available through Oracle Press at (415) 506-7000. To order *Oracle Magazine Interactive,* call (415) 506-9182.

Oracle Education

Whether to maintain proficiency in current technologies that are not a part of your current product mix, or to prepare for new technologies, Oracle's Education division offers over 100 different courses designed to fulfill customers' needs at a high level of satisfaction. Oracle Education boasts an impressive 97 percent Customer Satisfaction Index in surveys covering 12 evaluation criteria and the overall course rating. Courses are offered in 26 cities. A total of 85 classrooms are in the system, with more added each year. About 100 classes are presented each week.

Oracle Education customers' needs are met by targeting skills required to excel at job functions and achieve performance goals. A comprehensive set of job functions to which the courses are tuned is shown here:

Database administrators	Application developers
Designers/developers	Systems analysts
Network administrators	Nontechnical managers
End users	Technical sales representatives
Presales consultants	Consultants and implementers

Oracle Education alone is authorized to provide Oracle Masters Training. This program is specifically designed to produce the top Oracle talent in the business. Beyond that, Oracle Education provides Train-the-Trainer programs for large groups. This enables organizations to have members of their own staff certified as Oracle instructors facilitating quality internal training programs. In addition, to best achieve the goals of its customers and the students, Oracle Education provides its courses through a variety of delivery options, as shown here:

Individual classes at an Oracle Education center	Conveniently located and comfortable
On-site training	To minimize disruption and avoid travel budget crunches
Customized instruction	Tuned for your organization's needs
Media-based training	Computer-based audio and video training
The Oracle Channel	Live instruction at or near your location via satellite

Oracle Education's offerings strive to train to the appropriate level. Subject mastery is defined by Oracle Education as the following levels: orientation, understanding, skill, and expert. By targeting each subject and desired level of mastery, Oracle Education can tailor educational programs to the individual, work group, or organization. But this is only the scope of the training programs. Oracle Education also offers services and technology that enable customers to build training mechanisms right into their applications. Using Oracle's Electronic Performance/ Learning Support Systems (EP/LSS), customers may limit their support and training costs by providing users with both on-the-spot answers to application questions and application-related exercises for integrated hands-on and on-the-job training.

Oracle Services

Just because you are an expert doesn't mean you can do it all. It's okay to need a hand. For those times when you need the most current expertise from the company that created the technology or to shore up limited resources, Oracle Services, Oracle's consulting services arm, is ready to help. Oracle Services can provide assistance from its staff of over 3,500 members worldwide. From pinpoint expertise in a new technology to global design and rollout of Oracle-based solutions, Oracle Services may serve your needs.

Oracle Services provides resources to aid in the following tasks:

Organizational Change Services

Management Advisory Services

* Business Process Reengineering (BPR)
* Open Systems Transformation

Application Development Services

* Custom Application Development
* Application Implementation
* Field-Developed Applications

Technology Services

* Emerging Technologies
* Enterprise Groupware Services
* Computer-Aided Systems Engineering (CASE)
* Core Technologies Services

At the heart of these services are the basic tools of the Oracle consultant:

■ *The Oracle method*   Oracle's full life-cycle, service integration method. Rather than a linear solution path, Oracle can cut development time and enforce greater management controls over your project using the Oracle Method's captured best practices solutions.

■ *Industry templates*   Reliance on standard Industry-hardened and -proven templates for application development and life cycle management.

■ *Open systems transformation labs*   A state-of-the-art testbed for prototyping your organization's change management policies and techniques.

■ *The Oracle applications repository*   With each year that passes, additional information is stored in the repository by Oracle consultants worldwide. Then, when your problems are being solved, your Oracle consulting team can span years of experience and the world to bring you proven solutions.

■ *Automated delivery tools*   Including AIM Advantage. Based on Oracle's proven Application Implementation Method (AIM), AIM Advantage provides a comprehensive toolkit for implementing any Oracle applications package.

Alliances Marketing

Oracle's Alliances Marketing is the group concerned with supporting all of Oracle's vendor-channel relationships. These include independent software vendors (ISVs), consultants, systems integrators, and other associated providers of Oracle-related technology. Alliances Marketing strives to provide up-to-date marketing information and support to those whose jobs depend on timely Oracle information to complete their projects and close deals. This includes sales support, pre-sales technical support, product literature, and special reduced-price development licenses for technology evaluation and new product development.

Business Alliance Programme (BAP)

Oracle's Alliances Marketing runs the Business Alliance Programme. The progam supports the activities of all of Oracle's business partners including systems integrators, worldwide partners, and application providers. BAP partners alone are authorized to sell Oracle products and services. In return, BAP members enjoy access to Alliance team members, who provide timely assistance and support of BAP members sales activities.

BAP members also participate in specially designed courses from Oracle Education that are tailored to the needs of Oracle's solutions partners. For the

Oracle product and services provider, the BAP program opens additional pathways to information and internal Oracle resource access.

Oracle Integrator
Alliances Marketing publishes its own magazine, called *Oracle Integrator: The Journal for Oracle Solutions.* It is a bimonthly publication that provides technology overviews, addresses marketing issues, includes technical articles for the developer community, and provides synopses of all of Oracle's press releases. A key benefit of *Oracle Integrator* is that it provides information on the integration of third-party technologies with Oracle products. To order, contact Oracle Alliances Marketing at (415) 506-7000.

Oracle Developers' Conference
Each year Alliances Marketing, in conjunction with Oracle Global Events, stages the Oracle Developers' Conference. Held in San Francisco each spring, the conference provides over four days of technical and marketing breakout sessions, plenary presentations featuring new product announcements, and product launches where new technologies and marketing strategies are unveiled.

Oracle WorldWide Customer Support

You get what you pay for. Oracle WorldWide Customer Support (WWCS) provides the best source of information you can buy. When you need a timely answer from those in the know, there is no substitute. Support is provided flexibly through a variety of media and to suit a variety of needs. These include read-only, delayed question-and-answer, real-time interactive, and even on-site support products. Once available only through their own bulletin board system, they can now be reached through CompuServe and the World Wide Web. WWCS is constantly evaluating new delivery channels to ensure every customer can receive the support they need.

Installation support is free for 30 days for most products in the United States. There is even free electronic 90-day-trial-period support for the Workgroup/2000 products. After the initial support period, customers may choose to purchase either incident-based or contract-based support. And for those on Metal Level support contracts, there is no substitute for the wealth of resources made available. The differences between the levels are illustrated in Figure 15-8.

DEFINITION
Meta Level: In addition to incident-based support, where you pay a flat rate per contact, or *incident*, Oracle provides ongoing Metal Level support contracts in three categories: Bronze, Silver, and Gold. Interestingly, although "medal" appears to be a more appropriate moniker, "metal" is the term used to look up this type of support within Oracle's own SupportLink system.

ORACLE CUSTOMER CARE MATRIX

	Oracle Gold	Oracle Silver	Oracle Bronze	Oracle SupportLink
Software Releases/Updates				
Product Updates and Patches	✔	✔	✔	
Electronic Services				
Oracle SupportLink	Q&A	Q&A	Q&A	read only
Online Access to Problem fix Database	✔	✔	✔	
Online Access to Support System	✔	✔	✔	
Online Alerts	✔	✔		
CD-ROM SupportNotes™	✔	✔	$	$
Add'l Subscriptions to SupportNotes™	$	$	$	$
Mail Server	✔	✔	✔	
Telephone Assistance				
5 Days/Week, M-F 5am-6pm PST	✔	✔	✔	
7x24 Telephone Coverage	✔	✔		
Toll free 800 Number	✔	✔		
Proactive Support				
Proactive Alerts	✔	✔		
Technical Newsletter and Bulletins	✔	✔	✔	$
Scheduled Onsite Support[†]	$	$		
Full-time Onsite Support[†]	$			
Personalized Support				
Priority Processing/Routing	✔			
Designated Support Team	✔			
Account Management Reports				
Automatic	✔			
On-demand	✔	✔		
Database Center of Expertise[†]	$			
Additional Options/Requirements				
Education	rec	rec	rec	rec
Consulting				
Oracle7™ installation	$	$	option	
Oracle V6 to Oracle7™ Upgrade	$	$		
DATABASE Audit Service	$			
Documentation	$	$	$	$

LEGEND

✔	Bundled At No Additional Charge
$	Option Available At An Additional Charge
blank	Not Available
[†]	Limited Release

FIGURE 15-8. *Metal Level support matrix*

Free Installation Support

In the case of Workgroup/2000 products, support during the 90-day trial period is available in three forms:

Via World Wide Web:	**http://www.oracle.com/support/support.html**
	http://www.oracle.com/support/feedback.html
Via Faxback Service:	U.S. and Canada: (415) 506-8438.
	Outside U.S. and Canada: +1.415.506.8438
Via Bulletin Board:	U.S. and Canada: (407) 888-1234.
	Outside U.S. and Canada: +1.407.888.1234

With most other Oracle products in the United States, once you purchase a product, you receive 30 days of free Installation Support from Oracle. This support is available either through Oracle's SupportLink forum on CompuServe or over the telephone. Customers outside the United States should contact their local Oracle sales office for information on technical support. In the United States, telephone support is obtained by calling (415) 506-1500. You will be asked to provide your Oracle Product Registration Number, which is usually found on the back of the Customer Support Information Booklet provided with each product. An even better choice is SupportLink.

SupportLink is Oracle WorldWide Customer Support's private forum on the CompuServe Information Service (CIS). Although the Oracle support is provided free, normal CompuServe connect charges still apply. Don't have CompuServe? No problem, along with every product sold, Oracle includes a brochure explaining how to get online with CompuServe and receive an initial number of hours for free. In most cases the brochure is accompanied by the Windows version of CompuServe's Information Manager, called WinCIM.

SupportLink Quick Start   Once you are online with CompuServe, you must send a mail message to Oracle WorldWide Customer Support requesting access to the forum to establish your free support period. Attempts to visit the forum will not yield access as it is available by invitation only. To send the message, perform the following steps:

1. From WinCIM, select Mail.

2. Select Create Mail.

3. Enter the Oracle WWCS Name and CompuServe ID as shown in Figure 15-9.

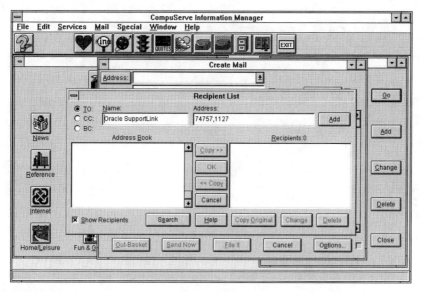

FIGURE 15-9. *Addressing a mail message to WWCS on CompuServe*

4. Click on the Add button. This automatically adds it to the recipient list on the right. You will probably also want to press the Copy button to add it to your permanent CompuServe address book.

5. Click on the OK button in the center of the dialog box to complete recipient selection.

6. Figure 15-10 shows the mail creation dialog box along with the text you must enter to register. You must enter both the line tags or descriptions up to and including the colon. After each colon, press TAB and then enter the required information.

The components of the message are described in Table 15-1.

Once on SupportLink, you can communicate with other users and support analysts, and receive timely information on Oracle products and services. Best of all, this is direct electronic contact where you can exchange code, screen prints, and other information without intermediaries or media conversions.

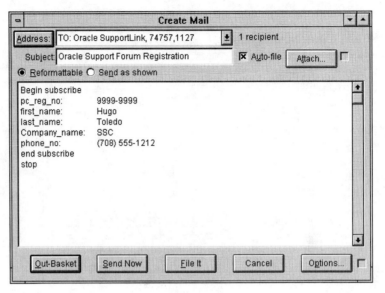

FIGURE 15-10. *Formatting your access request*

`Begin subscribe`	This is required by Oracle's auto-registration software.
`pc_reg_no`	This is your Product Registration Number, found on the back of the Customer Support Information Booklet.

`first_name`
`last_name`
`Company_name`
`phone_no`
	This is the authorized contact under which support is registered.

`end subscribe` `stop`	These two lines are required by Oracle's auto-registration software.

TABLE 15-1. *Formatting Your Access Request*

Oracle Alerts   Once you are under SupportLink contract, you will receive
Oracle Alerts. Alerts are mail messages sent to all supported users notifying them of
important information regarding their supported products. Here is an example of
one such alert:

```
From: Reem  Adranly  <radranly@us.oracle.com>
To: 72700.1705@compuserve.com
Subject: ALERT: NETWARE ONLINE BACKUPS AND 3RD PARTY UTILITIES.
Content-Type: text
Content-Length: 2180


Document ID:9073823.61
Title:ALERT:        NetWare Online Backups and
                   3rd Party Utilities.
Creation Date:     28 August 1995
Last Revision Date: 28 August 1995
Revision Number:   1
Product Version:   6 & 7
Platform:          NetWare
Information Type:  SOLUTION
Impact:            HIGH
Abstract:          This document contains ORACLE ALERT
                   Oracle6 & Oracle7 on NetWare - On-
                   line Hot Backups using 3rd Party
                   Utilities.
Keywords:          NETWARE; ORACLE; DATABASE; ALERT;
                   ONLINE; BACKUP; CORRUPT
-------------------------------------------------------------


                   ORACLE ALERT
Oracle6 & Oracle7 on NetWare - Online Hot Backups using 3rd Party
Utilities.

The recommended method to perform online/ hot backups is to issue
the "ALTER TABLESPACE BEGIN BACKUP" command.  Both hot backups
AND cold backups should be performed regularly.  Remember that
you must first shutdown the database before performing cold
backups.  It is also recommended that all backup and recovery
```

procedures be fully tested before deploying into mission critical/ production environments.

Please exercise extreme caution if you are using 3rd Party Backup Utilities to perform online/ hot backups of your Oracle database. There are some serious and known issues such as corruption to redo log files in which the only recourse is to restore the database from the latest full cold backup. Please call your Backup Utilities software vendor (i.e. Cheyenne, Palindrome, Arcada, Legato, etc.) to confirm whether or not they are able to provide reliable backup and recovery of Oracle Servers for NetWare.

Oracle Product Line Management is currently investigating anomalies with the Backup Utilities software vendors. Specifically, Cheyenne has identified problems with Archserve DB Agent version 1.0. Their latest release is version 1.2. There is a desire so set up a more formal certification program.

```
------------------------------------------------------------
                            Oracle WorldWide Customer Support
```

Real-Time Support System (RTSS)
In order to stay current, you can even dial in directly and access Oracle's RTSS 24 hours a day. Once there you have timely access to the vast repository of information Oracle's support personnel use to diagnose and resolve problems. You can even enter your own Technical Assistance Requests (TARs), update your own support records, view the RTSS bulletin board, submit product enhancement requests, and view the Product Change Request database to learn more about work in progress on Oracle's technologies.

SUPREQ
SUPREQ provides Metal Level support customers with a convenient e-mail–based means of accessing the RTSS bulletin board, submitting and updating TARs, and otherwise conducting all other support-related business without having to get onto a bulletin board, commercial service, or dial up customer support.

SupportNotes
For faster, offline access, each quarter much of the information found on RTSS is provided on the SupportNotes CD-ROM. In Oracle Book format, SupportNotes contains information on product patches and fixes, General Maintenance releases, and updates to documentation. Additionally, SupportNotes contains the latest

version-level information on all Oracle products so that you know where you stand with regard to updates and enhancements.

SupportNews

Finally, each quarter, Metal Level customers receive *SupportNews*. This is Oracle WorldWide Customer Support's newsletter providing highlights of product offerings and including information on not-yet-released products.

Extra-Oracle Information Sources

Beyond Oracle's campus, a fertile source of Oracle information awaits as well. The following sources, independent of Oracle Corporation, offer equally useful information.

Commercial Online Services

For less cost to the end user, commercial services such as CompuServe and America OnLine provide a forum for users and providers alike to share information and assist each other. Most have similar means of access but vary widely in content, ease of use, and target audience. In the case of CompuServe, considered the provider of choice for commercial users and business professionals, the International Oracle Users Group-Americas (IOUG-A) maintains both public and private areas exclusively devoted to the Oracle community.

CompuServe offers users several access methods. It can be reached via the Internet using Telnet, dialed up using a local number via CompuServe's own network, or through one of several national and international packet networks such as Tymnet. It is reachable at speeds up to a full v.34 28.8 Kbps. It will be available nationwide eventually.

Interface choices include simple terminal emulator and WinCIM, CompuServe's own Windows and Macintosh interface software, shown in Figure 15-11. Once there you can interact with other users in several different ways:

- Message areas
- Library sections
- Online Conferences
- Electronic mail

TIP
WinCIM V2 now provides access through CompuServe's own IP network. This means you can access CompuServe and the Internet at the same time. In fact, you can launch the web browser of your choice right from WinCIM.

FIGURE 15-11. *IOUG-A forum on CompuServe's GUI front-end, WinCIM*

Message Areas

Message areas are often the first line of information. Organized by topic, each section consists of various subject threads, or conversations. Here you can see if others are dealing with the same problem you have. In the message sections users post new messages, reply to others, and read both. Messages addressed to an individual will result in that user being notified of the posting when logging on, and all users will see the posting. Figure 15-12 shows a recent snapshot of the message area contents.

The message counts shown are those you have not yet read. In this manner, you are looking at a dynamic bulletin board. After some time, old messages will "scroll off." If you want to save a message for future reference you can capture it or, under WinCIM, store it in your file cabinet, a database maintained on your local machine. Figure 15-13 shows some of the threads you could find in the Desktop-PC,Mac,NLM section.

In Figure 15-14, a single message from the message thread is displayed. You see you can then select the next message or continue to the next thread. You may also post a reply to the message while here. You also can update your address list with either the From or To addresses, and you can save the message in your file cabinet on your computer.

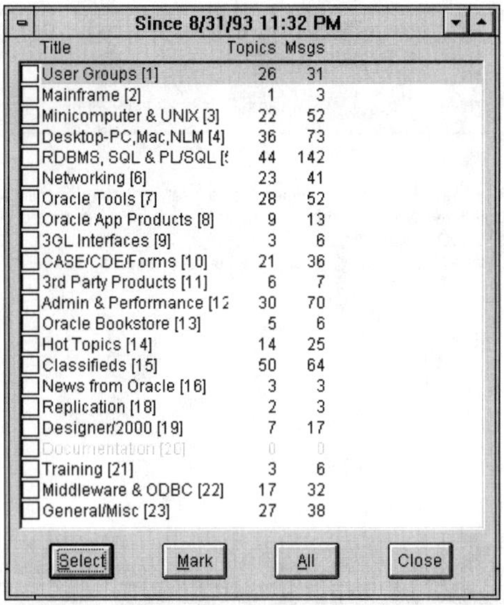

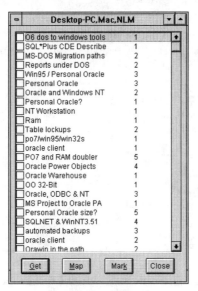

FIGURE 15-12.   *IOUG-A CompuServe forum message area*

FIGURE 15-13.   *Desktop message section threads*

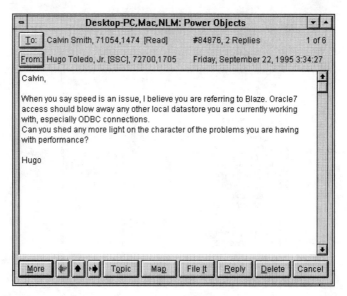

FIGURE 15-14. *CompuServe Forum message*

CompuServe also provides for message searches by description or message number. In the following illustration, you see the message search dialog. You can specify the number of the message, or more likely, search for a word found in the subject or title of the message. Message searches may also be constrained by date. Be aware, however, that messages eventually "scroll off" or are deleted once too many are in the system. This occurs on a per-forum basis, and on some forums messages are short-lived due to their high level of activity. When a message does scroll off, if it was addressed to you, CompuServe will mail you the message to ensure you see it.

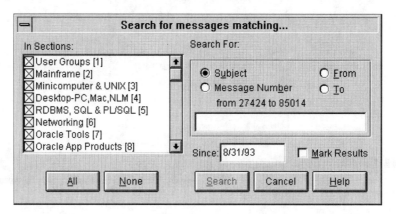

Library Sections

The Oracle User Forum library sections are generally grouped by the same topics as are the messages. Here you will find software, press releases, and even old message threads edited and saved by the sysops for future reference. The forum can also be used to notify others of commercial opportunities in the appropriate section. These include help wanted, consultant available, and new product announcements. Figure 15-15 shows the IOUG-A library area.

As with messages, the library sections may be searched as well. In the next illustration you see that a greater number of selection criteria are provided. These include filename, submitter ID, and keywords along with the date range of the submission and the selection of library areas to search.

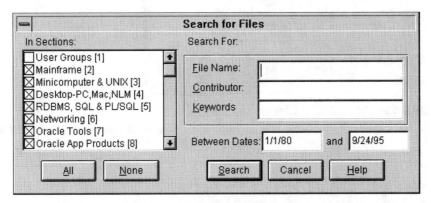

Here is a recent offering from the Admin and Performance library section. As shown in Figure 15-16, they identify the CompuServe user who uploaded the file, the filename and size, the date it was uploaded, and the number of times it had been downloaded—80 times in the case of the first file. Also provided are keywords that, as with messages, may be used to search for files.

Online Conferences

Another feature is the Online Conference. In these interactive sessions you can hear from and ask questions of those in the know. Conference dates and times are announced each time a user visits a forum. When the conference is in progress, users log into the conference and then see other conferees' input displayed. Depending on the type of conference, all users may be able to interact asynchronously. However, more organized conferences utilize a moderator who coordinates questions and responses in order.

FIGURE 15-15. *IOUG-A library sections*

Title	Size	Date	Accesses
Tune & troubleshoot the O7 Da	170101	9/21/95	80
R*LogLab redo log reader and	3820	9/13/95	25
R*SQLab SQL Analyzer and Ap	5256	9/13/95	26
RDB ODBC Driver For DEC Alp	746537	9/12/95	19
Info on Flex/ODBC Driver for D	4939	9/11/95	7
RDB ODBC Driver for Intel Wint	206763	9/10/95	316
RDB ODBC DRIVER FOR WIN	841317	9/10/95	947
New 32 Bit ODBC driver for Wi	1018050	9/8/95	95
Process status incrementor	663	9/6/95	80
VB API ODBC Prototype Applic	58378	8/31/95	123
MSVC MFC/C++ Prototype	85341	8/25/95	58
C++ Class Libraries for Oracle	43694	8/25/95	57
Quick & Dirty SQL for Windows	120706	8/23/95	94
PowerBuilder Catalog Tables	1579	8/10/95	34
Oracle Corporation Press Rele	219263	8/3/95	1003
SQLTool V 1.2 for Windows	1790633	8/2/95	92
Learning Oracle Forms 4.5: A	606	8/1/95	168
C-Shell script to check trace fil	2286	7/24/95	193
Designer/2000 and PO7 Instal	6504	7/24/95	277
Oracle Power Objects Educati	1303	7/21/95	159
Text file parser reports require	5651	7/17/95	109
Oracle Forms 4.5 Tutorial	830	7/10/95	452
PL/SQL Package: Sub-second	16617	6/20/95	347

Description Mark Retrieve View Close

FIGURE 15-16. *IOUG-A library file entry example*

Conference logs may be collected. To do so from WinCim, prior to entering the conference, select Special|Preferences|Forums|More. The resulting dialog box is shown here:

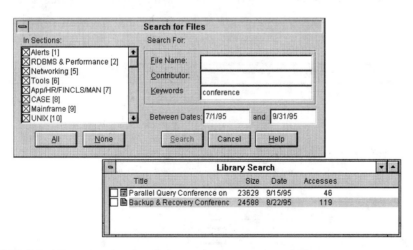

In the case of broad interest conferences, the sysop will save a log in the library for future reference. An example of one such log of a conference held in the Oracle SupportLink forum featuring Rama Velpuri, is shown in Figure 15-18. Figure 15-17 shows how to search for and display the conference log using the library search features described previously.

FIGURE 15-17. *Conference log search*

The conference log identifies the speakers and their text. Note the use of signal words like "over" to indicate that it is okay for another to speak. Without such signals, the display is overrun with many intertwined conversations. Signal words are the standard for moderated conversations.

Electronic Mail

CompuServe's mail system can communicate with others on CompuServe, the Internet, MCI Mail, and other mail systems including those of rival commercial service providers. You can attach files to your messages and receive them as well. This is most useful when you need to receive or provide binary information.

An important benefit of electronic mail is that it allows you to significantly expand your contact space. It is simple to manage groups of contacts so that you may easily update them all with information. Also, the fact that the person you wish to contact does not need to be there to take your call further enhances its utility. This is not a small thing for those of us who prefer to work at odd hours to the rest of the world!

Independent BBSs and Local Users Groups

Around the world are bulletin board systems (BBS) catering to the Oracle community. Some are maintained by the local Oracle Users Group. Others are privately maintained but may be used by several organizations. Many BBSs cooperate in the dissemination of public information by providing the initial download from a corporate source such as Oracle and then making it available for no fee to its local

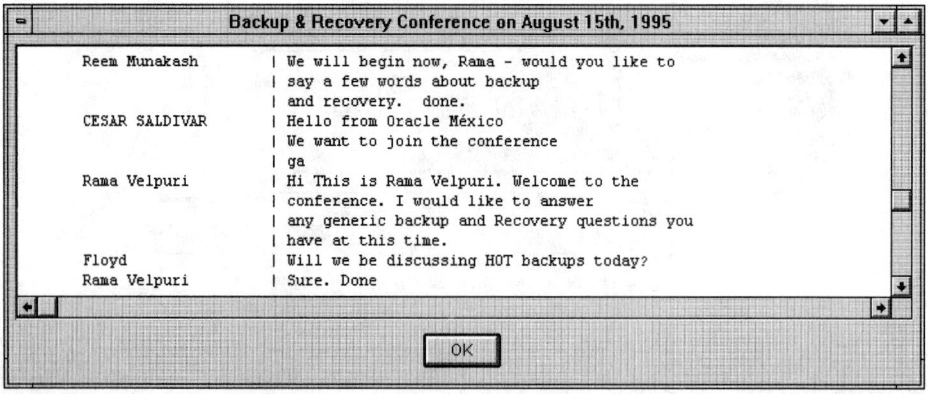

FIGURE 15-18. *Rama Velpuri conference log*

users. Thus, users avoid paying to retrieve information. BBSs may also participate in one of several BBS networks such as FidoNet. They rely on agreed-upon standards for sharing information, including mail and news among BBS users.

The quality of information found on BBSs depends on the amount of interaction. Successful user groups tend to have more motivated members. However, they often spend their time on the Internet or CompuServe. What is most useful about BBSs is that they foster regional networks of users. The users groups can then leverage their size to influence key players to provide information on corporate direction and even on-site demonstrations of product.

TIP
Visit IOUG-A (**http://www.ioug.org/**) on the Internet for a list of users groups in your area.

The Internet

Finally, there is the Internet. In fact, the Internet encompasses commercial service providers and some bulletin board systems that may provide e-mail gateways or even simple front-ends to other services on the Internet. Additionally, on the Internet you can belong to a mailing list, access Usenet newsgroups, or use a web browser such as Oracle's PowerBrowser, to traverse the World Wide Web (WWW).

World Wide Web (WWW)

As was discussed thoroughly in Chapters 12–14, the World Wide Web supports the protocols primarily used for browsing and retrieving information across the Internet. Oracle's Power Browser, the Oracle browser of choice and part of Oracle's WebSystem, plays a key role in the collection and management of sites maintained on your *hotlist,* your list of important and frequently visited sites.

Many web browsers such as Power Browser now provide access to non-HTML-based resources including WAIS databases, FTP archives, Gopherspace, Usenet, and even e-mail.

E-mail and Mailing Lists

The Internet offers a richer set of features for electronic mail than those found on the commercial service providers. Indeed, CompuServe can use Internet gateways to route mail. One feature available on the Internet is mailing list servers. These allow groups of users with an interest in a particular topic to automatically notify each member of others' communications on that topic. Generally newsgroups are formed when a mailing list begins to get very big.

There are a number of excellent mailing lists on the Internet. Foremost is *Oracle-L,* the Oracle users mailing list. It is a bit more savvy group than those found on the Usenet. It also consists of many folks who have no other access to the

Internet than through mail. Figure 15-19 shows a recent sample of issues discussed on the Oracle-L mailing list. The mailing list generates about 50 messages a day.

To subscribe to Oracle-L, submit an e-mail message from the address to which you want your messages sent. It is sent to **listserv@ccvm.sunysb.edu** with the body **SUBSCRIBE ORACLE-L** *your email address.* No subject line is necessary. Make sure you suppress your signature lines if they are added automatically to your outgoing mail.

For a complete list of commands, send the body message **INFO REFCARD** to that same address. The commands provide a host of opportunities to alter the way you use the list. For example, should you wish to receive a digest of messages instead of one at a time, you may instruct the list manager to do so. You may also choose to retrieve the digest periodically rather than continually receive messages.

A mailing list devoted to Oracle WebSystem is *Oraweb-L.* To subscribe send a message to **majordomo@labyrinth.net.au.** As with Oracle-L, the body should be **SUBSCRIBE ORAWEB-L** *your email address.* For a list of available commands, send the message **HELP** to **majordomo@labyrinth.net.au**.

Another mailing list of interest to Oracle users is *www-rdb.* Hosted out of CERN, the European High Energy Particle Physics Lab, this mailing list covers the integration of relational databases and the WWW. In fact, it was members of this mailing list who created and distributed the initial products that comprised some of

	listserver: ORACLE-L			
•	Scott Stout	08:23 AM 9/25/95	3	Re: Why does EXPLAIN PLAN give 0 cost
•	Eric Siglin	09:05 AM 9/25/95	3	Re: question about the [space leak] error
•		09:02 AM 9/25/95	2	Re: question about the [space leak] error
•	Morse, Don (SMAR	06:33 AM 9/25/95	3	Final: Do we want job listings
•	Martin Purbrook	02:40 AM 9/25/95	3	Optimization of UNION
	David White	10:11 AM 9/25/95	3	Algorithm for Primary Key?
	David Kent	10:54 AM 9/25/95	4	Re: Hoping to Identify ORACLE DBAs in Philadelphia Nex
•	Kayne Grau	11:01 AM 9/25/95	4	Re: question about the [space leak] error
R	Bill Conner	07:53 AM 9/25/95	1	test
•	Helena Whitaker	10:40 AM 9/25/95	3	Re: question about the [space leak] error
•	David White	12:36 PM 9/25/95	3	Re[2]: Algorithm for Primary Key
•	Kenneth Komoto	10:08 AM 9/25/95	2	Re: RPT conversion
•	Paul Dorsey	01:46 PM 9/25/95	2	Re: Re[2]: Algorithm for Primary Key
•	Paul Dorsey	01:41 PM 9/25/95	2	Re: Algorithm for Primary Key?
	Netserf, DUDE	11:32 AM 9/25/95	6	FAQ 2 of 3, was http://www.bf.rmit.edu.au/Oracle/conte
	Netserf, DUDE	11:28 AM 9/25/95	9	FAQ stuff: 1 of 3, was http://www.bf.rmit.edu.au/Oracl
	Netserf, DUDE	11:37 AM 9/25/95	11	FAQ 3/3Re: http://www.bf.rmit.edu.au/Oracle/intro.html
•	Frank Bowers	11:28 AM 9/25/95	2	Re: question about the [space leak] error
•	Neil Gwillym <ng	04:08 PM 9/25/95	4	Re: Algorithm for Primary Key?
•	Martin Bradburn	11:20 AM 9/25/95	2	Re: Algorithm for Primary Key
•	Tara Hinkle, UNH	11:21 AM 9/25/95	4	Re: Algorithm for Primary Key?
	Nagarajan Ravi	04:12 PM 9/25/95	2	Sqlnet 2.1.6 - Database Connection not established.
	Morse, Don (SMAR	04:59 PM 9/25/95	2	Re: Sqlnet 2.1.6 - Database Connection n
•	Hutchinson, Scot	10:37 AM 9/26/95	2	Running Forms4 for MAC from fileserver
•	Subramaniam, Sri	01:03 PM 9/26/95	2	RE : .err files after generation in FORMS 4.5

FIGURE 15-19. *Oracle-L messages*

the key components in Oracle's WWW SDK. To subscribe to www-rdb, send a message to **listproc@info.cern.ch** with the message **SUBSCRIBE WWW-RDB**.

Often, mailing lists will also mirror themselves on Usenet newsgroups using a mail archiver. This software program collects mailing list correspondence and aids in organizing it. For more information on mail archivers, check out the Piero Serini's Mail Archive Server software list. It is available in the **comp.answers newsgroup**, or via anonymous FTP. Its universal resource locator (URL) is

ftp://ftp.netcom.com/pub/wu/wuapub/archive servers/FAQ

Usenet Newsgroups

At Duke University in the early 1980s Tom Truscott and others developed Usenet, which preceded the Internet itself. This was an agreed-upon protocol for exchanging messages among the members of what was growing out of ARPANET and would become the Internet. Little did we know that from a small group of servers, a map of which would fit on two letter-size pages, this vehicle would grow to encompass tens of millions of users on millions of computers. You see, the newsgroups are now accessible to anyone on the Internet, CompuServe, Prodigy, and most other commercial service providers.

Newsgroups are like CompuServe's message sections. This means of information exchange is being further encouraged by workgroup tools such as Lotus Notes, which uses a similar hierarchy in its basic messaging scheme. You post documents to which others may respond. The responses themselves may also be responded to. These are organized by topic within subject area.

The tools used to access newsgroups were once limited to character-based metaphors. Now, most web browsers support newsgroups and provide better means of tracking their hierarchical nature. This includes not necessarily suppressing previously read messages but merely dimming them to indicate their status. Also, the management of the thousands of newsgroups is better managed with a hierarchical browser as is now provided in most news readers.

Table 15-2 lists newsgroups relevant to those looking for Oracle networking answers.

comp.databases.oracle	Primary source of Oracle information
comp.dcom.*	Encompasses about 20 other newsgroups related to data communications, including networking
comp.infosystems	Newsgroups related to WWW, Gopher, WAIS, and other Internet-based information systems technologies
comp.client-server	Client/server computing issues

TABLE 15-2. *Oracle Networking-Related Newsgroups*

Figure 15-20 shows a recent view of the first page of threads in
comp.databases.oracle. Note how the information is shown hierarchically. More
than one article shown in a sublevel indicates a response to the original article.

TIP
Did you forget to save something you saw posted on
comp.databases.oracle? Check out ASKNPAC on the Web at
http://asknpac.syr.edu/. This site uses Oracle technology to archive
the **comp.databases.oracle** newsgroup and many others. You can
search by combinations of keyword, date, and sender.

User Groups and Conferences

It is not enough to just read about solutions. It is important to meet others and
benefit from the unique experience of conversation. Fortunately, there are a
number of opportunities each year for members of the Oracle community to come
together, discuss problems, have fun, and acquire additional T-shirts!

International Oracle User Week (IOUW)
Sponsored by the International Oracle Users Group-Americas (IOUG-A), this is the
major Oracle conference. Alternating coasts of the United States for each year's

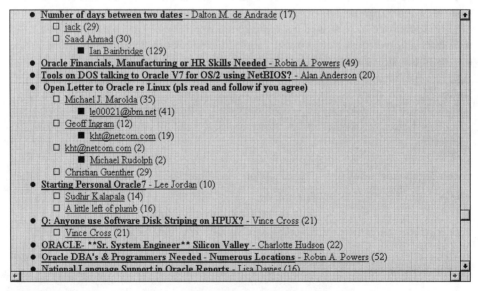

FIGURE 15-20. *Some comp.databases.oracle threads*

venue, IOUW is an important conference where new technologies are launched. In recent years, IOUW was where users first saw Power Objects, Project X at the time, and Oracle Power Browser. The conference proceedings are provided to every attendee and are available in both mammoth multivolume hard copy and in CD-ROM format for viewing with Oracle Book. Information on IOUW is available from the IOUG-A CompuServe Forum, GO ORAUSER, or by writing to IOUG-Americas Headquarters, 401 North Michigan Avenue, Chicago, IL 60611-4267, USA. The IOUG-A telephone number is (312) 245-1579. To e-mail IOUG-A, the address is **73144.1777@compuserve.com**.

Europe, Middle East, and Africa Oracle User Group (EOUG) Conference

The EOUG has held a week-long conference much like IOUW annually since 1983. Now slated to alternate only between Amsterdam in the northwest of Europe, and Vienna in the southeast, the conference runs alongside Europe's largest Database Product and Services Exhibition. A special feature of recent EOUG conferences is that they also run concurrently with The Internetworking Event (TIE). TIE is the combination of the former LanWorld, EuroComm, and Mobile Networking Conferences.

To get more information on EOUG, you may write EOUG Headquarters, Brigittenauer Lände 50-54, 1200 Vienna, Austria. You may telephone them at +43-663-017045. To e-mail EOUG, use **100520.631@compuserve.com** for Beate Zidisinova and **100130.502@compuserve.com** for Petra Smulders.

Oracle Developers' Conference (ECO)

The most informative and effective technical presentations are continually heard at the Oracle User Resource's (OUR) Oracle Developers' Conference. The annual ECO conference, formerly the East Coast Oracle (ECO) Conference, is held each spring. It continually draws very high-quality speakers from the Oracle user community and from Oracle Corporation itself. Information on the ECO conference is available from (910) 452-0006 or by writing Your Conference Connection, 1417 S. College Road, Wilmington, NC 28403.

Osborne/McGraw-Hill's Oracle Press Series

You already know about Osborne/McGraw-Hill's Oracle Press series. You are consuming one of its products right now. This is only one book in a library covering the breadth of Oracle's technologies. Titles include

- *Oracle Power Objects Developer's Guide*   The most comprehensive sourcebook for Oracle's cross-platform visual application development environment

■ *Oracle: The Complete Reference* The single most comprehensive sourcebook for the Oracle RDBMS

■ *Oracle DBA Handbook* What every systems administrator needs to know for effective and efficient database management

■ *Tuning Oracle* Your ultimate resource for making Oracle reach its full potential

■ *Oracle: A Beginners Guide* A thorough introduction for first-time users

■ *Oracle Workgroup Server Handbook* The one authoritative book on the platform for users and administrators alike, as well as many others listed in the back of this book

Other Oracle Press titles are listed at the back of this book.

The Fourth Estate

Finally, there are the continuing sources of current information: the Oracle journals. There are two regularly published sources dedicated to providing timely Oracle information: Informant Communications Group's *Oracle Informant* and Pinnacle Publication's *Oracle Developer.* On the horizon are more, including Miller-Freeman's *Oracle Technical Journal (OJT),* which released an issue to coincide with the 1995 International Oracle User's Week and is expected to be published quarterly.

Oracle Informant
Published by Informant Communications Group (ICG), *Oracle Informant* is a monthly magazine covering Oracle issues and highlighting products in the Workgroup/2000 suite. Each issue contains reviews, regular technical columns, and a floppy disk containing code samples. It is the Oracle version of ICG's Delphi and Paradox Informant magazines.

ICG maintains a forum on CompuServe featuring discussions on articles and offering examples of code from the articles available for download. This author's Oracle networking features appear regularly in *Oracle Informant.* For more information, on CompuServe GO ICGFORUM. You may also call ICG at (916) 686-6610. ICG is also on the Web, at **http://www.informant.com**.

Oracle Developer
Published by Pinnacle Publications, *Oracle Developer* is a monthly developers journal providing technical information from such industry luminaries as Steven Feuerstein and Ed Kosciuszko. It is edited by Tony Ziemba, founder of the Oracle User Resource (OUR) and the East Coast Oracle Developers' Conference (ECO).

Oracle Developer comes with a floppy disk containing software examples and supporting material for the articles. Pinnacle Publishing may be reached at (206) 251-1900. Their home on the Web is **http://www.pinpub.com**.

Anything Missing?

If you find any other sources you think should be included in future editions of this book, contact the author on CompuServe at 72700,1705 or on Internet at **hugo@mcs.net**.

Index

A

Abstract Notation Syntax 1, network
    management implementations,
    201
Access Manager, 29-30, 31
        transaction integration
            technology, 149
access to
        legacy data and code, 142
        non-Oracle7 databases,
            122-123

non-Oracle7 procedures from
    Oracle applications,
    125-126
Oracle7 data from non-Oracle
    applications, 123-124
Oracle7 stored procedures
    from non-Oracle
    applications, 124-125
accounting management, ISO
    network management framework,
    200
ACME PLC, 16-18
Administrator, ODBC (Open
    Database Connectivity), 131-132

agents
  intelligent, 207
  master, 201
  Oracle Mobile. *See* OMA
  Oracle Web. *See* OWA
  SNMP, 201
  wowstub, 261
Alliances Marketing, 319-320
  BAP (Business Alliance
    Programme), 319-320
  Oracle Developer's
    Conference, 320
  Oracle Integrator, 320
annotations, Hypertext Help,
  311-312, 323, 324
anonymous FTP (File Transfer
  Protocol), 243
API errors, SQL*Net OPEN, 95
API functions, SQL*Net OPEN,
  93-95
application interfaces, 119-136
  bridging technologies, 121-126
  heterogeneous access means,
    126-136
  heterogeneous access needs,
    120-121
  native drivers, 130-131
  OCI (Oracle Call Interface),
    126-127
  ODBC (Open Database
    Connectivity), 131-136
  precompilers, 128-129
  SQL*Module, 129-130
Archie Internet service, 243-245
architecting connectivity, TNS
  network design and deployment,
  154-156
ARPANET, history of Internet,
  237-239
asset management
  ISO network management
    framework, 198

management stations, 203
  OEM (Oracle Enterprise
    Manager), 213
audit trails, problem resolution
  policy, 174
authentication, basic and digest for
  WebServer 1.0, 270
Authentication Adapters, TNS
  applications, 89-90
automated discovery tools for
  topology mapping
  management stations, 204
  OEM (Oracle Enterprise
    Manager), 211-212

B

BAP (Business Alliance Programme),
  Alliances Marketing, 319-320
basic authentication, WebServer
  1.0, 270
BBSs (Bulletin Board Systems),
  sources of information on Oracle
  products, 334-335
bit-orientation, defined, 42
blocking operations, Windows and
  Windows for Workgroups
  problems, 190
bookmarks
  Hypertext Help, 315
  PowerBrowser, 297
bridging technologies, 121-126 *See
  also* middleware
  access to non-Oracle7
    databases, 122-123
  access to non-Oracle7
    procedures from Oracle
    applications, 125-126
  access to Oracle7 data from
    non-Oracle applications,
    123-124

access to Oracle7 stored
procedures from non-Oracle
applications, 124-125
heterogeneous
communications, 121-122
browsers *See also* PowerBrowser
World Wide Web, 250

C

capacity planning
management stations, 204
OEM (Oracle Enterprise
Manager), 212-213
centralized management stations,
205
CGI (Common Gateway Interface),
254-256
GET method, 255-256
POST method, 256
security and, 255
change management
management stations, 204
OEM (Oracle Enterprise
Manager), 212-213
client applications
confirming loopback, 53-54
OMA (Oracle Mobile Agents),
227
client profile encryption parameters,
SNS (Secure Network Services),
87, 88
client/agent/server overview, OMA
(Oracle Mobile Agents), 226-229
client/server components, SQL*Net,
40
client/server limitations, OMA
(Oracle Mobile Agents), 222-223
client/server processing,
middleware, 3-5

close operations, SQL*Net, 43-44
CMP (Common Management
Protocol), network management
implementations, 202
columns, SQL (Structured Query
Language), 6
commercial Internetworking, 239
COMMIT/ROLLBACK, Open Client
Adapter for ODBC (OCA/ODBC),
183
Common Gateway Interface. *See* CGI
Common Management Protocol
(CMP), network management
implementations, 202
Communities tab, Oracle Network
Manager, 111
community cost value, MPI
(MultiProtocol Interchange), 85
community involvement, TNS
network design and deployment,
154-156
compound documents, defined, 249
CompuServe, 327-334
e-mail, 334
IOUG-A forum, 328, 330
library sections, 331, 332
message areas, 328-330
message searching, 330
online conferences, 331-334
conferences
CompuServe, 331-334
Europe, Middle East, Africa
Oracle User Group, 339
International Oracle User
Week, 338-339
Oracle Developers', 339
configuration management, ISO
network management framework,
198
configuring
flat-hierarchy, single-protocol
networks, 108-109

listeners, 112-113
Oracle Names servers, 78-79
Oracle Native Naming
Adapters, 83
SQL*Net. *See* Easy
Configuration (SQL*Net)
configuring interchanges, MPI
(MultiProtocol Interchange), 84-85
configuring parameters
Oracle SNMP, 91
SNS (Secure Network
Services), 87-89
conformance level, ODBC drivers,
180
connection descriptors, Oracle
Names, 72
connection operations, SQL*Net,
43-44
connectivity architecture, TNS
network design and deployment,
154-156
connectivity products, 15-34
ACME PLC, 16-18
heterogeneous networked
environments, 34
native drivers and OCI, 24-25
ODBC (Open Database
Connectivity), 25-26
Open Gateway Technology,
27-29
OpenDoc and OLE, 33-34
Oracle Access Manager,
29-30, 31
Oracle Mobile Agents (OMA),
30-31
Oracle Open Client Adapter
for ODBC, 26-27
Oracle XA library, 29, 30
SQL*Net, 18-24
TCP/IP, 32

connectivity troubleshooting. *See*
troubleshooting connectivity
problems
consulting, Oracle Services, 318-319
cookie utilities, OWA (Oracle Web
Agent), 283

D

data management
management stations, 204
OEM (Oracle Enterprise
Manager), 212
data operations, SQL*Net, 44
data pumps, MPI (MultiProtocol
Interchange), 85-86
database administrators, TNS
network design and deployment,
156
database aliases, Easy Configuration
(SQL*Net), 55-56
Database Creation tab in Listener
dialog box, Oracle Network
Manager, 113, 114
database technology, distributed
processing, 10-11
databases
hierarchical, 146-147
network, 147
relational, 147
Date's 12 rules for distributed
databases, 12-13
DDL statements, Open Client
Adapter for ODBC (OCA/ODBC),
184
DDO. *See* Dynamic Discovery
Option
decentralized management stations,
205

DECOUX gateways, WWW
Interface Kit, 257
dedicated server processes
listeners, 48
prespawned, 49-51
defining nodes, Oracle Network
Manager, 109-112
dependency management, ISO
network management framework,
198
device management
management stations, 205
OEM (Oracle Enterprise
Manager), 209-210
digest authentication, WebServer
1.0, 270
discovery tools for topology
mapping, automated, 204,
211-212
distributed data management, 4
distributed database systems, 11
distributed databases, Date's 12
rules for, 12-13
distributed logic, 4
distributed management stations,
205
distributed presentation, 4
distributed processing, 1-13
client/server processing, 3-5
database technology, 10-11
distributed database systems,
11
Gartner Group's definition of,
4-5
local database systems, 10
middleware, 2-5
ODBC (Open Database
Connectivity), 9
open systems, 5-10

Oracle7 Servers, 11
remote database systems, 10-11
SNMP (Simple Network
Management Protocol), 9-10
standard LAN and WAN
protocols, 8-9
Dither Images checkbox,
PowerBrowser, 293
DLL errors, Oracle Objects for OLE
(OO4O), 185
DLLs, Windows and Windows for
Workgroups problems, 189
documentation
problem resolution policy,
171-172
product, 309-317
documents, compound, 249
domains
Dynamic Discovery Option
(DDO) and, 80
Oracle Names, 73-74
DRDA (Distributed Relational
Database Architecture) Servers,
migration technologies, 150
drivers
native. *See* native drivers
ODBC. *See* ODBC drivers
Dynamic Discovery Option (DDO),
79-80
domains, 80
regions, 80
TNS network design and
deployment, 163
well-known Oracle Names
servers, 80
dynamic web pages, 253-254
CGI (Common Gateway
Interface), 254-256
server-side includes, 254

E

e-mail
 CompuServe, 334
 Internet sources of information
  on Oracle products, 335-337
Easy Configuration (SQL*Net), 55-58
 adding database aliases, 55
 choosing database aliases, 56
 choosing protocols, 57
 confirming adding database
  aliases, 58, 59
 dialog box, 57
 exiting, 58, 59
 TCP/IP Host Name and
  Database Instance, 57, 58
EDA/SQL, transparent gateways,
 145, 146
encryption and Secure Network
 Services (SNS), TNS (Transparent
 Network Substrate), 47
end-user support, TNS network
 design and deployment, 156
Enterprise Manager. See OEM
 (Oracle Enterprise Manager)
Enterprise Naming Services, Oracle
 Native Naming Adapters, 82-83
error messages, ODBC drivers,
 181-182
error stack, problem resolution
 policy, 173-174
errors See also troubleshooting
 connectivity problems
  SQL*Net OPEN API, 95
Europe, Middle East, Africa Oracle
 User Group, conferences, 339
event management
 management stations, 203
 OEM (Oracle Enterprise
  Manager), 211-212

events, ISO network management
 framework, 197
exception operations, SQL*Net, 44
executable archives, defined, 289

F

fault management, ISO network
 management framework, 197
faults, ISO network management
 framework, 197-198
field force automation, OMA
 (Oracle Mobile Agents), 219-220
applications, OMA (Oracle Mobile
 Agents), 220-221
File Transfer Protocol. See FTP
firewall strategies, PowerBrowser,
 292
flat files, transparent gateways, 146
flat name spaces, Oracle Names, 73
fleet applications, OMA (Oracle
 Mobile Agents), 220
FTP (File Transfer Protocol), 242-243
functions
 PL/SQL. See PL/SQL functions
 SQL*Net OPEN API, 93-95

G

gateways
 Common Interface. See CGI
  (Common Gateway
  Interface)
 Open Gateway Technology,
  27-29, 142-150
 procedural, 28-29, 148
 transparent. See transparent
  gateways

WOW, 259-263
WWW Interface Kit, 257
GET method, CGI (Common
    Gateway Interface), 255-256
Gopher, 247-249
    Veronica and, 248
GPFs (General Protection Faults),
    Windows and Windows for
    Workgroups problems, 190

H

heterogeneous access means,
    application interfaces, 126-136
heterogeneous access needs,
    application interfaces, 120-121
heterogeneous communications,
    bridging technologies, 121-122
heterogeneous networked
    environments, connectivity
    products, 34
hierarchical databases, transparent
    gateways, 146-147
hierarchical name spaces, Oracle
    Names, 74
HTML (HyperText Markup
    Language), 251-252
        LiveHTML, 282
        WebServer Developer's
            Toolkit, 273-275
HTTP (HyperText Transfer Protocol),
    251
hypertext, defined, 250
Hypertext Help, 311-315
        annotations, 311-312, 323, 324
        bookmarks, 315
        customizing, 313-315
        printing, 315

I

image map utilities, OWA (Oracle
    Web Agent), 283
in-band breaks, SQL*Net, 44
indexed files, transparent gateways,
    146
information on Oracle products. *See*
    sources of information on Oracle
    products
installation support, WorldWide
    Customer Support (WWCS), 322
installing the WWW Interface Kit,
    258-259
instrumentation management
        management stations, 203
        OEM (Oracle Enterprise
            Manager), 210
INTCTL, MPI (MultiProtocol
    Interchange), 86
intelligent agents, OEM (Oracle
    Enterprise Manager), 207
interchanges. *See* MPI
    (MultiProtocol Interchange)
interfaces. *See* application interfaces
International Oracle User Week
    conference, 338-339
Internet, 235-263, 335-338 *See also*
    World Wide Web
        Archie, 243-245
        commercial Internetworking,
            239
        e-mail, 335-337
        FTP (File Transfer Protocol),
            242-243
        Gopher, 247-249
        history of, 237-239
        mailing lists, 335-337
        MIMEs (Multipurpose Internet
            Mail Extensions), 249
        NSFnet, 239

protocols, 239-256
standards, 239-240
Telnet, 240-241
Unix and Usenet, 238
Usenet newsgroups, 337-338
WAIS (Wide Area Information
Search), 245-247
World Wide Web, 249-254,
335
WWW Interface Kit, 236,
256-259
inventory management
management stations, 203
OEM (Oracle Enterprise
Manager), 213
IOUG-A forum, CompuServe, 328,
330
ISO network management
framework, 196-200
accounting management, 200
asset management, 198
configuration management,
198
dependency management, 198
events, 197
fault management, 197
faults, 197-198
license management, 198-199
performance analysis, 199
railway system metaphor,
196-197
security management, 199

J

Java, WRB (Web Request Broker),
282

L

LANs, protocols, 8-9
libraries
extended PL/SQL function,
282-283
XA, 29, 30
library sections, CompuServe, 331,
332
license management
ISO network management
framework, 198-199
management stations, 204-205
OEM (Oracle Enterprise
Manager), 213
listeners, 48-51
configuring, 112-113
dedicated server processes, 48
multi-threaded servers (MTS),
48-49, 50
prespawned dedicated server
processes, 49-51
troubleshooting failed
SQL*Net connections, 62-64
WebServer 1.0, 267-271
LiveHTML, WRB (Web Request
Broker), 282
local database systems, distributed
processing, 10
local user groups, sources of
information on Oracle products,
334-335
location transparency, TNS
(Transparent Network Substrate),
46-47
locking, Open Client Adapter for
ODBC (OCA/ODBC), 183
logging, problem resolution policy,
173
logging onto SQL*Net, 65-66
logic, distributed, 4

LONG columns, Open Client
Adapter for ODBC (OCA/ODBC),
183-184
loopback
confirming client, 53-54
confirming server, 52-53
troubleshooting failed SQL*Net
connections, 64-65

M

Macintosh, troubleshooting
connectivity, 191
mailing lists, 335-337
Oracle-L, 335-336
www-rdb, 336-337
managed devices, network
management implementations,
200-201
Management Information Base. *See*
MIB
management stations
centralized, 205
decentralized, 205
distributed, 205
network management
implementations, 201
network management
technology, 203-206
network manager checklist,
205-206
topology, 205
Map views, Oracle Network
Manager, 115, 116, 117
master agents, network management
implementations, 201
media independence, TNS
(Transparent Network Substrate),
47

message areas, CompuServe,
328-330
message gateways, OMA (Oracle
Mobile Agents), 228-229
Message Manager, OMA (Oracle
Mobile Agents), 227-228
message-based applications, OMA
(Oracle Mobile Agents), 224
Meta Level support, WorldWide
Customer Support (WWCS), 320,
321
method name errors, Oracle Objects
for OLE (OO4O), 187
MIB (Management Information Base)
network management
implementations, 201
Oracle SNMP, 90
middleware, 2-5 *See also* bridging
technologies
client/server processing, 3-5
defined, 3
migration considerations, TNS
network design and deployment,
165-167
migration technologies, Open
Gateway Technology, 149-150
MIMEs (Multipurpose Internet Mail
Extensions), 249
PowerBrowser, 295-297
Mobile Agents. *See* OMA (Oracle
Mobile Agents)
MPI (MultiProtocol Interchange),
83-86
community cost value, 85
configuring interchanges, 84-85
data pumps, 85-86
INTCTL, 86
preferred connection
managers, 85
SQL*Net, 21
MTS (Multi-Threaded Servers),
listeners, 48-49, 50

N

name spaces, Oracle Names, 72-74
NAMESCTL, Oracle Names, 81-82
naming services. *See* Oracle Names
National Language Support (NLS),
    defined, 42
native drivers
    access to non-Oracle7
        databases, 122-123
    application interfaces, 130-131
    OCI and, 24-25
Native Naming Adapters, TNS
    applications, 82-83
NetConv utility, Oracle Network
    Manager, 105, 106
NetFetch utility, Oracle Network
    Manager, 106-107
NetPrint utility, Oracle Network
    Manager, 105, 106
NetWare, troubleshooting
    connectivity problems, 190-191
network components, 17
    TNS applications, 70-71
network configuration files, Oracle
    Network Manager, 102-103
network databases, transparent
    gateways, 147
network management
    implementations, 200-203
        Abstract Notation Syntax 1, 201
        CMP (Common Management
            Protocol), 202
        managed devices, 200-201
        management stations, 201
        master agents, 201
        MIB (Management Information
            Base), 201
        Object IDs, 201
        RMON (Remote Monitoring),
            202-203

SNMP, 200
SNMP agents, 201
SNMP management stations,
    201
SNMP V2, 202
network management technology,
    194-206 *See also* OEM (Oracle
    Enterprise Manager)
    ISO framework, 196-200
    management stations, 203-206
    reasons for, 195-196
network manager checklist,
    management stations, 205-206
network transparency, TNS
    (Transparent Network Substrate),
    46
networks, TNS. *See* TNS network
    design and deployment
newsgroups, sources of information
    on Oracle products, 337-338
NLS (National Language Support),
    defined, 42
nodes
    defining via Oracle Network
        Manager, 109-112
    TNS network design and
        deployment, 163
notes, Hypertext Help, 311-312,
    323, 324
NOWAIT clause for locks, Open
    Client Adapter for ODBC
    (OCA/ODBC), 183
NSFnet, history of Internet, 239
NVT (Network Virtual Terminals),
    Telnet, 241

O

Object IDs, network management
    implementations, 201

OCA/ODBC. *See* Open Client
    Adapter for ODBC
OCI (Oracle Call Interface)
    application interfaces, 126-127
    native drivers and, 24-25
ODBC (Open Database
    Connectivity), 9, 25-26, 131-136
    access to non-Oracle7
        databases, 123
    adding Oracle7 connections,
        132-133, 134
    Administrator, 131-132
    Open Client Adapter for,
        26-27, 182-184
    QuickStart for Windows, 131
    SQL*Net and, 131
    TNS network design and
        deployment, 166
ODBC drivers
    conformance level, 180
    error messages, 181-182
    Oracle7 caveats, 134-136
    performance problems, 180
    TNS network design and
        deployment, 166
    troubleshooting connectivity
        problems, 180-182
OEM (Oracle Enterprise Manager),
    206-213
    automated discovery tools for
        topology mapping, 211-212
    capacity planning, 212-213
    change management, 212-213
    components, 208-209
    data management, 212
    event management, 211-212
    instrumentation management
        and reporting, 210
    intelligent agents, 207
    inventory and asset
        management, 213
    operations, 209-213

problem, workload, and device
    management, 209-210
software and license
    management, 213
summary, 214
OFA (Optimal Flexible
    Architecture), TNS network
    design and deployment, 164
OLE. *See* Oracle Objects for OLE
    (OO4O)
OMA (Oracle Mobile Agents),
    30-31, 217-232
    agents, 229
    application components,
        225-226
    application design, 223-225
    application types, 219-221
    client applications, 227
    client/agent/server overview,
        226-229
    client/server limitations,
        222-223
    field force automation, 219-220
    field sales applications,
        220-221
    fleet applications, 220
    limitations of mobile
        computing, 229
    limiting client/server
        interaction, 224-225
    message gateways, 228-229
    Message Manager, 227-228
    message-based applications,
        224
    messages, 227
    mobile links, 228
    OPO (Oracle Power Objects)
        and, 230-231
    system structures, 225-229
online conferences, CompuServe,
    331-334

online services, CompuServe, 327-334

ONM. *See* Oracle Network Manager

OO4O. *See* Oracle Objects for OLE

OPEN, SQL*Net. *See* SQL*Net OPEN

Open Client Adapter for ODBC (OCA/ODBC), 26-27
    troubleshooting, 182-184

Open Database Connectivity. *See* ODBC

Open Gateway Technology, 142-150
    components of, 143
    migration technologies, 149-150
    procedural gateways, 28-29, 148
    transaction integration technology, 149
    transparent gateways, 28, 143-148

open operations, SQL*Net, 43-44

open systems, 5-10
    defined, 2
    SQL (Structured Query Language), 5-8

OpenDatabase method, Oracle Objects for OLE (OO4O), 187-188

OpenDoc and OLE, 33-34

operating system-specific problems, 188-191

OPO (Oracle Power Objects), OMA (Oracle Mobile Agents) and, 230-231

Oracle
    Access Manager, 29-30, 31, 149
    application interfaces, 119-136
    bridging technologies, 121-126
    connectivity products, 15-34

connectivity troubleshooting, 169-191

distributed processing and, 1-13

Enterprise Manager, 206-213

FTP (File Transfer Protocol) and, 243

Internet and, 235-263

mobile agents. *See* OMA (Oracle Mobile Agents)

MPI (MultiProtocol Interchange), 21

network components, 17

Network Manager. *See* Oracle Network Manager

Power Objects. *See* OPO (Oracle Power Objects)

PowerBrowser, 287-303

precompilers, 128-129

sources of information on products, 305-341

SQL*Module, 129-130

SQL*Net, 18-24, 37-67

TNS applications, 69-96

TNS network design and deployment, 153-167

transparent gateways, 139-148

troubleshooting, 169-191

Web Agent. *See* OWA

WebServers, 265-284

WWW Interface Kit, 236, 256-259

Oracle Access Manager, 29-30, 31
    transaction integration technology, 149

Oracle Alerts, SupportLink, 325-326

Oracle Authentication Adapters, TNS applications, 89-90

Oracle Book, product documentation, 315-316

Oracle Call Interface. *See* OCI

Oracle Corporation (sources of
information), 308-327
  Alliances Marketing, 319-320
  Oracle Education, 317-318
  Oracle Services, 318-319
  product documentation,
    309-317
  WWCS (WorldWide Customer
    Support), 320-327
Oracle Developer, sources of
  information on Oracle products,
  340-341
Oracle Developers' Conference, 339
  Alliances Marketing, 320
Oracle Education, Oracle
  Corporation, 317-318
Oracle Enterprise Manager. *See* OEM
Oracle Informant, sources of
  information on Oracle products,
  340
Oracle Integrator, Alliances
  Marketing, 320
Oracle Magazine, product
  documentation, 316-317
Oracle Mobile Agents. *See* OMA
  (Oracle Mobile Agents)
Oracle Names, 71-82
  configuring servers, 78-79
  connection descriptors, 72
  domains, 73-74
  Dynamic Discovery Option
    (DDO), 79-80
  flat name spaces, 73
  general parameters, 79
  hierarchical name spaces, 74
  name spaces, 72-74
  NAMESCTL, 81-82
  Oracle Network Manager,
    77-78
  resolving service names, 72,
    75-76
  scalability, 76-77

SQL*Net, 21-22
  TNS (Transparent Network
    Substrate), 47, 71-82
  TNSNAMES.ORA, 75-76
  well-known servers, 80
Oracle Native Naming Adapters,
  TNS applications, 82-83
Oracle Network Manager, 99-117
  Communities tab, 111
  configuration validation and
    generation, 113-114
  configuring flat-hierarchy,
    single-protocol networks,
    108-109
  Database Creation tab in
    Listener dialog box, 113, 114
  defining nodes, 109-112
  listener configuration, 112-113
  Map views, 115, 116, 117
  NetConv utility, 105, 106
  NetFetch utility, 106-107
  NetPrint utility, 105, 106
  network configuration files,
    102-103
  Oracle Names, 77-78
  overview, 100-102
  protocol communities, 110-111
  QuickStart, 107-117
  ROS (Resource Object Store)
    Database Scripts, 104
  saving caveat, 112
  Service Address tab in Listener
    dialog box, 113
  SQL*Net, 20
  storage choices, 104
  Tree views, 115, 116
  views, 115-117
  walk-through feature, 108
Oracle Objects for OLE (OO4O)
  DLL errors, 185
  missing or incorrect files, 186

missing or incorrect OLE files, 185

OLE initialization and automation errors, 185

OpenDatabase method, 187-188

OpenDoc and OLE, 33-34

property and method name errors, 187

redistributable files, 186

registration database missing OLE2 data, 185-186

registration database missing OO4O data, 186

slow or hung connections, 188

troubleshooting connectivity, 184-188

Oracle Open Client Adapter for ODBC, 26-27

troubleshooting, 182-184

Oracle Power Objects. *See* OPO (Oracle Power Objects)

Oracle PowerBrowser. *See* PowerBrowser

Oracle.Press, product documentation, 316-317

Oracle Press series, sources of information on Oracle products, 339-340

Oracle Protocol Adapters, TNS (Transparent Network Substrate), 48

Oracle Services, Oracle Corporation, 318-319

Oracle 7 Servers

adding ODBC connections to, 132-133, 134

distributed processing, 11

driver caveats, 134-136

WebServer 1.0, 275

Oracle SNMP, 90-91 *See also* SNMP

configuring parameters, 91

MIB (Management Information Base), 90

Oracle WebServers. *See* WebServers

Oracle XA library, 29, 30

Oracle-L mailing list, sources of information on Oracle products, 335-336

ORAYWWW gateways, WWW Interface Kit, 257

Osborne/McGraw-Hill's Oracle Press series, sources of information on Oracle products, 339-340

out-of-band breaks, SQL*Net, 45

OWA (Oracle Web Agent), 271-275

extended PL/SQL function library, 282-283

OWA.CFG configuration file, 272-273

services, 271-273

WebServer Developer's Toolkit, 273-275

P

partitioning, TNS network design and deployment, 165

pattern matching utilities, OWA (Oracle Web Agent), 283

performance analysis, ISO network management framework, 199

Personal Server, PowerBrowser, 297-299

ping programs

confirming network availability with, 52-54

TNSPING program, 58-60

PL/SQL blocks, Open Client Adapter for ODBC (OCA/ODBC), 184

PL/SQL compilers, WWW Interface
    Kit, 258
PL/SQL extensions, WOW Gateway,
    262-263
PL/SQL functions
        extended library, 282-283
        WebServer Developer's
            Toolkit, 274-275
        WRB (Web Request Broker),
            282
platforms, transparent gateway, 145
PLC. *See* ACME PLC
polling, problem resolution policy,
    177-178
polymorphism, WebServer
    Developer's Toolkit, 274
POST method, CGI (Common
    Gateway Interface), 256
PowerBrowser, 287-303
        bookmarks, 297
        Cache tab, 293-294
        Dither Images checkbox, 293
        firewall strategies, 292
        helper applications, 295-297
        MIMEs (Multipurpose Internet
            Mail Extensions), 295-297
        New User dialog box, 290
        Personal Server, 297-299
        preferences, 291-297
        Preferences dialog box, 291
        programming, 299-303
        proxies, 292
        QuickStart, 289-297
        Setup dialog box, 290
        TCP/IP connectivity products,
            32
        URL history list, 297
        User tab, 292-293
        WIZARD.SCR, 299-303
precompilers
        application interfaces, 128-129

transaction integration
    technology, 149
preferred connection managers, MPI
    (MultiProtocol Interchange), 85
prespawned dedicated server
    processes, listeners, 49-51
printed media, product
    documentation, 309, 310
printing Hypertext Help, 315
proactive measures, problem
    resolution policy, 172-178
problem management
        management stations, 203
        OEM (Oracle Enterprise
            Manager), 209-210
problem resolution policy, 170-179
        audit trails, 174
        documentation, 171-172
        error stacks, 173-174
        logging, 173
        polling, 177-178
        proactive measures, 172-178
        problem solving strategies, 179
        reactive measures, 178-179
        tools, 178
        tracing, 174-177
procedural gateways *See also*
    transparent gateways
        Open Gateway Technology,
            28-29, 148
product documentation, 309-317
        Hypertext Help, 311-315
        Oracle Book, 315-316
        Oracle Magazine, 316-317
        Oracle Press, 316-317
        printed media, 309, 310
        README files, 311
        release notes, 310
products, information on Oracle.
    See sources of information on
    Oracle products

property and method name errors,
Oracle Objects for OLE (OO4O),
187
Protocol Adapters, TNS (Transparent
Network Substrate), 48
protocol communities, Oracle
Network Manager, 110-111
protocol independence, TNS
(Transparent Network Substrate),
47
protocols
Easy Configuration (SQL*Net),
57
Internet, 239-256
standard LAN and WAN, 8-9
TNS network design and
deployment, 163
proxies
PowerBrowser, 292
WebServer 2.0, 280

Q

QuickStart
Oracle Network Manager,
107-117
PowerBrowser, 289-297
SQL*Net, 52-66
Windows ODBC, 131

R

railway system metaphor, ISO
network management framework,
196-197
reactive measures, problem
resolution policy, 178-179

README files, product
documentation, 311
Real-Time Support System (RTSS),
WorldWide Customer Support
(WWCS), 326
redistributable files, Oracle Objects
for OLE (OO4O), 186
redundant, defined, 237
regions, Dynamic Discovery Option
(DDO), 80
registration database, Oracle
Objects for OLE (OO4O),
185-186
relational databases, transparent
gateways, 147
release notes, product
documentation, 310
remote data management,
distributed processing, 4
remote database systems, distributed
processing, 10-11
Remote Monitoring (RMON),
network management
implementations, 202-203
remote presentation, distributed
processing, 4
replication, TNS network design and
deployment, 165
resolving service names, Oracle
Names, 72, 75-76
RMON (Remote Monitoring),
network management
implementations, 202-203
ROS (Resource Object Store)
Database Scripts, Oracle Network
Manager, 104
rows, SQL (Structured Query
Language), 6
RSFs (Required Support Files),
Windows and Windows for
Workgroups problems, 189

RTSS (Real-Time Support System), WorldWide Customer Support (WWCS), 326

S

saving caveat, Oracle Network Manager, 112
scalability, Oracle Names, 76-77
schemas, SQL (Structured Query Language), 7-8
search engines, WWW Interface Kit, 257-258
Secure Network Services. *See* SNS
Secure Sockets Layer. *See* SSL
security
    CGI (Common Gateway Interface), 255
    ISO network management framework, 199
    TNS network design and deployment, 160
segmentation, TNS network design and deployment, 165
sequential files, transparent gateways, 146
server profile checksumming parameters, SNS (Secure Network Services), 88, 89
server-side includes, dynamic web pages, 254
servers
    confirming loopbacks, 52-53
    dedicated processes, 48
    multi-threaded (MTS), 48-49, 50
    Oracle Names, 71-82
    PowerBrowser Personal, 297-299

prespawned dedicated processes, 49-51
Service Address tab in Listener dialog box, Oracle Network Manager, 113
shell scripts, WOW Gateway, 261
SNMP (Simple Network Management Protocol), 9-10 *See also* Oracle SNMP
    agents, 201
    management stations, 201
    network management implementations, 200
    SQL*Net, 23-24
    V2, 202
SNS (Secure Network Services), 86-89
    client profile encryption parameters, 87, 88
    configuring parameters, 87-89
    server profile checksumming parameters, 88, 89
    SQL*Net, 22-23
    TNS (Transparent Network Substrate), 47, 86-89
software developers, TNS network design and deployment, 156
software management
    management stations, 204
    OEM (Oracle Enterprise Manager), 213
Solaris, troubleshooting connectivity problems, 191
sources of information on Oracle products, 305-341
    BBSs (Bulletin Board Systems), 334-335
    commercial online services, 327-334
    electronic, 307-308
    Internet, 335-338
    local user groups, 334-335

nonelectronic, 308
Oracle Corporation, 308-327
Oracle Developer, 340-341
Oracle Informant, 340
Osborne/McGraw-Hill's
  Oracle Press series, 339-340
types of, 307-308
user groups and conferences,
  338-339
SQL (Structured Query Language),
  5-8
    schemas, 7-8
    statements, 8
    tables, rows, and columns, 6
SQL*Loader, transaction integration
  technology, 149
SQL*Module, application interfaces,
  129-130
SQL*Net, 18-24, 37-67
    checking configurations, 58-60
    client/server components, 40
    configuring, 54-60
    confirming client loopback,
      53-54
    confirming network
      availability, 52-54
    confirming server loopback,
      52-53
    connection operations, 43-44
    data operations, 44
    described, 38
    Easy Configuration, 55-58
    exception operations, 44
    functions of, 39-40, 42-45
    how it works, 40-52
    in-band breaks, 44
    listeners, 48-51
    logging on, 65-66
    MPI (MultiProtocol
      Interchange), 21
    multiprotocol network, 39

ODBC (Open Database
  Connectivity), 131
open and close operations,
  43-44
OPEN. See SQL*Net OPEN
Oracle Names, 21-22
Oracle Network Manager, 20
out-of-band breaks, 45
QuickStart, 52-66
Secure Network Services,
  22-23
SNMP (Simple Network
  Management Protocol),
  23-24
TNS network design and
  deployment, 166
TNS (Transparent Network
  Substrate), 45-47
TNSPING program, 58-60
troubleshooting failed
  connections, 60-65
Two-Task Common, 42
User Programmatic Interface
  (UPI), 41-42
SQL*Net OPEN, 92-96
    API errors, 95
    API functions, 93-95
    application development,
      92-93
    sample applications, 95-96
SQL*Plus, WOW Gateway, 260
SSL (Secure Sockets Layer),
  WebServer 2.0, 279
SupportLink
    Oracle Alerts, 325-326
    WorldWide Customer Support
      (WWCS), 322-326
SupportNews, WorldWide
  Customer Support (WWCS), 327
SupportNotes, WorldWide
  Customer Support (WWCS),
  326-327

SUPREQ, WorldWide Customer
  Support (WWCS), 326

T

tables, SQL (Structured Query
  Language), 6
TCP/IP
  connectivity products, 32
  history of Internet, 238
  Host Name and Database
    Instance, 57, 58
telecommunications architects, TNS
  network design and deployment,
  156
Telnet, 240-241
  NVT (Network Virtual
    Terminals), 241
text manipulation utilities, OWA
  (Oracle Web Agent), 283
TNS (Transparent Network
  Substrate), 45-47
  applications. See TNS
    applications
  encryption and Secure
    Network Services (SNS), 47
  location transparency, 46-47
  network design and
    deployment. See TNS
    network design and
    deployment
  network transparency, 46
  Oracle Names, 47
  Oracle Protocol Adapters, 48
  protocol, media, and topology
    independence, 47
TNS applications, 69-96
  MPI (MultiProtocol
    Interchange), 83-86
  network components, 70-71

Oracle Authentication
  Adapters, 89-90
Oracle Names, 71-82
Oracle Native Naming
  Adapters, 82-83
Oracle SNMP, 90-91
SNS (Secure Network
  Services), 86-89
SQL*Net OPEN, 92-96
TNS network design and
  deployment, 153-167
  assessing present status,
    157-158
  comfort, 160-161
  community involvement,
    154-156
  connectivity architecture,
    154-156
  construction requirements, 159
  customer needs, 159
  customer requirements,
    161-162
  database administrators, 156
  design process, 162-163
  Dynamic Discovery Option
    (DDO), 163
  end-user support, 156
  flexibility, 160
  goals, 158-162
  implementation, 165-167
  maintenance requirements, 160
  migration considerations,
    165-167
  natural flow, 159-160
  nodes and protocols, 163
  ODBC drivers, 166
  OFA (Optimal Flexible
    Architecture), 164
  partitioning, 165
  planning, 157-163
  reliability, 160
  replication, 165

security, 160
segmentation, 165
software developers, 156
SQL*Net release 2.0 nodes, 166
techniques, 164-165
telecommunications architects, 156
user community representatives, 155-156
WAN dispersal, 166-167
TNSCLOSE(), SQL*Net OPEN API functions, 94-95
TNSNAMES.ORA, Oracle Names, 75-76
TNSOPEN(), SQL*Net OPEN API functions, 93
TNSPING program, checking SQL*Net configurations, 58-60
TNSRECV(), SQL*Net OPEN API functions, 94
TNSSEND(), SQL*Net OPEN API functions, 93-94
topology, management stations, 205
topology independence, TNS (Transparent Network Substrate), 47
topology mapping, automated discovery tools for, 204, 211-212
TP monitors, Oracle XA library, 29, 30
tracing, problem resolution policy, 174-177
transaction integration technology, Open Gateway Technology, 149
transparent gateways, 143-148 *See also* procedural gateways
access to legacy data and code, 142
caveats, 147
EDA/SQL, 145, 146

hierarchical databases, 146-147
indexed files, 146
network databases, 147
Open Gateway Technology, 28, 142-150
platforms, 145
relational databases, 147
sequential files, 146
Transparent Network Substrate. *See* TNS
Tree views, Oracle Network Manager, 115, 116
troubleshooting connectivity problems, 169-191
Macintosh, 191
NetWare, 190-191
ODBC drivers, 180-182
Open Client Adapter for ODBC (OCA/ODBC), 182-184
operating system-specific problems, 188-191
Oracle Objects for OLE (OO4O), 184-188
problem resolution policy, 170-179
products, 179-188
Solaris, 191
steps to, 179
Windows NT and Win95, 190
Windows and Windows for Workgroups, 189-190
troubleshooting failed SQL*Net connections, 60-65
confirming database starts, 60-62
confirming listeners, 62-64
verifying database server TNS loopback, 64-65
Two-Task Common, SQL*Net, 42

TXX demo search engine, WWW Interface Kit, 257-258

U

Unix, history of Internet, 238
UPI (User Programmatic Interface), SQL*Net, 41-42
URL history list, PowerBrowser, 297
URLs (Uniform Resource Locators), 252-253
Usenet
history of Internet, 238
newsgroups, 337-338
user community representatives, TNS network design and deployment, 155-156
user groups, sources of information on Oracle products, 334-335, 338-339
User Programmatic Interface (UPI), SQL*Net, 41-42

V

Veronica, Gopher and, 248
views, Oracle Network Manager, 115-117
VSAM Transparency technology, migration technologies, 150

W

WAIS (Wide Area Information Search), 245-247

walk-through feature, Oracle Network Manager, 108
WAN dispersal, TNS network design and deployment, 166-167
WAN protocols, 8-9
Web Agent. *See* OWA (Oracle Web Agent)
Web Listener, WebServer 1.0, 267-271
web pages, dynamic, 253-254
Web Request Broker. *See* WRB
WebServers, 265-284
WebServer 1.0, 267-278
application optimization, 276
basic authentication, 270
components of, 267, 268
converting WOW applications to, 276-278
Developer's Toolkit, 273-275
digest authentication, 270
file access management, 268-270
IP address and domain name restriction, 271
limiting access, 270-271
Oracle7 servers, 275
OWA (Oracle Web Agent), 271-275
Web Listener, 267-271
WebServer 2.0, 267-278
proxy support, 280
SSL (Secure Sockets Layer), 279
WRB (Web Request Broker), 281-282
WebServer Developer's Toolkit, 273-275
polymorphism, 274
WebSystem, TCP/IP connectivity products, 32
well-known Oracle Names servers, Dynamic Discovery Option (DDO), 80

Wide Area Information Search (WAIS), 245-247
Windows NT and Win95 problems, 190
Windows and Windows for Workgroups problems, 189-190
    blocking operations, 190
    DLLs, 189
    duplicate or missing files, 189
    GPFs (General Protection Faults), 190
    RSFs (Required Support Files), 189
WIZARD.SCR, PowerBrowser, 299-303
WORA gateways, WWW Interface Kit, 257
workload management
    management stations, 204
    OEM (Oracle Enterprise Manager), 209-210
World Wide Web, 249-254 *See also* Internet; PowerBrowser; WebServers; WWW Interface Kit
    browsers, 250
    CGI (Common Gateway Interface), 254-256
    dynamic web pages, 253-254
    HTML (HyperText Markup Language), 251-252
    HTTP (HyperText Transfer Protocol), 251
    hypertext, 250
    Interface Kit. *See* WWW Interface Kit
    server-side includes, 254
    URLs (Uniform Resource Locators), 252-253
WorldWide Customer Support (WWCS), 320-327
    free installation support, 322
    Meta Level support, 320, 321

RTSS (Real-Time Support System), 326
SupportLink, 322-326
SupportNews, 327
SupportNotes, 326-327
SUPREQ, 326
WOW applications, converting to WebServer 1.0, 276-278
WOW Gateway, 259-263 *See also* WebServers
    components of, 259-260
    demonstration with SQL*Plus, 260
    limitations of, 263
    PL/SQL extensions, 262-263
    shell script, 261
    wowstub agents, 261
    WWW Interface Kit, 236, 257
WRB (Web Request Broker), 281-282
    Java, 282
    LiveHTML, 282
    PL/SQL functions, 282
WWCS. *See* WorldWide Customer Support
WWW Interface Kit, 256-259
    acquiring, 258
    gateways, 257
    installing, 258-259
    overview, 257-258
    PL/SQL compilers, 258
    search engines, 257-258
    WOW Gateway, 236, 257, 259-263
www-rdb mailing list, sources of information on Oracle products, 336-337

X

XA library, 29, 30

FUTURE CLASSICS FROM

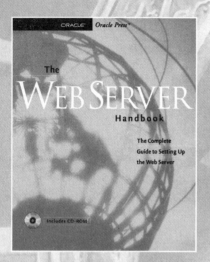

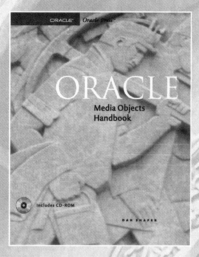

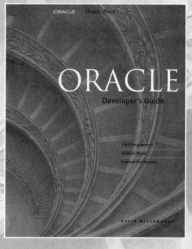

THE WEB SERVER HANDBOOK

by Cynthia Chin-Lee and Comet

Learn how to set up and maintain a dynamic and effective Web site with this comprehensive guide that focuses on Oracle's new Web solutions.

ISBN: 0-07-882215-7
Price: $39.95 U.S.A.
Includes One CD-ROM

ORACLE MEDIA OBJECTS HANDBOOK

by Dan Shafer

The power, flexibility, and ease of Oracle Media Objects (the cross-platform multimedia authoring tools) are within your reach with this definitive handbook.

ISBN: 0-07-882214-9
Price: $39.95 U.S.A.
Includes One CD-ROM

ORACLE DEVELOPER'S GUIDE

by David McClanahan

Loaded with code for common tasks, developers will find all the information they need to create applications and build a fast, powerful, and secure Oracle database.

ISBN: 0-07-882087-1
Price: $34.95 U.S.A.

ORACLE: THE COMPLETE REFERENCE

Third Edition

by George Koch and Kevin Loney

ISBN: 0-07-882097-9
Price: $34.95 U.S.A.

ORACLE DBA HANDBOOK

by Kevin Loney

ISBN: 0-07-881182-1
Price: $34.95 U.S.A.

ORACLE: A BEGINNER'S GUIDE

by Michael Abbey and Michael J. Corey

ISBN: 0-07-882122-3
Price: $29.95 U.S.A.

TUNING ORACL

by Michael J. Corey, Michael Abbey, and Daniel J. Dechichio, Jr.

ISBN: 0-07-881181-3
Price: $29.95 U.S.A.

DIGITAL DESIGN
FOR THE
21ST CENTURY

You can count on Osborne/McGraw-Hill and its expert authors to bring you the inside scoop on digital design, production, and the best-selling graphics software.

Digital Images: A Practical Guide
by Adele Droblas Greenberg
and Seth Greenberg
$26.95 U.S.A.
ISBN 0-07-882113-4

Scanning the Professional Way
by Sybil Ihrig and Emil Ihrig
$21.95 U.S.A.
ISBN 0-07-882145-2

Preparing Digital Images for Print
by Sybil Ihrig and Emil Ihrig
$21.95 U.S.A.
ISBN 0-07-882146-0

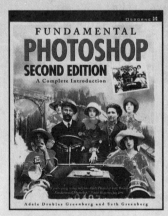

**Fundamental Photoshop:
A Complete Introduction,
Second Edition**
by Adele Droblas Greenberg
and Seth Greenberg
$29.95 U.S.A.
ISBN 0-07-882093-6

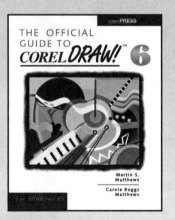

**The Official Guide to
CorelDRAW! ™6 for Windows 95**
by Martin S. Matthews and Carole Boggs Matthews
$34.95 U.S.A.
ISBN 0-07-882168-1

**The Official Guide to Corel
PHOTO-PAINT 6**
by David Huss
$34.95 U.S.A.
ISBN 0-07-882207-6

ORDER BOOKS DIRECTLY FROM OSBORNE/McGRAW-HILL

For a complete catalog of Osborne's books, call 510-549-6600 or write to us at 2600 Tenth Street, Berkeley, CA 94710

Call Toll-Free, *24 hours a day, 7 days a week, in the U.S.A.*
U.S.A.: 1-800-262-4729   *Canada: 1-800-565-5758*

Mail *in the U.S.A. to:*   *Canada*
McGraw-Hill, Inc.   *McGraw-Hill Ryerson*
Customer Service Dept.   *Customer Service*
P.O. Box 182607   *300 Water Street*
Columbus, OH 43218-2607   *Whitby, Ontario L1N 9B6*

Fax *in the U.S.A. to:*   *Canada*
1-614-759-3644   *1-800-463-5885*
                                      Canada
                                      orders@mcgrawhill.ca

SHIP TO:

Name _____

Company _____

Address _____

City / State / Zip _____

Daytime Telephone *(We'll contact you if there's a question about your order.)*

ISBN #	BOOK TITLE	Quantity	Price	Total
0-07-88				
0-07-88				
0-07-88				
0-07-88				
0-07-88				
0-07088				
0-07-88				
0-07-88				
0-07-88				
0-07-88				
0-07-88				
0-07-88				
0-07-88				
0-07-88				

Shipping & Handling Charge from Chart Below	
Subtotal	
Please Add Applicable State & Local Sales Tax	
TOTAL	

Shipping & Handling Charges

Order Amount	U.S.	Outside U.S.
$15.00 - $24.99	$4.00	$6.00
$25.00 - $49.99	$5.00	$7.00
$50.00 - $74.99	$6.00	$8.00
$75.00 - and up	$7.00	$9.00
$100.00 - and up	$8.00	$10.00

Occasionally we allow other selected companies to use our mailing list. If you would prefer that we not include you in these extra mailings, please check here: ❏

METHOD OF PAYMENT

❏ Check or money order enclosed (payable to Osborne/McGraw-Hill)

❏ AMERICAN EXPRESS   ❏ DISCOVER   ❏ MasterCard.   ❏ VISA

Account No. [ ][ ][ ][ ][ ][ ][ ][ ][ ][ ][ ][ ][ ][ ][ ][ ]

Expiration Date _____

Signature _____

In a hurry? Call with your order anytime, day or night, or visit your local bookstore.

Thank you for your order   Code BC640SL